SPECIAL NEEDS IN ORDINARY SCHOOLS
General editor: Peter Mittler
Associate editors: Mel Ainscow, Brahm Norwich, Peter Pumfrey,
Rosemary Webb and Sheila Wolfendale

Spelling

Titles in the Special Needs in Ordinary Schools series

Assessing Special Educational Needs
Management for Special Needs
Meeting Special Needs in Ordinary Schools (2nd Edition)
Reappraising Special Needs Education
Special Needs Provision: Assessment, Concern, Action
Working with Parents of Children with Special Needs

Concerning pre- and primary schooling:

Expressive Arts in the Primary School
Improving Children's Reading in the Junior School
Pre-School Provision for Children with Special Needs
Primary Schools and Special Needs (2nd Edition)

Concerning secondary education:

Secondary School Mathematics and Special Needs
Secondary Schools for All? (2nd Edition)

Concerning further education:

Further Opportunities: Learning Difficulties and Disabilities in FE
Opening Doors: Learning Support in Higher Education

Concerning specific needs:

Children with Hearing Difficulties
Children with Learning Difficulties
Children with Speech and Language Difficulties
Educating the Able
Improving Classroom Behaviour
Mobility for Special Needs
Spelling: Remedial Strategies

Forthcoming:

New Directions in Special Needs

Spelling

Remedial Strategies

Diane Montgomery

CASSELL

Cassell
Wellington House
125 Strand
London WC2R 0BB

PO Box 605
Herndon
VA 20172

British Library Cataloguing-in-Publication Data
A catalogue record for this book is available from the British Library.

ISBN 0-304-32972-X (hardback)
     0-304-32974-6 (paperback)

Typeset by Action Typesetting, Northgate Street, Gloucester
Printed and bound in Great Britain by Biddles Limited, Guildford and King's Lynn

Contents

Acknowledgements

My special thanks to all the pupils over the years who put up with my questions and games to help me test out ideas and put this book together. They knew that it would be too late to help them but they helped me in the belief that what we found out together might help some pupils in the future.

My thanks also to all the initial teacher education students, head teachers who gave me access to their schools, and teachers on in-service training courses who have helped me refine my ideas, tested things out in their classrooms and fed back their results and criticisms.

I am also particularly indebted to the former teachers at the Kingston Reading Centre – Lucy L. Cowdery, Paula Morse and Mary Prince-Bruce – with whom I enjoyed a collaboration extending over a ten-year period and to whose work I hope to have done justice.

All our thanks are due to Miss Hickey for her untiring work for dyslexics in the unfriendly climate of the 1970s and to her colleagues of that period, Beve Hornsby and Marion Welshman, who can also be considered to have been pioneers in their own right and who are still proactive.

Editorial foreword

When I was training as a psychologist, I was asked to provide 'extra spelling and personal support' to a highly intelligent 16-year-old pupil, whose school deducted half a mark for every spelling mistake she made in any piece of written work and who felt totally discouraged by the experience. She left this school at 16, took her A levels at a college of further education and embarked on a successful career as a teacher, despite continuing difficulties in spelling.

The response of the education system to pupils who experience spelling difficulties has not always been helpful. Some pupils are still penalized by teachers and exam boards for every spelling mistake but have received little constructive help. Spelling difficulties can be a poor relation in the list of special needs priorities.

We can all think of friends, relatives and colleagues for whom spelling is still an obstacle to written communication; at least some readers of this book will be amongst their number. Indeed, all university tutors know a small number of head teachers, teachers and educational administrators who attend advanced courses in education and whose spelling difficulties have proved resistant to intervention.

We know remarkably little about the process involved in learning to spell. While many pupils 'pick it up' almost spontaneously, others experience difficulties which may be minor and temporary or major and life-long and a source of considerable stress or embarrassment in later life.

Diane Montgomery's book is therefore both timely and constructive. It summarizes a wealth of information on what is currently known about learning to spell and ways of helping pupils for whom spelling continues to present a challenge. Her book will prove a rich source of ideas and support.

Professor Peter Mittler
University of Manchester
October 1996

Introduction

For almost a century spelling has been the poor relation in the literacy partnership between reading and spelling. In the last fifty years in particular many researches, surveys and reports have been published which have the word 'reading' in their title. Even if they do not, any reference to literacy is mainly to reading and reading standards. The National Curriculum has redressed this balance somewhat by defining targets for achievement in spelling and handwriting as well as in reading.

To a large extent it has been assumed that spelling is picked up during reading and reinforced in writing. Phonics activities have always played some part in literacy teaching, particularly with regard to reading, but in the case of poor spellers this knowledge has evidently not been transferred, even when there has been individual and direct teaching. It may seem puzzling but it is clear that some children learn to read and spell without ever having been taught; most become literate by a variety of methods after several years' apprenticeship in schools; a significant number remain well behind the rest, although they are not necessarily slower learners in general terms; and a few remain semi-literate or even illiterate into adulthood, despite in many cases being intelligent and having received extensive remedial support. There are also some individuals with very low test intelligence scores (IQ 40) who learn to read, although they understand little of it.

The view that standards of literacy are falling is often reiterated. Yet there are no survey results to draw upon to show that standards of spelling and handwriting have improved or declined, although some data exist. For many years it was not thought necessary to test a pupil's spelling even when he or she was being referred for specialist help.

Any consideration of standards needs to be made in context. Over the decades the spelling vocabulary children use grows and changes. Some standard spelling test words have become obsolete for most children, whose failure to spell them correctly seems to indicate falling standards.

Another significant factor is that nowadays industrial and business employers are drawing their employees from a different cadre. As the school leaving age was raised and the numbers entering universities and colleges expanded to 30 per cent, the more literate pupils were creamed off the employment lists featuring school leavers. The cry has thus gone up that they (school leavers) cannot spell and write as well as formerly. This ignores the fact that the 'they' are different.

The context has changed in other ways. Children who might previously have been preoccupied by books at home now spend much time on television and video games and have less time to practise their literacy skills, even were they so inclined. There are also more subjects to be learned at school. Whereas in the early decades of the century children might have been seen in neat rows chanting their spellings or rote-learning poems and sections of the Bible, they now have science, technology, history, geography, art and music to supplement the former diet of reading, writing, arithmetic and religious instruction. A 'return to basics', which is what critics usually call for, should and could not return this far.

Yet allowing that complaints about literacy may not always be based on realistic assessment, it is evident that there are many pupils who could benefit from being helped to achieve higher standards of literacy, the earlier the better. The purpose of this book is to reassert the important contribution that learning to spell and write makes to becoming literate. It seeks to show how an approach to the literacy curriculum that balances the emphasis on reading with due attention to writing and spelling can be beneficial and can enhance reading even more.

The first two chapters explain the nature of spelling, how it develops and how it may best be assessed. Chapters 3 and 4 focus upon developmental assessment and intervention combined in an assessment through learning and teaching model. The next three chapters deal with general remedial intervention which can support and promote spelling development in poor spellers or those who have missed crucial teaching input. The final chapter gives an outline of the nature and use of particular programmes which are effective and necessary for pupils with specific learning difficulties in reading and spelling, afterwards referred to as dyslexia.

HOW IMPORTANT ARE LITERACY SKILLS IN THE COMPUTER AGE?

How important are writing and spelling nowadays, when alternative means of communication, spoken and printed, are available, or becoming so, through new technology? On the next two pages are the views of some seven-year-olds on writing and spelling (examples are reduced in size). They think these skills are important, but also feel that they require a great deal of effort.

The acquisition of writing and spelling skills remains essential until such time as we all have voice-activated writing facilities and individual computers at home and school, when we shall only need to be able to read. Even then there will be a significant number of pupils who will need special help if they are to cope with the demands of the curriculum, unless we commit all text to audiotape as well and have read-back facilities on what they 'write'. Meanwhile 4 per cent (9 per cent in inner city areas) of children underfunction in schools because of inadequate literacy. This prevents them from accessing higher levels of curriculum knowledge and skill and from demonstrating their full range of intellectual abilities. It impedes their career progression and frustrates them. The more intelligent they are the more they will be frustrated by their inability to have mastered the basic skills of spelling and writing.

THE IMPORTANCE OF LITERACY FOR A GOOD EXPERIENCE OF SCHOOLING

Another reason for giving pupils early and effective support in literacy is that when severe reading and spelling problems are not identified within the first year (ideally the first month) in school those experiencing them can become set upon a career in school failure and disruption. Although pupils may receive help in other areas, they often fail to receive help with spelling. Without special help they cannot recover from this downward spiral. They become three- and four-time failures and feel hopeless, frustrated and worthless. They may defend themselves from further loss of self-esteem in various ways. This usually takes one of two forms: they may act out their problems and become disruptive, attention-seeking and abusive or they may withdraw. The real risk of such developments is emphasized for example in J. Edwards's book *The Scars of Dyslexia* (1994), in which she presents eight detailed case studies of pupils who have been failed by their ordinary

James

I cant write very neatly.
I quit like writing storys.
But I dont like writing storys
more than one page long.
I think that spalling is very
importent But I am not very good
at spalling.

Edmund

Writing can be used as a form
of self expression many things may
be expressed through writing. I
prefer poem wich are powerful
and can show something through words.
Words are beatiful if put together
properly, certainly important in our
daily lives. Words can show something
more than than pictures.

Stephanie
I find writing very boring but I
sometimes learn somthing from
it like spelling
I like sending messages in code

MATTHEW 13
I hate writing its so boring
sitting doing nothing apart
from moving your hand up
and down.

Claire

I think it is important to learn to write because it is a way to comunicate. When you write a long sentce or story your writing tends to get messy. I like writing letters but after 1 page or so I cant think what to put. If you couldnt read you couldnt write I guess so if i couldnt write I thint I would miss reading.

Shankar

I am afull at writting and Spelling and english I hate writting Comprehenchon and ereything involving copying I like writting story's

P.5
the spelling of all this is probely wrong but it is the best you WILL get out of me

schooling and have finally been sent to a special school. It is salutary to quote from this book:

> Four groups of totally unexpected experiences were registered:
> 1. Violence from teachers;
> 2. Unfair treatment/discrimination;
> 3. Inadequate help/neglect; and
> 4. Humiliation.

Edwards ascribed these experiences to the failure of teachers to acknowledge or understand dyslexia, and their readiness to label a child disruptive or dim (Edwards, 1994, p. 1).

She found that the emotional reaction of dyslexic students to their circumstances could be classified under nine headings: truancy/school refusal, psychosomatic pain, isolation/alienation from peers, lack of communication, lack of confidence, self-doubt/denigration of intellect, competitiveness disorders, sensitivity to criticism, and behaviour problems.

> Six of the eight experienced incidents of enduring pain connected with their treatment at school. All eight individuals lacked confidence, were highly sensitive to criticism, and had displayed behaviour problems. Two students only revealed lesser levels of resentment and damaged morale, owing to a milder degree of dyslexia or effective early identification. (ibid., pp. 1–2)

Boland (1995) in interviews with twelve dyslexics and their parents found similar consequences attending from a failure to diagnose the pupils' specific learning difficulties at an early stage. At the age of 5 years four of the children showed overt behavioural difficulties; at the age of 8 nine of them did. Their failure to learn induced stress both in themselves and in their families.

It is clearly very important that children's problems with spelling are taken seriously from an early stage. The chapters that follow analyse the problems and suggest practical strategies for improvement.

—1

Spelling: teaching and development

INTRODUCTION

From the 1950s until recently, spelling lessons have not featured in any significant manner in primary school practice in England and Wales. The conventional approach to teaching spelling in the period after the Second World War, according to Peters (1967), was that incidental learning during reading was the primary vehicle for spelling instruction. This reflected the view that reading and spelling were two sides of the same coin, with spelling parasitic upon reading. Successful schemes involving 'look and say' methods were developed in the USA in the 1920s. *Janet and John* was the first such scheme piloted in Britain in 1947, and it became very widely used. Preceding this, however, there was a long history of the teaching of spelling, reaching back into the Middle Ages, not enjoyed by the teaching of reading. The preoccupation with teaching reading and the research on this, to the exclusion of attention to spelling, is a twentieth-century phenomenon that has probably been to the detriment of both. Recently, however, a more balanced approach has evolved which has helped redress some of the problems.

SPELLING

At the simplest level spelling is the association of alphabetic symbols, called graphemes, with speech sounds, called phonemes (the smallest identifiable sounds in speech). In English we use 44 distinct phonemes out of the 70 or so which have been identified in human speech. The association of speech sounds with the alphabet symbols is called 'phonics'. Sometimes the association is direct, giving, in English, simple regular spellings, such as *d-o-g*, *ch-i-p* and *b-e-nd*, etc. It is thought that when the alphabet was first invented, several centuries BC, most words could be transcribed thus, but over time this simple correspondence between sound and symbol, called one-to-one correspondence, has, in many languages, gradually slipped. In this respect Turkish and Italian are more regular than Greek, which is more regular than English.

Then there are morphemes, the smallest meaningful elements of speech, represented in writing by single syllables or even letters, which in isolation or added to a word can be meaningful or change the original word's meaning. Examples are: *cat, I, a, -ing, -ed*. In English there is a conflict between the phonemic representation (writing the spoken word directly as it sounds now) and the morphemic (indicating meaning and often the historical origins of words which can involve different past pronunciation). It is the convention to preserve the history over the current sound: thus 'sheep herder' is spelt as *shepherd* rather than as *sheperd*. We may have pronounced sheep as 'shep', or we may have transcribed 'sheep' as *shep*, in those days – as some poor spellers might today. English spelling is rich in history of this kind and so methods of teaching which offer an understanding of the origins of the language as well as its basic phonemic representation are helpful. Yet other aspects of spelling knowledge obviously play a part – 'phonics' for example in the early stages of reading.

English is said to be a very irregular language to learn to spell, yet Hanna *et al.* (1966) claim it is possible to spell 85 per cent of the English language with a knowledge of phonics and some basic rules. These researchers found that it was possible to programme a computer to spell 17,000 basic words, using 300 rules plus a knowledge of how sounds are transcribed and represented by alphabetic symbols: i.e. phonics. However, they were dealing with rules governing letter order and frequencies (often called surface rules) rather than with deep structure rules concerning word and syllable structure, which are the province of linguistics. It has been argued that a much smaller number of deep structure rules can generate an even larger number of correct spellings. However true this may be, it is also the case that many people have learnt to spell accurately without knowing any linguistic rules.

In addition to recognizing spelling patterns in order to read, it is also necessary for members of a modern society to be able to commit these patterns to paper in order to communicate in writing. This is a rather more difficult task than recognizing all the letters when they are present in context. Spelling requires the recall of spellings from the memory store or lexicon of the brain in exactly the correct order and the ability to construct spellings that are not so stored. Prior to the introduction of the printing press, and even for some while afterwards, spelling by scribes and clerks was much more variable than it is now and such variation was accepted. Today only correct spelling is acceptable and poor spelling tends to be regarded, often quite wrongly, as indicative of poor intellectual ability or of carelessness. Poor spelling in job applications will often result in the applicant being screened out.

It has also been necessary until recently for the fine hand co-ordination movements and pencil grip to be learned in order to perform graphomotor squiggles accurately. Now it is possible for keyboard skills to be learnt and for text on computer to be spell-checked, or for voice input to be used for producing text. Nevertheless, for some time yet writing and spelling skills will still be required of pupils in schools.

Fluent writing requires that spellings are reeled automatically out of the brain's lexicon, guiding the pen as it moves across the page. Such fluency does not involve thinking about the process. Learning to spell, however, places demands on many areas of the brain, and the resulting messages have to be integrated and co-ordinated with the writing or transcription machinery. It is not surprising, therefore, that when children are learning to write and spell their communication sometimes becomes disrupted, disconnected and terse. If they were allowed to *tell* that same story it would be of a much higher quality in content and ideas. It is for such reasons that the word processor has become particularly valued for its redrafting and editing facilities and its use as a pairs scribing and teaching device.

Despite all the potential difficulties in learning to spell and write, there are many people who have never experienced any difficulties at all. These fortunate ones, often teachers, have learned happily and easily within their first eighteen months to two years of schooling by any method which their schools chose to use. Some children have even learned to read and write without ever seeming to have been directly taught before they arrive at school. It is often difficult for such successful learners to understand why a few children fail to learn to spell at all and a significant number of others make spelling errors even as adults.

The purpose of this book is to try to explain what causes difficulties in spelling for some people and to suggest how these can be addressed at an earlier stage than has been customary. After a brief section on the establishing of the alphabet, the history of spelling teaching will be outlined. In each approach described there will be found to be some information relevant to an eclectic approach to teaching spelling.

THE ORIGINS OF THE ALPHABET

Many writing systems have evolved throughout history. They have included hieroglyphs – sacred characters used in ancient Egyptian picture writing and picture writing in general; logographs – the use of single signs or symbols to represent words; syllabaries – a set of characters representing syllables; rebus – an enigmatic representation of a word or part of a word by pictures to give clues to its meaning; and the alphabetic system. It is maintained that the alphabet was only ever invented once (Diringer, 1962; Gelb, 1963), whereas the other systems have appeared in original forms in many cultures. The Phoenician traders were believed to have invented the first alphabet writing system (Gelb, 1963) in about the seventh century BC and perfected it for their commercial needs as a maritime trading nation. The Greeks are thought to have experimented with its use and added vowel symbols to adapt it to their Indo-European language, and by the fourth century BC a common Hellenic alphabet and language had been constructed. The Romans appeared to have acquired this alphabet from the Greeks (Delpire and Monory, 1962) and disseminated its 23 letters throughout their empire. The mediaeval Christians then added the definitive distinction between 'i' and 'j' and 'u' and 'v'. What is of interest and significance was that the alphabet was only invented once, presumably by some stroke of innovative genius. A second important feature in its development was that it was invented in the context of a consonantal (Semitic) language. The Phoenicians developed signs, based upon shapes of common objects, such as whips and horses' heads (Jarman, 1979), to fit the 22 sounds of their consonantal language. These consonants did not correspond to those of Greek, and Greek cannot be expressed without written vowels. Hence the principle was taken and the alphabet adapted to fit the new language. If the alphabet were to be invented today in English it would have to consist of a set of symbols which would represent the 44 sounds which make up all the words in this language. Pitman accomplished this in 1961 with his initial teaching alphabet (i.t.a.).

The significance of the alphabetic principle in spelling and reading difficulties will become apparent in later chapters especially in relation to the problem often referred to as 'dyslexia'.

METHODS OF TEACHING SPELLING

Alphabetic systems and the ABC method

In earlier centuries the traditional way to learn to read and spell was by an alphabetic method in which children had to master the criss-cross row or hornbook. This was a sheet of paper mounted on a board and covered with a thin layer of horn. There was a cross in the top lefthand corner and the alphabet was written in Roman letters, or 'black letter' (a mediaeval gothic form; see Figures 1.1 and 1.2), and italic. The alphabet was learned by the child pointing to each letter in turn and then naming it. Sounds were not introduced at this stage. Learning the alphabet was followed by learning the sounds of vowels and the punctuation marks. Knowing the sounds of the vowels helped the pupil in the next stage, which was to master the 'syllabarium'. The syllables were taught by first naming the letters, thus: *ay, bee, ab-ee, bee-eb* (Chalmers, 1976).

In rote order the pupils spelled the syllabarium through forwards and backwards, down, up and across until each meaningless syllable was fully memorized. A teacher could leave a monitor to hear groups and classes of fifty or more chanting the hours away. Most teaching then consisted of rote memorizing vast quantities of poetry, prose and the scriptures: a stultifying experience for any pupil and particularly so for the able learner. Failure to memorize could and frequently did bring about severe punishments.

Figure 1.1 *An example of black letter or Gothic*

minimum

Black letter is difficult to read and dots on 'i's were added to help overcome this problem.

Figure 1.2 *A problem with black letter*

More from the syllabarium:

ab eb ib ob ub
ba be bi bo bu
ca ce ci co cu
(and of course 'fah fee fi fo fum' was derived from this)

The last item in the hornbook was the Lord's prayer, which was spelled out word by word and read aloud. After this the pupils were 'ready' to spell out the words in the Bible. As can be envisaged, reading for meaning played little part in this system although whole-word recognition may have developed incidentally in the process. According to Diack (1965) this method remained largely unchanged from mediaeval times to the first half of the eighteenth century.

The persistence of the alphabetic method was apparently due to its suitability for learning black letter and because of the late introduction of Roman type for vernacular use (Chalmers, 1976). Although Barker's Bible had been reissued in 1612 in Roman type, 'black letter' was still to be found in cheap books well into the first half of the eighteenth century.

Although compilers of spelling books in the early eighteenth century, such as Dyche in 1707 and Dixon in 1728, used the hornbook as the basis for their books and began with the alphabet and lists of syllables to be spelled out, there was an increasing awareness of the importance of the sounds of the letters. Newer books combined simple phonic, alphabetic and syllabic methods. The books were intended for use by the parents and private tutors, for most reading teaching then took place in the home and in the Sunday schools. The Charity School Movement encouraged this trend.

At the beginning of the nineteenth century Mrs Trimmer's method and her book, *Teacher's Assistant*, was published. This still used the spelling method and rote learning but the Anglican catechism was used as the 'reading book'. The method was synthetic, involving extensive drill in the alphabet and breaking down words into syllables and letters to aid word recognition. The catechism was learned section by section using this method. Writing was only introduced when children could read competently. This is also of course quite different from today when reading and writing are introduced at the same time whether or not the children have the necessary fine motor co-ordination skills.

Although views on education had changed by the early eighteenth century, under the influence of John Locke and Jean-Jacques Rousseau, schoolbooks only began to reflect this change half a century later. The first signs appeared in the change of content to include children's stories and nursery rhymes to help teach children the alphabet. From 1770 hornbooks, which had often been used as bats, were superseded by 'battledores'. These were small three-leaved cards, costing about a penny, which could be folded into an oblong with a flap left over to form a handle. Battledores contained alphabets, numerals, easy reading lessons and woodcuts. Later nineteenth-century books not only contained these items but also included an extended syllable approach: sounds and simple rules governing syllable division and syllable and word structure. The more popular of these books were widely used and reprinted several hundred times.

Figure 1.3 *An example of the copperplate form*

The introduction of phonics methods

The ABC spelling method of teaching reading, which had dominated since educational records were first kept, began to give way during the late nineteenth century to a phonics and a rule-based method. However, even into the early twentieth century, alphabetic methods were still lingering in many country schools and extensive periods of the school day were spent in rote memorizing activities (Barnard, 1961). This form of education was associated with the teaching of copperplate handwriting (see Figure 1.3), and late nineteenth-century copy books for this abound (Jarman, 1979). The handwriting was so called because it derived from the script used by those etching into copper blocks. It was essential that the flow of the writing should be continuous and so a very precise and elaborate hand was produced.

Copy writing books also became a prime source of early reading material. The fundamental feature of the phonics approach was that the *sounds* of the letters singly and in combination became the overriding targets for children's learning. Alphabet learning took second place and, eventually, in more modern times it was often banned from the programmes. When it did appear it was introduced as capital letters for starting sentences. Even when the phonics approach became well developed in the twentieth century it was still linked to extensive rote learning and handwriting practice. In the early part of the twentieth century the pupils learned a modified form of cursive, joined writing, called 'civil service hand' (Jarman, 1979), which had fewer loops and curls and was thought to be easier for beginners. Characteristically the sounds of the lower-case (small) letters were introduced in alphabetical order but from the 1960s onwards it became common practice to introduce them in groups which it was believed had similar writing patters: *a c o e s*. However, the visual similarity was misleading and the shapes were not equally easy to make in handwriting. Under this scheme children who had not been taught the alphabet did not gain a sense of alphabetical order, which then needed to be separately learned.

When the sounds of the letters had been learnt they were used in a simple way to decipher text. A popular item was:

'The' c-a-t 'cat' s-a-t 'sat' o-n 'on' 'the' m-a-t 'mat'.

A very popular phonics-based scheme, using stories and fables, and including teaching notes and letter and blend cards which could be assembled to construct words, was introduced in 1929 by Fassett. This graded scheme, consisting of the New Beacons

Readers, was published by Ginn and could be found in schools throughout the country well into the 1950s.

Putting the sounds together to blend words – phonic synthesis – was somewhat restrictive for there are a limited number of words which can be treated in this way. It gave rise to the development of rather bizarre story lines such as: 'The pig with a wig did a jig in the bog'. It could take about six months of this phonics synthesis to teach the rudiments of spelling and reading sufficient to tackle more interesting text, and by then some children's motivation and interest might have waned. Able children with quick memories would not need the repetitive practice and could quickly become bored. The very slowest to learn stayed in the class with the beginners, repeating their lessons until they had sufficient skills to be moved up into 'Standard 2'.

The current pressure for a 'return to basics' and a 'back to phonics' approach must not be allowed to go this far back! Purely phonics methods ignore the true speed of eye and brain, which enable us simultaneously to 'spell by ear' and 'read by eye', using phonic knowledge to help us guess words from context, and building up whole-word memories as well as part-word knowledge.

The introduction of 'Look and Say'

From the 1950s, however, a revolution in literacy teaching began and a method called 'Look and Say' was introduced from the USA, where it had emerged in the 1920s. It was a graded scheme of reading books, exemplified by the *Janet and John* series, in which children learned a basic sight vocabulary by looking at words on cards and saying them aloud. After ten such sightings and sayings it was expected that most would be able to commit a whole word to memory and then be able to read it when they met it in the story line. This 'meaning emphasis' method quickly became widespread and replaced the phonics method in England and Wales. It was in use well into the 1980s (Grundin, 1980; Hinson and Smith, 1993). Systematic phonics teaching was almost eradicated in some reception classes and it became usual to introduce initial letter sounds after a basic vocabulary of fifty sight words had been learned. Few rules were taught, thus there was very little direct teaching to support early spelling development. The main method of cultivating this was copy writing. Yet as early as 1967 Chall's survey of teaching methods indicated that to delay the introduction of sound values in this way slowed down the acquisition of reading (and spelling) skills.

Copy methods for teaching spelling

In 1912 a simple print script, said to be suitable for infants, was introduced to a group of London teachers. This rounded unjoined 'infant print' gradually became very popular and children's stories and reading schemes were printed in it, as it was thought to be easier for little children to understand. The style became widely used. Although teaching alphabet sounds and blends had disappeared, copying whole words and sentences (now in infant unjoined print), in keeping with the meaning emphasis methods, was preserved. Rote methods of teaching spelling survived alongside whole-word, rote-learning methods for teaching reading. Even the Breakthrough to Literacy scheme introduced in the 1970s presented a list of 100 basic sight words for copying before encouraging segmentation into separate letters for word building. It was through the daily task of 'writing news' or writing 'stories' that spelling might be learnt. In reception class the child would tell the teacher his or her news, the teacher would write down a simple sentence about the event in the writing book, the child would draw a picture of it and then copy the sentence below the teacher's. Some teachers did not specifically teach the child how to make the letters but encouraged more and more careful copying over a period of time. When letters were taught these were presented in the simple unjoined script and not necessarily linked to spelling use.

Whereas once reading had been incidentally acquired through spelling and writing activities, in the twentieth century the reverse became the practice: spelling became incidentally acquired during reading and copying activities. Both methods illustrate extreme positions in literacy teaching, and were recognized as questionable, and during the 1970s 'mixed methods' gradually gained ground.

Whole-language approaches

There developed an increasing emphasis upon whole-language approaches, encouraged by the work of F. Smith (1971, 1973, 1985), whereby necessary reading and spelling skills were developed in context and in the process of reading and speaking. Learning to read was described by Smith as a psycholinguistic guessing game. Spelling, however, still tended to receive less attention than reading from teachers who had themselves most often been brought up in a 'look and say' environment and so did not always have the necessary knowledge to make appropriate interventions.

Peters and Smith (1986) reported that pupils entering secondary school unable to read were just as aware of their spelling as their reading difficulty. However, whilst there had been consistent pressure upon them to read, and they had been given support for their reading, the same kind of pressure had never been applied to their spelling. They might well have had several years of remedial 'phonics', with simple reading books and activity workbooks to help them and the teacher always there to give them the word and to correct their mistakes. Even so they had not learned to spell; nor had the remedial phonics been effective.

The constant instructions given to these pupils to 'Mind your spelling', 'Learn this word', 'Write this word out five times' and 'Use a dictionary' had been to no effect. Such pupils do not make spelling mistakes deliberately or out of laziness (Cotterell, 1974) and would use a dictionary if they knew how to spell the word in the first place. What can be observed in these individuals is *learned helplessness*. It was as a result of observing such difficulties that an analysis of spelling difficulties and their remediation began in 1979 and developed, in 1981 with Schools Council support, into the establishment of the Learning Difficulties Research Project.

Teaching and testing of spelling observed prior to the implementation of the National Curriculum

In 1983–5 cohorts of students on initial and in-service teacher education courses were placed in schools in several education authorities in inner London, northwest and southwest outer London and Surrey, and asked to record any methods of teaching and testing spelling observed over the period of a term. Although it had been popularly believed that schools were giving insufficient attention to basic skills (reading, spelling and numeracy) during the 1970s and early 1980s, the National Foundation for Educational Research (NFER) report by Barker-Lunn (1984) found to the contrary: teachers were found to be spending a high proportion of their time engaged in such pursuits and many gave regular spelling tests. (Spelling tests had been a weekly and often daily feature of the old phonics system.)

The data collected in the Learning Difficulties Research (LDR) Project showed that such spelling tests appeared to be organized on four main principles:

- By association: test words related to a topic under study.
- At random: words thought to be suitable for the age group selected at random, often made up on the spur of the moment and not selected from the 200 key words used by beginning spellers.

- By rule: words selected according to the rule they follow and thus having a similar pattern, e.g. late, fate, mate, which follow the silent 'e' rule.
- By letter patterns or letter strings: pupils are asked to learn weekly the next ten or twenty words listed in the selected spelling book, these lists being based on similar letter strings, e.g. brain, train, gain.

The first, second and fourth approaches have one feature in common: the basic method of learning is by rote. It was found that even in the rule-based method, the rule was usually rote-learned, rather than being explained until it was understood. Such a combination of rote learning and copy writing would seem to be inadequate for the purpose of achieving proficiency in spelling for the 10 per cent plus of the population identified by Tansley and Pankhurst (1981) as experiencing difficulties.

The methods of teaching spelling collected in the course of the LDR Project were:

- at first, extensive copy writing, especially in the reception class.

After this, when the pupils had learned a basic spelling vocabulary:

- some teachers taught *common letter strings*
- some teachers asked pupils to *guess the spellings, particularly the initial sound*, and would provide the correct spelling after this
- some teachers taught some *basic phonics and simple blending*
- many of the classes of children kept *personal word dictionaries* of the most common words – the ones they could spell or those they frequently used in open-ended story writing
- the *'look–cover–write–check'* system for correcting errors was becoming popular.

Once again the major underlying method observed was rote learning.

What successful readers actually do

It is of interest, when studying spelling as it is 'caught', to ask what successful readers are doing when they learn. Clay, in the early 1960s, shed light on the reading behaviour of pupils in their first year in school. In later research (Clay, 1979), she found that the behaviour of 'high progress' readers involved anticipating or predicting what can occur in meaning and language structure, searching for clues, self-correcting and forming intuitive rules that took them beyond what they already knew. She found that their reading was organized at the phrase and sentence level and their attention focused on meaning. They checked meaning cues against cues related to syntax. Also significant were punctuation and directionality, the visual impact of the print and sound-to-letter associations. With meaning as the goal, this integrated cue-searching behaviour enabled the reader to spot immediately when a mistake had been made and continue searching for an appropriate fit. This self-correction inevitably led to a greater independence in reading. The competent readers were behaving as problem solvers, using a range of cognitive strategies and skills which enabled them to gain more knowledge and skill.

Clay found that the 'low progress' readers organized their reading at the letter and word level and used a narrower range of cues. They tended to rely on remembering words by sight and their attention to letters was usually restricted to the first letter. The resulting 'fractured utterances' caused the reader to lose track of the text's message. When a mistake was made, he/she was often unaware of it and so self-correction did not occur and the pupil remained dependent on the teacher to give help to continue the reading.

Francis's (1982) research supported this picture of reading skills. She found that good beginning readers taught by the 'look and say' method nevertheless grasped the alphabetic principle and used this discovery in their word attack skills. The children of the group who later developed reading difficulties showed a tendency to become 'stuck' on the phonic strategy and tried to sound out every word they did not know. Since most of the new words could not be decoded by this strategy they quickly faltered and needed help from the teacher.

The complex combination of whole-word recognition, phonics and cognitive activities used by good readers and poor alike may not transfer to spelling. Nevertheless an approach to the teaching of reading which gives appropriate emphasis to each strategy can provide substantial opportunities for learning to spell, especially where the connections between reading and spelling are made clear. An overemphasis on copy writing and a pressure for accuracy without some direct spelling teaching can hinder or suppress the exploratory cognitive activity which would otherwise be aiding spelling development. (See Chapter 3 on developmental assessment and intervention for examples of this process.)

What successful spellers learn to do

If children relied wholly on the rote training for spelling described (pp. 11–12) it would be scarcely possible for most of them to become accomplished spellers, their main exposure being through reading and copying. The pressure for accuracy observed in many classrooms needs to be replaced by encouragement of exploration.

Creative spelling

The already mentioned work of Clay (1975, 1979, 1989), and that of Read (1975, 1986) has helped provide insight into what successful spellers are doing. These researchers have found that a child's first literate response is not to read but to write. They advocate that this natural tendency should be encouraged, starting with making marks on paper. This is the idea behind a method called 'emergent writing', 'developmental writing' or 'creative spelling', in which children are encouraged to write their messages and stories mustering any spelling skills they can. The teacher then teaches the spelling skills and strategies that will prove most useful in bringing the children's spellings closer to standard orthography. Ignoring most of the misspellings, the teacher supplies limited but helpful information on such matters as sounds not yet learnt and then gives rules if problems persist. The method needs careful explaining to parents, who usually like to see correctly spelled work. According to Read (1986), the children's 'creative spellings' may look bizarre at first but if the teacher persists with an analysis it can be seen that the spellings are based upon reasonable principles, such as: spellings represent sounds, and similar sounds may have similar spellings. Children may often be found to have a surprising amount of spelling knowledge when they enter school, which they have picked up from books, television and advertising in the street and in shops.

In addition to absorbing spelling information from the environment and from the teacher in the classroom it has become clear that the eye and brain are doing a considerable amount of additional processing work on their own. Thus children taught entirely by a 'look and say' method developed knowledge of letter sounds without ever being directly taught. Moreover, children taught by the phonics systems of earlier times learned to read and spell a much wider range of words than were presented to them in the schemes, including words which could not be sounded out phonically. There are clearly as many learning routes to spelling as to reading. An emphasis upon 'look and say' alone can hamper and slow down the learning but not actually cut it off (Chall, 1967; Francis, 1982).

An interactive approach using a judicious mixture of the best of the teaching approaches in both reading and spelling is obviously to be recommended, for this will facilitate the learning of the able and support that of the pupils with difficulties, teaching them the strategies which they have not inferred from contact with print. Using such an approach could well enable almost all children to meet the National Curriculum attainment targets for spelling at the appropriate level for their age and ability.

THEORIES OF SPELLING DEVELOPMENT

Only in recent years has the focus of research shifted from reading to spelling. It was always obvious that pupils do not suddenly move from a state of no spelling knowledge to one of complete spelling accuracy and success, but no one had tried to trace spelling progress and link it to a model, or models, of spelling development. The publication in 1980 of *Cognitive Processes in Spelling*, edited by Frith, marked a turning point. The nature of spelling, spelling development and spelling difficulties became a key area of investigation. Now there are a number of proposed theories and models, which are being refined or changed as new findings are published.

Theorizing, of course, arises within the context of a particular education system and teaching method. Research findings relating to spellers in a 'look and say' regime might not be quite the same as those relating to spellers using 'whole language' and phonics schemes. This variety in findings can lead to different emphases in hypotheses on early development.

Information-processing models

Simon and Simon (1973) proposed an information-processing model of spelling in which, once the spellings of skilled writers were phonetically accurate, a number of alternative phonemic spellings were generated and the correct one selected by comparison with partial information in visual memory.

Marsh *et al.* (1980) found, however, that very proficient spellers made heavy use of visual information and even mediocre spellers were able to use their visual information store to spell new words, and non-words, by analogy with already known words. This led these researchers to propose a series of developmental stages in spelling for the normal reader: (1) a *sequential encoding* strategy, in which a word is processed in a left to right serial order when spelling unknown words; (2) a later *hierarchical coding* strategy, based upon conditional rules, which would develop more slowly over a longer period of time, reaching a ceiling by about 5th grade (10 years). Examples of conditional rules would be the softening of 'c' before 'e', 'i' and 'y', or the effect of the silent 'e' at the end of a syllable, which lengthens the preceding vowel (makes it 'say its name') as in 'late', 'rote', etc. (3) Finally, the use of *analogy*, that is, spelling unknown words by comparing their sound with wholes and parts of already known words and selecting the most likely combination. This developmental shift towards the use of analogy strategies appeared to affect both reading and spelling between second and fifth grade (7–10 years) (Marsh *et al.*, 1977).

More recently Goswami (1992, 1994) has shown that beginning readers and spellers also use analogy strategies, or can do so if encouraged. This discovery led her to reject the notion of a stage theory and to promote a teaching strategy incorporating analogy to beginning readers. This strategy, using onsets (initial sounds) and rimes (endings of syllables, such as 'ig' in pig, fig and wig), has been called the phonological approach to teaching.

Developmental stage models

The theories outlined above identify information processing strategies which are available or could be made available to both beginning and proficient spellers. A somewhat different approach has been developed by Frith (1982). She identified different stages at which spellers arrive as they accumulate spelling information and skill. These could be indicative of the invariant mental structures which Gibson and Levin (1975) proposed were built from contact with print. Her theory thus reflects the products of learning as well as the processes. Initially Frith's model was three-stage:

1. *Logographic stage*: an instant recognition of familiar words. A range of graphic features may act as cues in this process. Letter order is generally ignored and phonological considerations are secondary – the pupils pronounce the words *after* they have recognized them. They usually refuse to respond if they do not recognize the word.
2. *Alphabetic stage*: letter order and phonological considerations now play a crucial role. Pupils begin to use a systematic approach, decoding grapheme by grapheme. They may use these strategies to pronounce new and nonsense words, although they may not do this correctly.
3. *Orthographic stage*: the instant apprehension of words as orthographic units, without phonological conversion. Strategies at this stage are systematic and non-visual and operate on larger than phonological units – for instance

morphemic (meaningful) units or simply letter strings. The possible variation of focus can depend on the strategy emphasized in teaching, when teaching is taking place.

In 1985 Frith redeveloped this basic framework as a six-step model (see below). She proposed that in normal development reading and spelling proceed out of step, with each of the three stages divided into two, in which either reading or spelling may be the pacemaker. In logographic reading stage 1a the skill is presented in a very basic form, at level 1b it is ready to be adopted for writing. At stage 2a in reading the strategy may continue to be logographic and only at the next step, 2b, become alphabetic, whereas writing at 2a becomes alphabetic at a simple level, continues into 2b and on into 3a before developing into the orthographic mode. Her rationale for the six-step model was that the alphabet is tailormade for spelling rather than for reading and that in acquired disorders, phonological reading is always accompanied by phonological spelling but not vice versa. In general, progress in literacy skills in normal subjects she regards as 'an alternating shift of balance between reading and spelling. Reading is the pacemaker for the logographic strategy, writing for the alphabetic strategy, and reading again for the orthographic one' (1985, p. 313). It is possible to use this framework to assess the level of a pupil's spelling development and plan further analysis and intervention.

Frith's (1985) six-step model of stages in reading and writing acquisition		
Stage	Reading	Spelling
1a	Logographic	(Symbolic)
1b	Logographic	Logographic
2a	Logographic	Alphabetic
2b	Alphabetic	Alphabetic
3a	Orthographic	Alphabetic
3b	Orthographic	Orthographic

From the six-step model Frith (1985) identified the classic developmental dyslexic's problem as a failure to proceed to the alphabetic stage, quoting Makita (1968) on the relative absence of developmental dyslexia in Japan, where the Kanji script involves logographic and syllabic but not alphabetic skills. Makita's survey of 9,195 schoolchildren had revealed an incidence of reading disabilities of any type of 0.98 per cent.

It is interesting that this proportion of about 1 per cent closely approximates the proportion of pupils who, after Clay's Reading

Recovery programme, still needed specialist help, and the 1.5 per cent of children needing remedial teaching discovered by HMI (SED, 1978) in their Scottish schools survey. These percentages compare favourably with the 4 per cent identified by Rutter *et al.* (1970) in their Isle of Wight survey, which was taken to be representative of the position in England and Wales excluding inner city areas, where Rutter *et al.* (1979) found more than 9 per cent of pupils were in need of special support.

In 1992 Makita's results would seem to have been challenged by Amano, whose research revealed a larger number of failures (often drop-outs) than had Makita's. These failures were, however, imputed to the lock-step progression through the Japanese curriculum, with extensive memorizing required at all levels and children spending many hours in the evenings and at weekends in private 'crammer' classes. In order to achieve basic literacy 2000 characters have to be learned by very young children, many of whom are failing to do this at the pace expected of them. In addition they are also expected later to transfer to Kana, which is a more alphabetically based script. However, failure to learn because of an inappropriate education system cannot be equated with failure that is due to a problem in development of literacy skills.

To return to Frith's six-step model. This does help explain how one can come across a beginner who reads logographically but spells alphabetically and can write correctly some simple regular words which he or she cannot read (Bradley and Bryant, 1980). With more experienced readers, it is possible to find competent orthographic reading accompanying spelling that remains alphabetic (Frith, 1980). Frith (1985) argued that achievement of orthographic competence in reading is not in itself sufficient for attainment of this level in spelling and did indeed identify a group of subjects who were average, and even good, readers but disabled spellers (Frith, 1978). As will be seen, this is not an uncommon problem.

Frith (1985) made connections between her three-stage model and methods of teaching reading. The logographic stage she connected with the 'look and say' method, which was applied to the first stage of reading acquisition, and resulted in the acquisition of a sizeable sight vocabulary. The alphabetic stage she linked with the 'phonics' approach, noting (p. 309), in reference to Chall's 1967 survey on the subject, that 'It is generally agreed that a "phonics" stage in reading is of great importance and cannot simply be skipped'. The orthographic stage she related to the morphemic approach in 'structural reading' of Stern and Gould (1965) and to the later stages of the Gillingham–Stillman (1956) programme.

Comparable to Frith's model of developmental stages are the five levels of spelling development proposed by Gentry (below), based on an analysis of the writing of normal children, and the levels of spelling development proposed in the National Curriculum (see p. 19).

Gentry's (1981) levels of spelling development

Precommunicative: scribble writing in which children may tell a story as they scribble and draw.
Prephonetic: the creative or invented spelling stage, in which a single letter may represent a word or a group of letters, e.g. H or h for 'high'.
Phonetic: letter by letter transcriptions of sounds, e.g. 'hi'.
Transitional: the spellings look more like standard spelling influenced by origin and rules, e.g. 'hye'.
Correct: standard spelling, e.g. 'high'.

Levels of spelling attainment in the National Curriculum (DES, 1989)

Level 1
- Pupils begin to show an understanding of the difference between drawing and writing, and between numbers and letters;
- can write some letter shapes in response to sounds and letter names;
- use single letters or pairs of letters to represent whole words or parts of words.

Level 2
- Pupils produce recognizable (though not necessarily always correct) spelling of a range of common words;
- know that spelling has patterns, and begin to apply that knowledge in order to attempt the spelling of wider range of words;
- spell correctly words in regular use in their own writing which observe common patterns.

Level 3
- Pupils spell correctly less common words which are important in the learning context in which they occur (e.g. technical vocabulary in science);
- show a growing awareness of word families and their relationships;
- check their own writing for accurate spelling;
- recognize and use correctly regular patterns for vowel sounds and common letter strings of increasing complexity.

Level 4
- Pupils spell correctly words which display the other main patterns in English spelling, including the main prefixes and suffixes.

Level 5
- Pupils spell correctly words of some complexity, including words with inflectional suffixes (e.g. -ed, -ing), consonant doubling, etc; and words where the spelling highlights semantic relationships (e.g. sign, signature).

Theories and levels of spelling development compared

Frith, 1980	Gentry, 1981	National Curriculum
Logographic	Precommunicative	Level 1
	Prephonetic	Level 2
Alphabetic	Phonetic	Level 3
Orthographic	Transitional	
	Correct	Level 4/5

The levels of spelling development are not definitive but do offer guidelines from which to assess a pupil's general level when the method of introductory teaching of reading and spelling is taken into account. For example, the impact of a 'phonics only' approach will be different from a 'look and say' one, with more alphabetic knowledge evident in the writing at an early stage.

SPELLING DIFFICULTIES AND DYSLEXIA

Not all pupils with a spelling problem have difficulties severe enough to need special provision or can be referred to as dyslexic.

Origins of spelling difficulties

Children who have general learning difficulties may develop both reading and spelling difficulties which are consistent with their slower profile of development across a range of skills and abilities. However, they should not always be expected to be lower in standard and may even have good reading and copying skills. The key factor is their much poorer comprehension of what they read. An intelligence quotient is not a stable predictor of reading ability, for groups of subjects with IQs as low as 40 have been taught to read fluently. They fail, however, to comprehend what they read (similar studies are not available for spelling).

Some poor spellers and readers have been subject to poor teaching, have missed key aspects of early schooling, or have suffered from a range of different teachers or transfers from one school to another (SED, 1978). These factors have disrupted some, but not all, pupils' literacy learning and they need opportunities to catch up or to receive the teaching, if somewhat compacted, that they may have missed.

There are also a small number of pupils who have failed to read and spell by any method and who have severe difficulties, often in the presence of average or above average intellectual abilities. These pupils may have experienced very good teaching provision in reception class and Year 1. They may also have been given in-class remedial support for their reading and spelling, which has failed. They may then have been referred for specialist withdrawal provision as well as in-class support and over a five-year period may have made little or no progress.

It is such pupils who are now referred to as 'dyslexic'. Dyslexia is only one of a number of different *specific learning difficulties*. These include attention deficit hyperactivity disorder (ADHD), perceptuo-motor difficulties and clumsiness, developmental language difficulties and so on.

Developmental dyslexia

This is a severe difficulty in learning to read *and* spell. It is rare to find a dyslexic who does not have not only a severe reading difficulty but an even more severe problem with spelling. However, many books still only refer to dyslexia as a 'reading difficulty'.

Developmental dysorthographia

This is a severe difficulty in learning to spell in the absence of a similar difficulty with reading. The pupil may have learned to read very early at the age of two or three or may have had a reading difficulty which has cleared up. The major signs of this earlier difficulty will be in slow reading, particularly with the more complex texts in the sixth form and in higher education.

Dyslexic difficulties may result in the pupil's referral for special help, whereas in the case of a spelling problem alone there may be no referral even though this pupil is equally in need of help if he or she is to succeed in later academic and professional studies. Without help they will be unable to achieve recognized qualifications which are consistent with their intellectual abilities in the so-called academic areas, and their contribution to the work force will be lost.

What are often associated with a failure to help dyslexic and dysorthographic pupils are secondary emotional and behavioural difficulties (Montgomery, 1995; Edwards, 1994). In addition to these specific learning difficulties more than 30 per cent of the referrals for remedial support to a dyslexia centre were initially referred for their handwriting problems (Montgomery, 1994).

Developmental dysgraphia

This refers to developmental difficulties in handwriting where there is a motor co-ordination problem in the fine skills of penmanship. There need not be any lack of reading and spelling skills. Where handwriting difficulties are severe then the lack of success leads the child to withdraw from writing activity wherever possible, and this can result in lack of spelling practice and ultimately in spelling difficulties (Cripps, 1988). The number of children with handwriting difficulties has been assessed as from 10 to 15 per cent of the school population (Alston, 1993).

The term 'dyslexia'

The term 'dyslexia' is widely used in the research field. It is a shortened version of the term 'developmental dyslexia' which is used to refer to individuals who have an unexpected difficulty in learning to read and spell at a level in accord with their intellectual ability. It is not a popular term in education for a number of reasons, such as an aversion to medical-sounding terms, avoidance of potentially stigmatizing labels and reluctance to commit funds to remedial provision. However, dyslexics and their parents are greatly relieved to have this diagnosis given, for it helps them feel less at fault.

Definitions of dyslexia

An early definition which became widely accepted in the dyslexia field, based upon the researches of Clements (1966), was as follows:

> A disorder manifested by a difficulty in learning to read despite conventional instruction, adequate intelligence and socio-cultural opportunity. It is dependent upon fundamental cognitive disabilities which are frequently constitutional in origin.

Here can be seen the focus upon reading only and the medical notion of a disorder. More recently an expert group established to advise the British Psychological Society (1989) offered the following definition:

A specific difficulty in learning, constitutional in origin, in one or more of reading, spelling and written language, which may be accompanied by a difficulty in number work. It is particularly related to mastering and using written language (alphabetic, numerical and musical notation) although often affecting oral language to some degree.

The British Dyslexia Society (1990) offered a more fundamental definition thus:

Discrepancy in a person between his/her good understanding of conceptual ideas and the ability to express that understanding using standard verbal, numerical and perceptual symbols.

These last two definitions give a better general idea of the dyslexic's problems than the first and provide the framework and context for the final chapter in this book, which deals with the remediation of dyslexic, as opposed to ordinary, spelling problems.

Use of terminology

The term 'learning disabilities' is frequently used to refer to dyslexia in the USA. In the UK 'specific learning difficulties in reading and spelling' is often incorrectly shortened to 'specific learning difficulties' (SpLD), a term which includes many other conditions (see p. 21), or 'specific reading difficulties', which, given the nature of the problems, is plainly wrong. For brevity the term 'dyslexia' will be used in this book.

SUMMARY

This chapter has given an outline of the nature of spelling and how it has been taught over the centuries to the present. Within the context of literacy teaching the strategies that good readers and spellers develop and use were identified to show what may need to be directly taught to poorer spellers.

Theories of spelling development were discussed and matched to National Curriculum levels. The points at which errors might occur were indicated, particularly the failure of dyslexics to enter the alphabetic stage despite a large amount of 'remedial phonics' teaching.

In addition to developmental spelling errors spelling 'problems' were identified in three separate groups. These were spelling errors due to missed opportunities, spelling errors due to slowness in ability to learn standard orthography and spelling errors made by dyslexics.

When these spelling difficulties become so severe that they prevent or retard the development of knowledge and skills in the content curriculum then they become a problem. Similarly, when the messages written by poor spellers fail to communicate their intent, then this also constitutes a problem. How these errors and problems may be addressed will be discussed after the next chapter on assessment.

Assessment

INTRODUCTION

Many changes have taken place in the area of assessment since the 1981 Education Act was implemented in April 1983. Prior to that, assessment of spelling hardly figured in the formal process. Even where it was included it was as additional information secondary to reading test data and usually recorded as 'spelling age'. Some local education authorities (LEAs) screened children in the first year of schooling for indicators of learning difficulties, some screened at 7 years of age and others at 8. Many LEAs preferred to adopt a referral system in which schools would put forward the names of children about whom they were concerned to the consultant adviser and then the educational psychologist to observe and assess. Gradually it became clear that classroom observation was a necessary part of this profile, as was the teacher's report.

The results of technical assessment very often made little contribution to the teacher's understanding of how to deal with the children's difficulties. This was not surprising because programmes of training for teachers and educational psychologists did not at that stage include a detailed and up-to-date analysis of the teaching of reading and spelling, or an assessment of the relative merits of different intervention techniques. A closer relationship existed between research on behavioural approaches to learning, such as task analysis, and courses for teachers in behaviour modification theory and practice. This had potential benefit for the management of emotional and behavioural difficulties, but not much to offer on how to improve literacy teaching.

Recently progress has been achieved in spelling assessment and intervention mainly through links being made between experimental researches in psychology and in-service teacher education courses that use research findings to underpin their recommendations on teaching and remedial methods. Conferences involving contributions from experimental psychologists, teacher educators and remedial teachers have proved highly fruitful in disseminating research and having it field tested.

With the implementation of the 1981 Act there was a requirement on all LEAs and schools to develop both informal and formal procedures for assessment leading to statementing. The procedure was based upon the recommendations in the Warnock Report (1978), which laid down that a statement of special educational need should have five sections in which there would be a report from the school, specialist reports from the educational psychologist and speech therapist, if relevant, medical reports and social services reports and finally a contribution from the parents. The final document had a summary statement written by an official of the LEA defining the pupil's special educational need(s) and the provision which would be offered to meet it or them. Drawing up such a statement could take a great deal of time. Whereas some LEAs managed the procedure in eighteen months others were taking an average of up to three years. As some LEAs also laid down that no child should be referred for statementing before the age of eight, and then many of these pupils had to wait for three years for a statement, they could have suffered with spelling difficulties for five years before anything was done to help them. By this stage they had missed an extensive amount of learning through reading and writing and many were found to have developed 'challenging behaviour' or emotional and behavioural difficulties (Edwards, 1994; Montgomery, 1995; Boland, 1995).

As funding was not associated with the implementation of the 1981 Act the additional administration costs had to be absorbed at local level; this is still the case. Some small education authorities had not appointed advisers for special educational needs to guide the policies and co-ordinate responses and then were required to do so, incurring additional expense. According to Cox (1985), the definition of special needs given in the 1981 Act was such that LEAs could provide as little or as much assistance as they chose, which does in fact appear to have happened. A review of numbers statemented by different LEAs (Pumfrey and Reason, 1991) showed that they varied from 4 in one LEA to 400 in another. A recent survey by the Office for Standards in Education (OFSTED, 1996) found that one London borough had been able to bring its statementing period down to under six months, the average period was closer to eighteen months, and for some authorities it was twice as long.

Whole-school and LEA-wide policies are not simple to define, even in an area such as spelling. Spelling also involves writing, often extensively for long periods, in both primary and secondary schools. The policy-maker has to determine when making spelling mistakes becomes severe enough to warrant calling on additional expertise and/or resource materials. In either case a price has to be attached to the proposed provision. If the severest of spelling difficulties is seen in cases of dyslexia, it might be assumed that this, at least, would be an easy case to deal with: the diagnosis of dyslexia would entail provision. This might be so if it were agreed by all LEAs that dyslexia as a condition at all really exists. In the 1980s it was not uncommon for the word to be banned and any pupil with reading and spelling problems that might qualify for the banned description to be placed in a so-called remedial group with slow learners and others with challenging behaviour. In the past there have been some crucial attitudes and prejudices from all levels of administration and professional life which have had a detrimental effect on the life chances of these special pupils. This situation has not been helped by the range of available definitions, not all of which had validity.

DEFINITIONS WHICH HAVE AFFECTED ASSESSMENTS OF NEED IN DYSLEXIA

Definition by exclusion

A disorder manifested by a difficulty in learning to read despite conventional instruction, adequate intelligence and socio-cultural opportunity. It is dependent upon fundamental cognitive disabilities which are frequently constitutional in origin.

This definition by Clements (1966) is a prime example of definition by exclusion, and has been used over the years by educational psychologists and clinicians to guide them when referring pupils for specialist remedial help. It was Lerner (1971) who identified it as a definition by exclusion, meaning that when no neurological, pedagogical, or other such intellectual definition for the problem can be found, then it may be labelled 'dyslexia', and special tuition becomes appropriate. Since the definition itemizes those circumstances under which reading and spelling problems cannot be considered to be dyslexic rather than addressing the actual nature of dyslexia, it is difficult to conclude what type of special teaching should be provided. Not only this, but each of the exclusion categories immediately becomes a subject of debate.

Definition by statistical means: discrepancy formulae

The DES (1972) recommended that a discrepancy of 20 per cent between IQ and reading quotient (RQ) should be the guideline for referral for specialist remedial help, indicating that severe decrement in RQ in the absence of low intelligence would warrant special attention. This guideline of 20 per cent discrepancy was adopted by a number of local authorities; some stipulated that 15 points discrepancy between IQ and RQ on a screening test should warrant more detailed diagnosis, and 10+ points discrepancy should put pupils on a special register for annual review. In defining suitable research subjects, Rutter and Yule (1973) advocated that there should be a decrement between mental age and reading age of some two years four months, whilst Vellutino (1979) recommended at least two years. More recently, since decrement is a function of increasing age, it has been suggested that for children under 10 there should be a decrement of at least 18 months and for children over 10 of at least two years. Similar guidelines have been indicated by regression equation predictors (Yule, 1967).

In many early studies of 'dyslexia', the decrements selected were variable, ranging from a few months to several years but giving an overall mean of about one year or more. In cases where the discrepancy is only of a few months, it can be argued that the accuracy of the reading and intelligence tests in specifying age levels and quotients is not sufficient to justify distinguishing such subjects from normal, slightly low-scoring readers and spellers.

Miles (1993) questioned whether even large discrepancies between IQ and RQ scores were sufficient to indicate dyslexia and suggested that other indicators need to be present, for which he devised the Bangor Dyslexia Test.

Despite such variations and uncertainties, the percentage discrepancy definition is still used by educational psychologists in many local authorities to identify pupils for statementing for specialist remedial tuition. The policy adopted is that the pupil should show at least a 20 per cent decrement between intellectual ability and *reading* attainment (rarely spelling attainment, which is often worse) before any consideration be given to learning support. Additional behavioural problems usually need to exist before a statement is prepared. This means that fewer girls may be referred; other inequalities of provision may also exist. In those LEAs which did not recognize dyslexia as a distinct phenomenon, the attitude tended to be that this kind of severe reading and/or spelling difficulty was the result of general backwardness in reading, probably exacerbated by the over-anxious attention of neurotic parents: typically a 'middle-class disease'. In those authorities which did recognize 'severe literacy problems', 'severe reading retardation', and 'dyslexic-type difficulties', the tests often used were the NFER tests of verbal reasoning, Young's non-readers intelligence test, and Young's oral verbal intelligence test. One of the difficulties with these group tests is that they have a lower ceiling (top score) than individual tests. They are also less sensitive at their extreme ends, giving discrepant and unreliable scores. The problem is made particularly acute when the IQ group test given demands reading skills. This immediately handicaps poor readers who are also poor spellers, making them appear less able so that the discrepancy between reading and IQ is not suffi-ciently great to warrant referral.

Clinical definitions

By clinical it is understood that apart from generalized perfor-mance decrements noted on reading tests in relation to age and/or ability, there are characteristic patterns of difficulties or deficits in performance which may be observed at interview or on tests in pupils referred to clinicians and psychologists.

The syndrome given by clinicians and psychologists as charac-teristic of developmental dyslexia is:

- A severe retardation in reading general material and on tests (Critchley, 1970; Naidoo, 1972; Nelson and Warrington, 1974; Thomson, 1984, Snowling, 1987, Miles, 1993, amongst many others).
- Spelling which is more severely retarded than reading, observ-able in dictations, open-ended story writing and on tests (Orton, 1937; Boder, 1971; Vellutino, 1979; Pollack, 1975; Naidoo 1972; Miles and Miles, 1990).
- Directional confusions or order errors in reading, spelling and writing; similar confusions in identifying left and right in rela-tion to self and others; possibly also difficulties in reciting tables and in basic number skills, in sequencing the days of the week and months of the year (Orton, 1937; Critchley, 1970; Miles, 1983).
- Characteristically, but not invariably, a decrement in perform-ance on certain sub-tests (e.g. digit span, coding, arithmetic, and information) in standardized tests such as WISC-R (Wechsler Intelligence Scale for Children – Revised) and BAS (British Ability Scales) (Thomson, 1984).

It is thus maintained that deficits other than reading and spelling problems occur with some regularity, but that not all subjects experience all the problems or display the same pattern of deficits. There is a great deal of conflicting evidence about the different clusters of decrement on the sub-tests (Bannatyne, 1971; Nelson and Warrington, 1974; Thomson, 1984) except that they all involve reading and spelling difficulties.

Theoretical definitions of dyslexia

It is now over 100 years since the term 'dyslexia' was first coined and over 75 years since Hinshelwood (1917) defined it as 'congenital word blindness' resulting in a severe difficulty in learning to read and spell. Since that time, a series of such unitary deficit theories have been propounded: visual-perceptual (Bender, 1957); visuo-motor (Frostig and Horne, 1964); intersensory integration (Birch, 1962); sequencing difficulties (Bakker, 1972); and phonological processing problems (Vellutino, 1979). The narrow view taken within the unitary theory (e.g. Hinshelwood, 1917) specifically implicates a critical mental operation only involved in learning to read and write. The broad view proposes the implication of several cognitive processes which are essential to reading and writing but are also involved in other activities. The broader view has become predominant recently.

Many students, teachers and remedial teachers mention deficits in visual perception when questioned about dyslexia. Others emphasize a sequential processing or temporal order problem. This may have been indicated by pupils' pronunciation reversals in reading and/or letter reversals in spelling. Although such errors do occur, they are not present in significant numbers, according to Nelson and Warrington (1974), to qualify definitively as causal; they may be correlative. Sequencing deficit received experimental support when Pavlidis (1978) found random eye movements in dyslexics asked to observe a pattern of lights. He explained these results as related to an underlying deficit in sequential ordering processes permeating a wider range of activities than just reading and spelling – the broad unitary theory approach. Subsequent researches by Rayner (1986), however, showed that research on eye movements and perceptual span identified only a small subgroup of dyslexics with perceptual-spatial difficulties. A much larger group of dyslexics, who had what were called 'language deficits', did not show random eye movements except as normal readers do when text becomes too difficult. He suggested that Pavlidis was dealing with a particularly select sample and because of his special interest was having such cases referred to him. This kind of

sampling and methodological problem has frequently characterized research on dyslexia.

The group which Rayner identified with perceptuo-spatial difficulties showed symptoms of minimal neurological dysfunction
which would place them according to Clements (1966) outside the
defined dyslexic group and make them part of a much wider
group with learning disabilities.

Subtypes in dyslexia

Kinsbourne and Warrington (1963) first offered evidence for
subtypes of dyslexia, which had previously been considered to be
a unitary disorder. They demonstrated two different neuropsychological syndromes in children referred for retardation in reading.
One group showed relatively inferior skills on the verbal, as
opposed to the performance, scale of WISC. These pupils were
usually male and found to have been slow to develop language.
They showed subtle impairment of verbal comprehension and
their spelling errors predominantly showed choice of the wrong
letters, lacking even phonetic correspondence to the sounds in the
words. The other group showed no such signs of language disorder but showed a performance deficit on WISC, especially in the
block design and object assembly subtests. They also showed
arithmetical difficulties and had more difficulty in spelling than
reading, making order errors and reversals in each. Failure on tests
of finger order sense suggested a sequential processing problem
(analogous to the Gerstmann syndrome). Pirozzolo (1979) also
found that such subjects had difficulty in left to right sequential
eye movements and with the return sweep to the line underneath.
Kinsbourne and Warrington (1963), however, were indicating
clear-cut extremes and did not claim to be able to subdivide the
large middle group of backward readers (spellers) into either one
of these two subtypes.

Boder (1971), on the basis of reading and spelling tests, identified two subtypes of dyslexia, which she classified as dysphonetic
and dyseidetic. Dysphonetic referred to those who could not apply
phonic knowledge or applied it wrongly and dyseidetic referred to
those who applied phonic knowledge appropriately but lacked
whole-word pattern knowledge or 'visual identification' skills.
The dysphonetic group was a much larger one, making up over
60 per cent of the whole, and was comparable to the language-
disordered subtype of Kinsbourne and Warrington. The dyseidetic
group was much smaller (15 per cent) and similar in characteristics
to groups identified by Myklebust (1965) as having visual versus

auditory weaknesses. It is possible that we can see here a developmental continuum between dysphonetics and dyseidetics, with the former being the most severely affected.

Frith (1985) identified a separate subgroup, i.e. apart from those with severe reading *and* spelling retardation: those who have a *spelling only* problem in the presence of average or even good reading skills. This has substantiated the views of remediators who argued in favour of special tuition for those with spelling problems alone, but were not able to demonstrate that such a target group existed.

Definition by classroom observation and on-task analysis of literacy skills

There is now strong pressure amongst teachers and remediators who have some expertise in the teaching of language and literacy to abandon the foregoing systems of definition and regard the child's performance on the reading (and spelling) task as giving the clearest indication of progress and the definition of need. Since the implementation of the 1981 Act there has been pressure within the education field to move from a diagnostic remedial model, which is regarded as medical in origin, towards an ecological model of special need (Mittler, 1990). This ecological model stresses the interactive nature of the origin of many special needs and the fact that the child does not 'own the problem', i.e. many difficulties are the result of a complex constellation of problems not always of the child's making. Under the influence of this view the roles of adults, school, pedagogy and curriculum in the special needs career of the individual were closely re-examined. Proponents of this approach advocated careful classroom and on-task analysis of pupils' skills and abilities. Teaching could then be developmental or remedial according to individual need. The teaching thus needed to take place in the setting in which the difficulties were observed (i.e. children would not be withdrawn), which introduced many training implications.

Classroom observation exemplified: Reading Recovery Programme

In the area of reading and writing these approaches were well illustrated and documented by Clay (1972, 1979, 1989) in New Zealand with the Reading Recovery Programme (1972, 1979), which aimed to identify reading difficulties early (before children reached age 6) and provide early remediation.

The Reading Recovery Programme involved first of all the early detection of reading difficulties by means of a diagnostic survey, which could be undertaken by a teacher. After that the teacher was advised to:

- Observe precisely what the pupils are doing and saying in the classroom, in everyday classroom activities or classroom-type activities.
- Observe what the pupils have been able to learn, not what they have not learnt.
- Find out what reading behaviours they now need to be taught by analysing their performance whilst reading (not on pictures and puzzles or from reading test scores). In other words, hear them read and analyse this. (I would add: observe them writing and spelling and analyse this.)
- Shift the reading behaviour from less to more adequate by training them on reading tasks (not on visual perception or auditory discrimination). (To this I would add: shift the spelling behaviour by training them on spelling tasks.)

If after the diagnostic survey and recommended measures there are some pupils who by their sixth birthday are not making good reading progress, these pupils should be given special attention and support.

The survey aimed to identify pupils with both mild and hardcore problems. The results of the survey were used to develop remedial programmes for those pupils who needed further support for reading. There remained 1 per cent of pupils who did not respond to Reading Recovery methods even after the support. Yet fifteen years after the introduction of Reading Recovery, the New Zealand government are still concerned by the lack of literacy of a significant number of their young adults (Ridehalgh, 1995).

In 1991 the British government funded a series of pilot studies whereby LEAs set up schemes and offered training in Reading Recovery methods. Evaluation of the schemes (Dombey, 1994; Wright and Prance, 1993) has shown variable results, for the evaluation methodology used was insecure and in the end there was no firm evidence that the results obtained could not have been gained if regular individual tuition had been offered on such a scale, using any number of different programmes.

The paradigm shift

Recent research has shown that the underlying difficulty in the vast majority of cases of dyslexia is a verbal processing deficit, in particular a phonological processing problem in which the dyslexic has difficulty in establishing and using any form of verbal code. These underlie our use of the alphabet system, arithmetical calculations, musical notation, recall of digits and so on (Liberman, 1973; Golinkoff, 1978; Vellutino, 1979, 1987; Frith, 1980; Snowling, 1985; Bradley and Bryant, 1985; Goswami and Bryant, 1990; Brown and Ellis, 1994). The turning point was the publication by Vellutino in 1979 of the book *Dyslexia: Theory and Research*, in which he reviewed all the existing theories and appraised their background research. In this book can be seen, after more than one hundred years, a paradigm shift in the research field from regarding dyslexia as a visual perceptual problem to a verbal processing one. Although specialist remedial programmes such as that of Gillingham *et al.* (1940) and Gillingham and Stillman (1956) had actually reflected this paradigm it had not been part of the programmes' supporting theory. This shift has only now permeated the remedial/support for learning field. Thus there is a growing awareness of necessary phonological skills and these are being built into current programmes.

The ACID profile

This merely refers to the four subtests on, in particular, the WISC-R test, at which dyslexics usually, but not always, do poorly: arithmetic, coding, information and digit span. Underlying each of these subtests is a need for verbal processing or use of verbal codes in recall, at which dyslexics are poor because of their proposed disability. In fact there are many IQ tests that also require proficiency in verbal processing etc. and so any IQ score which includes results of such tests is likely to be an underestimate of the real position. When there is a discrepancy of more than 15 to 20 points between performance and verbal quotients it is regarded as an indication of neurological difficulties which depress the scores on one or other of the hemisphere activities.

The Code of Practice (DfEE, 1994)

This code formalized a staged model of assessment which schools were to adopt by September 1994. By that time all schools were to have drawn up a special educational needs policy. The role of governors was made more significant, especially the role of the governor responsible for special needs. The Code stated that schools were free to develop their own policies in the light of their duties and functions with regard to pupils with special needs. Under the Code there was a statutory duty that all pupils with a special need must be placed in one of five stages defined in the assessment process and individual education plans (IEPs) must be written for them at Stage Two.

> **The stages of assessment of special educational need, as required by the Code of Practice (DfEE, 1994)**
>
> **Stage One**: Class or subject teachers identify or register a child's SEN and, consulting the SENCO, take the initial action.
> **Stage Two**: School SENCO takes lead responsibility for gathering information and for co-ordinating the child's special educational provision.
> **Stage Three**: Teachers and SENCO are supported by specialists from outside the school.
> **Stage Four**: LEA considers the need for a statutory assessment and, if appropriate, makes a multi-disciplinary assessment.
> **Stage Five**: LEA considers the need for a statement of special educational need and, if appropriate, makes a statement and arranges, monitors and reviews provision.

At all stages the parents must be consulted about their child. The special needs co-ordinator (SENCO) and the governor responsible for oversight of special needs must be named. Every school must have an SEN policy statement and supporting documents, linked to the school development plan. Between February 1994, when the draft code was introduced, and September 1994, when it was formally introduced, a large amount of work had to be done, mainly by the SENCO who, in small primary schools, might also have a curriculum leadership role and a full teaching load. Documents had to be evolved with colleagues, committed to formal statements, staff training had to be undertaken and all the children with identified special needs had to be placed at one of the five stages, and an individual IEP drawn up. A vast amount of paper work was involved. The SENCOs and other special needs staff were also committed to interviewing every child with special needs, and their parents, on a termly basis. Although those who wrote the Code of Practice did so with the best of intentions the practical results included not only teacher stress and overwork, but the removal of the SENCO's expertise from the pupils who most needed it, for SENCOs became administrators. Even after the initial problems of documentation development have been resolved, there will still be a heavy administrative burden, especially in schools where there are large numbers of pupils with special needs. These schools are likely to be in the less well-resourced and more disadvantaged areas. The co-ordinator will be kept busy writing IEPs, preparing reports for governors, collating the returns on each pupil from a range of staff, resulting in perhaps 100 pieces of paper on one individual flying to and fro. Already the results of this have begun to show in failures to resource the pupils with appropriate learning materials, failures to implement the recommendations in the IEPs, or in SENCOs and their assistants teaching during the day and doing administration at night and weekends. In the SEN field there are many dedicated teachers who are risking their own health to support an overstretched system. These insights into the current working of the system are based on the self-reports of over 100 SENCOs and teachers of pupils with special educational needs in a wide range of schools and LEAs.

It is also noticeable that in a climate of contract funding, in which statements must specify necessary resources and hours of specialist tuition, particularly for spelling and reading, the statements are growing more and more non-specific. There is a reluctance to refer children until as late as possible for specialist help and a reluctance to refer children with complex and specific learning difficulties to special, usually independent, dyslexia schools.

Boland (1995) found that in 11 out of 12 cases, independent educational psychologists recommended special school placement for dyslexic pupils who, a few months earlier, had not been recommended for this by educational psychologists employed by the LEA. The twelfth case did not need a referral. We have to ask whether parents who cannot afford to have a private assessment and special schooling can get fair treatment and appropriate educational provision for their children's needs.

Even when an IEP has been drawn up and 'specialist' teaching implemented what is observed is not always that 'special'. It can often be more of the same at which the pupil has already twice failed. It may bring about a modest improvement in literacy skills which do not transfer back in the ordinary classroom. It may bring about improvement in the behaviour and social skills of the pupil and give the class or subject teacher a rest. Very careful monitoring of progress needs to be undertaken and even then it may be found that the progress in reading or spelling age and written work is more imagined than real. This is particularly true of general remedial programmes applied to specific dyslexic problems (Ridehalgh, 1996). A study of some results from such programmes will be discussed in the final chapter.

Writing IEPs may in itself be an inappropriate approach in a fair number of cases, for it can be the teacher's teaching methods which are placing the pupils at risk (Montgomery, 1990, 1996).

Here in-service training for groups of staff may be the real answer. An IEP once again locates the problem 'within the child', a model which the SEN world sought to leave behind in the 1980s.

The staged model of SEN assessment in the Code of Practice

The staged model of assessment recommended in the Code is an assessment through teaching model:

TEACH – EVALUATE – PLAN – TEACH – TEST

This type of practice is part of a teacher's normal process of curriculum planning and teaching at the micro level. The classroom teacher observes the pupil on task. If there are problems seen in comparison with peers and in relation to the achievement of National Curriculum targets which ordinary interventions and support do not clear up then the SENCO will be consulted. Tests and diagnostic activities will then be used to help identify the barriers to learning and to plan intervention procedures. These are then evaluated further and a cycle of planning, teaching and evaluation is entered into which might result in calling in the help of specialists and drawing up a statement of special needs. An example follows which shows the process for a pupil with spelling and handwriting difficulties up to Stages Four and Five, the implementation of the statementing procedures.

Example of a special needs assessment for a pupil at primary school under the Code of Practice

PRELIMINARY

* Pupil has difficulty accessing some areas of the curriculum.
* Has spelling and handwriting difficulties.
* Often becomes irritable and frustrated with own efforts.

* Class teacher is becoming concerned at lack of progress in written work.
* Previous records show similar difficulties but, as reading was adequate for age, no special concern was expressed.
* Class teacher checks knowledge of initial sounds, alphabet and basic phonics. Devotes a few minutes each day to X individually to teach/reinforce basic phonics.

STAGE ONE

* Pupil continues to have difficulty with curriculum areas.
* Pupil fails to progress in spelling.
* Often seeks attention.
* Clowns about and chatters continuously; avoids written work if possible.

* The parents are consulted.
* The class teacher discusses the pupil's needs with the SENCO.
* Extra attention is given to spelling and writing, using the Spelling Made Easy scheme in consultation with SENCO.
* Daniels and Diack spelling and reading tests are given at outset so that progress can be monitored.

STAGE TWO

* Despite extra help the pupil still has the difficulties referred to in Stage One.
* Pupil needs some specialist teaching.

* The pupil has been carefully monitored.
* The parents have been informed.
* An individual education plan (IEP) is drawn up by SENCO.
* Two hours in-class support for learning is provided by school.

STAGE THREE

* Despite the interventions the pupil's difficulties continue.
* Little progress appears to have been made: spelling age has augmented one month in twelve.
* Challenging behaviour is now evident in a range of curriculum areas.
* Pupil requires specialist SpLD tuition.

* Pupil needs specialist help.
* The parents have been consulted.
* Central SEN support services have been consulted.
* An IEP has been drawn up with the advice of the support service.
* The school will fund one hour of specialist tuition from the support service and give two hours of in-class support with spelling and help with behaviour management.

A multisensory spelling, reading and handwriting teaching programme is introduced which teaches remedial cursive. One hour's specialist withdrawal support for this is arranged in the company of no more than one other child, using the TRTS or Hickey programme.

STAGE FOUR/FIVE	
* Despite the specialist help with spelling and follow-up support, progress has been slow; five months in twelve. * Pupil will find it difficult to cope with secondary school curriculum as yet. * Challenging behaviour still present but improving.	* The parents are consulted. * The educational psychology services are consulted. * A statement of special educational need may need to be drawn up to ensure continuity of provision. * Pupil needs two to three hours of specialist remedial tuition programme per week.

What is evident from the quoted assessment is that the severity of the child's problems was not acknowledged soon enough. The specialist programme plus the handwriting training should have been introduced at the outset, as soon as Stage One was reached. This might well have meant that Stage Three, or even Two, would never have been reached. As the child goes through the years there is a diminishing amount of time devoted specifically to reading and writing, as they become practised through the medium of other subjects in the curriculum. The need for early intervention in literacy areas, while it is still possible to devote time in the school day to practice in reading and writing, is pressing.

As far as one can see, the handwriting difficulty was not addressed until far too late. Spelling was supported by giving extra attention and worksheets during other lesson time at Stage One. Probably the least effective method of 'teaching' is the use of worksheets. Even after they have been completed children with difficulties can seldom remember what they were about and, if they do, it lasts with them only a short time.

At Stage Two we see that the pupil has probably had more of the same with a mentor on hand to give the correct spellings if needed and help to fill in and improve concentration upon the work sheets.

At Stage Three we might infer that a small concession to withdrawal has been made and the pupil is given one hour of tuition and two of support. It would have been wiser to invest at this point in two hours of specialist tuition and half an hour of liaison with the class teacher to enable him or her to reinforce the programme in the classroom.

If there is no continuity of provision we can predict that after a few months in the secondary school the behaviour and literacy skills of this pupil will have deteriorated to such an extent that a whole cavalcade of expensive specialists will need to expend their energies drawing up reports, giving batteries of tests, and holding case conferences to address what has become an almost intractable problem for the mainstream school. Because the pupil, though of average ability, is becoming disturbed and unmanageable he or she may finish up in the LEA special school for pupils with moderate learning difficulties, or in a unit for behaviourally disturbed adolescents, bound for a career in deviance.

All of this will be at a huge cost to the LEA, and then to society at large when an angry and disillusioned young person is let loose from the 'education' system. These are not idle words but based upon observation of many such unhappy and unfortunate young people and their careers in schools. Supporting evidence can be found, for example, in Edwards (1994) and Boland (1995).

HOW TEACHERS CAN ASSESS PUPILS' SPELLING DIFFICULTIES

As a result of Clay's work (see pp. 32–3) and developments within the field in this country the *informal reading inventory* became a popular diagnostic approach. Over the intervening period and despite the implementation of the National Curriculum and its assessments tasks in reading for 7- and 11-year-olds, the view put forward by Clay (1989) still holds support. This recommends observation of the pupil *on the reading task* as the best means of finding out skills and abilities and next learning needs, with normative tests being regarded as only an indirect method of assessing individual learners' needs. This observational approach to reading also needs to be adopted in relation to spelling. Pupils' spelling on classroom tasks, as well as in tests, should be used to analyse their difficulties and define their learning needs.

Clay (1989) has maintained, despite her training as a pyschometrist, that tests of intellectual abilities have marginal value in understanding and helping pupils with reading difficulties. The psychological test and its significance was accorded greater significance in the past than is now the case. However, teachers still expect such tests to be given – even though the results may tell them no more than what they already know. There is, of course, a vested interest by professional psychologists in retaining a testing role in the multi-million pound industry of special needs and such tests may provide supporting evidence in the legal cases (growing in number) in which provision offered is being disputed.

There is nonetheless a role for testing of intellectual ability:

checking the ability level of a pupil who is failing to learn to write can be helpful in determining the type of support which it might be appropriate to offer. For example, a highly able non-speller could profit more from a rapid and condensed programme of intervention than a less able pupil with general learning difficulties. The slower learners will have global difficulties in memory, language and thinking (Montgomery, 1990) which will influence the type and amount of provision which they can use. For more able learners a concentrated, short-term remedial intervention to bring them up to cohort or year level would be appropriate whereas less able learners would need a programme of support built into their whole school programme, i.e. a *developmental approach* rather than a *support for learning* one.

Proposed assessment strategies

When assessing spelling and spelling development it is essential to build up a profile of the pupil's development by sampling a range of spelling activities at regular points, for example open-ended writing and scribble, spelling to dictation, spelling from the pupil's own reading book, or a standardized diagnostic or age-graded test. Standardized tests should not be repeated within six months and different forms can be used, to avoid a practice effect.

An outline of a general assessment strategy for six-year-olds and upwards follows. A special format is recommended for obtaining samples from five-year-olds, who are often unaware that they can spell or are resistant to trying in case they make a mistake. Fear of making errors may also inhibit the open-ended writing of older pupils, who need to be encouraged to spell using any skills they can muster.

For contextual reference, record:

Reading ability and reading progress, using:
• a word recognition test (e.g. Schonell)
• a sentence- or prose-reading test (e.g. Salford, Macmillan)
• a reading comprehension test (e.g. Neale (revised), Macmillan)
• a miscues analysis of progress on current reading book
Pupil's handwriting profile-fluency (see style – print or cursive)
• accuracy of letter formation
• pencil/pen hold
• sample of writing, as in the open-ended writing for spelling
• example of copy writing
Evidence of emotional or behavioural difficulties
Note frequency and circumstances, e.g. as soon as writing tasks are presented.

Some children enter school with a range of spelling skills and spelling knowledge. Some of the them have no knowledge but quickly begin to develop it as they come into systematic contact with the environment of written words. Once the children have settled in to their new environment it is important for the teacher to find what spelling knowledge they possess so that those who fail to acquire any can quickly be identified as 'at risk' and given extra help through some direct teaching.

Testing spelling at 5 years old

The sort of spelling knowledge which children have acquired can be recorded in a very easy way and that is to ask them to settle down, a group at a time, and think of a message or a story they would like to tell. Give them paper and pencils and then ask them to 'write', i.e. make signs on the paper which will tell their story. The title is 'My First Story'. Do not give them any spelling support but do sit with the group and watch how they hold their pencils, place their paper and approach the task.

Anyone who cannot think of a message can be helped to construct one. Explain that each one is going to be kept and every now and then new stories will be put in the book. Pictures can be drawn afterwards and stuck in once the message/story has been written. No one is to mind about spelling – it must come from inside their own heads so that later they can look back and see how much they have learned.

The work produced on such an occasion should be kept in individual folders and added to once a month. Alternatively the children might have a special story book of their own in which they write. This should be kept separate from copy work or supported writing. Each new story should have their name written by them without help on the page somewhere so that progress in its form and shape can be observed. Within the same week as the story is constructed the teacher or one of the classroom assistants trained for the purpose should check the following:

- ability to name or give the sounds of any letters of the alphabet;
- ability to clap to the rhythm or syllable beats in own and others' names and in longer words;
- ability to appreciate rime (not rhyme necessarily), e.g. given the word 'dog' be able after the onset 'd' to give the rime 'og'; 'f'-'og' and then 'fog', etc.

Bradley and Bryant (1985) found the ability to appreciate onset and rime was a good predictor of the development of good literacy skills. In studies by Golinkoff (1978) and Montgomery (1990) the ability to sound or name letters of the alphabet presented randomly was an indicator of the potential for good spelling development. Randomized letters of the alphabet for presentation are to be found, for example, in the Aston Index though they are not recommended for test use by the authors, Newton and Thomson (1976), until the 7-year-old level! Yet good readers and spellers develop this knowledge in the pre-school and early stages of reception class learning, even when they are not directly taught. Children who do not demonstrate a smattering of such alphabetic knowledge are seriously at risk from future reading and spelling failure (Montgomery, 1990, 1994). The researches of a range of experimental psychologists, such as Liberman and Shankweiler (1972), Frith (1985) and Snowling (1987), confirm the inability of 'dyslexics' to acquire alphabetic knowledge. Poor spellers will show very slow progress in the acquisition of alphabetic knowledge whereas 'dyslexics' appear to have a '*disability*' in the acquisition of such material and will need special strategies for them to get over this barrier.

Studies in the Learning Difficulties Project have shown that direct teaching strategies such as those described in Chapters 3 and 8 can protect children from this very early learning failure. If this can be achieved in the first six months of schooling, the 'dyslexic' condition will be moderated considerably and in some children will not develop. What is of the essence is to begin the intervention programme at the earliest age with those who need it, *not all* the class.

This is not a plea for a return to phonics teaching but for the incorporation of the teaching of initial letter sounds and names at the earliest stage. Many teachers have already found the benefit of this and use Letterland (Wendon, 1984), based on the original pictogram system, to do it. The Letterland approach is helpful, for the peculiarities of the 26 letters of the alphabet are not so great as to be easily memorable and the link between symbols and their sounds is so arbitrary as to be distinctly *un*memorable, particularly to those children with learning difficulties – unless they have very good visual memories. In this case any such spelling problems may only emerge at about 8 years of age (Year 3), when the vocabulary the children are exposed to and need to use becomes suddenly much wider in range than it was at the infant stage.

If difficulties are found in learning letter sounds ... Dos and Don'ts

- *Do* start with one letter, the first letter of the child's forename.
- *Do* teach spelling – saying and writing the letter until it can always be picked out in a word and written and used to start new words.
- *Do* then teach the next letter which will make up a meaningful sound or word, e.g. *at, to, up, ib, sa.*

- *Don't* give repeated sessions of teaching and drill.
- *Don't* start from the beginning of the alphabet and work through.
- *Don't* teach all the vowels in a group first.
- *Don't* teach all the letters in a visually 'similar' group: *c a o d.*
(These methods all cause confusion.)

Severe hearing loss as a factor in learning difficulties

Severe hearing loss can create secondary literacy difficulties. The panel below indicates aspects of performance to look out for when trying to assess whether a child has this disability.

- A pattern of immaturity across a wide range of language skills can be observed.
- Vowel sounds may be distorted.
- Consonants and word endings may be omitted.
- Speech rhythms may be slow and laboured.
- Breath control may be poor.
- Words are acquired more slowly.
- Syntax appears more slowly although it appears to follow the normal patterns.
- By school age some children with severe hearing impairment have the sentence structure of a hearing two-year-old (Gregory, 1988).
- Metaphoric language is not understood until much later than normal, e.g. 'What is the time?' will be understood, but 'Have a good time' may confuse.
- Simple active declarative sentences will be understood whereas complex sentence structure, for example using the passive tense, may not. In a sentence such as 'Jan hit the dog' the syntax (subject, verb, object) is easy to follow, whereas 'The dog was hit by Jan' can easily be misunderstood.

Children with normal hearing bring to reading a knowledge of a wide range of vocabulary and complex sentence structure. Deaf children at 5 or 6 years of age may have the language skills of a

2-year-old and will be at a significant disadvantage when beginning to read. The likelihood is that they will not only have to learn the written symbols of print but also the meaning of the words expressed and the sentence structures presented.

Deaf children are often proficient spellers, for they seldom have problems remembering the patterns of words. They do have difficulty with reading and writing as they try to understand and use sentence patterns outside their experience.

CASE STUDY: BRIAN

Brian was a seemingly highly intelligent 6-year-old with severe hearing impairment in a unit for 5- to 11-year-old deaf children that favoured oral communication.

Brian seemed incapable of lip-reading and was showing difficulties learning to spell, read and acquire any spoken vocabulary. He communicated by gesture and mime, often in a most amusing way. The unit leader insisted on lip-reading, while his teacher felt that sign-supported communication would be more appropriate, and this situation began to result in frustration and behaviour problems from Brian. The teacher began to doubt his intelligence when test results on the Derbyshire Language Scheme (Knowles and Masidlover, 1982) and LARSP – Language Assessment, Remediation and Screening Procedure (Crystal *et al.*, 1976) – showed he had made no progress. When, however, Raven's Progressive Matrices (colour version)* were used he was found to have a visual-perceptual intelligence level in the top 2 per cent of the population.

It was concluded that Brian was a highly intelligent child with a double handicap. He not only had a hearing impairment but also an oral language learning difficulty. He was thus responding to the signing system which his teacher in desperation was using to make contact with him.

*Raven's tests present a set of flag-like patterns with one out of the set blank. Underneath the set are further flag patterns from which to choose one to supply the blank and thereby complete the set. The matrices tests can be used by teachers with the Crichton or Mill Hill Vocabulary scale to give general estimates of intelligence. The tests are available from NFER-Nelson Educational Test Division.

Testing spelling in years 1–10 and beyond

Most children and young adults will have acquired some spelling knowledge. The extent of this can easily be judged by examining the open-ended writing of the class group of their peers. A range of ability will be seen from 90 per cent inaccurate to 95 per cent accurate. As they grow older the inaccuracies are found in smaller and smaller numbers of scripts. The testing strategies below are recommended.

- Take a sample of timed open-ended writing. This time give a subject or title for the writing (e.g. 'All about me', 'How to play —', 'The day I went to —') or show the class/group a picture, discuss it and then ask them to describe what they saw or guessed was happening in the picture (Myklebust's 1965 Picture Story Language Test technique).
- Give a dictation suitable for the age group from a common reading book or specialist source, e.g. *Dictations for Years 3–6* in Peters and Smith (1993, pp. 69–70)
- Look at the handwriting. If the pupil has only been able to write a sentence, give some copywriting to do:
  (a) copying below the words
  (b) copying from the blackboard
- Give a standardized spelling test. There are several that are currently available:
  (a) Aston Portfolio Assessment Checklist (uses Schonell Spelling Test A).
  (b) Cassell's Linked English Tests (includes spelling test).
  (c) Daniels and Diack Spelling test for ages 5–12. It has a slow gradient with a large number of regular words (Daniels and Diack, Collins Educational, 1979).
  (d) Diagnostic and Remedial Spelling Manual (Peters, 1983; and Peters and Smith, revised).
  (e) Graded Word Spelling Test (Vernon; Hodder & Stoughton).
  (f) Hunter–Grundin Literacy Profiles (Test Agency).
  (g) Parallel Spelling Tests (Young; Hodder & Stoughton).
  (h) Schonell Spelling Test. This has a faster gradient and gives a more extended test of spelling skills from 5–15 years and there are two equivalent forms: Graded Spelling Tests A and B (Schonell and Schonell, 1970).
  (i) SPAR (Spelling and Reading Tests) (Young; Hodder & Stoughton).
  (j) Vincent and Claydon's Diagnostic Spelling Test A and B (1982; NFER-Nelson).

A well-known test from the USA frequently used and referred to in research studies is:

- Boder Test of Reading and Spelling (Boder and Jarrica; Grune & Stratton)

Most of the tests in this list are normative and give only a *spelling age* or a *spelling quotient* in which a child's test score can be compared to the scores of other children of a similar age and background. As already noted, if the *errors* made on tests are noted and analysed (a miscues approach) the skills shown and the lack of knowledge exhibited can be very informative and can help the development of an intervention and teaching programme. Some test constructors have begun to grapple with this issue, as can be seen in the next section.

- Keep the record of the pupils' misspellings; these will enable you to make a *diagnostic analysis* of errors even from the Daniels and Diack or Schonell tests. Spelling ages are of little help without diagnosis and intervention. Other diagnostic tests/assessments are by Peters and Smith (1993).
- Give a reading test such as Neale Reading Analysis (Revised) or the Macmillan Reading Test. This will enable you to obtain a reading comprehension age or estimate. If reading comprehension age is *higher* than reading fluency or skill then you have an able learner with a specific difficulty.
- If you wish to discover if there is a wider associated pattern of difficulties with the spelling problem, give the Bangor Dyslexia Test (Miles, 1983, 1993).
- Check alphabet knowledge where there are signs of multiple misspellings.
- Evaluate pupils' progress in relation to the National Curriculum attainment targets.

Now the Key Stage assessments in English in the National Curriculum at 7, 11 and 14 years will enable screening and intervention to be made and monitored at appropriate intervals and in between so that programmes can be evaluated and modified on an LEA wide, if not a national, basis.

Alphabet knowledge

The subject of whether or not to teach children the alphabet has often been controversial. Some teachers would not teach it at all, others would only teach it in Year 2. Yet more would teach it differentially as the children's needs in sentence writing begin to require it.

Despite resistance to teaching the alphabet and the complete omission of attention to alphabet skills in some classrooms, many children come to school 'knowing the alphabet'. It has been family tradition for grandparents to drill their grandchildren in the alphabet and this duty is frequently passed down to parents too. Children may learn to chant segments, or even the whole alphabet, forwards and backwards or sing it to a tune. This is probably from an oral tradition going back to the last century and the alphabetic methods then in use. This form of 'knowing the alphabet' is, however, of little use in spelling. These children are also most often taught to write their names in capital letters, to the chagrin of their teachers who want them to learn the sounds of letters and the lower case forms which are more frequently encountered and used.

Poor spellers and dyslexics alike in adulthood can often only write coherently in capital letters. It is known that in cases of brain damage suffered by adults to the left hemisphere areas responsible for literacy skills, one of the few skills left intact may be the recognition and production of capital letters. My hypothesis for this is that the formation of these letters was learned in the pre-school period using that part of the brain that is employed in learning to draw pictures. The shapes were not linked to sounds and so the left hemisphere never became involved. The memories reside in and are organized by the right hemisphere and so remain when the left hemisphere processes are interrupted.

Learning the alphabet in this way *does have its uses* if it is incorporated in the learning of the lower case letters with their corresponding sounds. Thus we should teach:

l (the letter form): 'l' the letter sound
and
L (the capital letter): L the name of the letter

When in the early stages of reading and spelling we ask the child to decode (analyse or break a word down for reading) or encode (synthesize or put parts of the word together for spelling) it is appropriate and helpful to say, 'Try the letter's name if it does not sound sensible.' For example, ăble (˘ breve signifying short vowel sound) makes the sound 'abble', which would not make sense in the sentence: She was *able* to see two dogs.

If we try instead using the letter's name, āble (¯ micron signifying long vowel sound), the word can be read aloud, the child hears it and understands it in the sentence context. A similar process can take place in spelling when knowledge of A /ā/ can produce the correct grapheme. This strategy is particularly useful for decoding or encoding the vowels, which all have these short and long sounds. Such instruction can precede the teaching of syllable structure and the short and long sounds, for which some children at reception stage may not be quite ready.

The alphabet is also useful for dictionary work and for the use of indices and lists and so *does need to be learned* at some point, and in

its correct sequence. Failure to begin to learn the alphabetic information should be a cause for concern and attract remedial support,
not at 7 and 8 years of age but *after a few weeks* in the reception class.

Diagnostic spelling tests

The Diagnostic Spelling Test by Vincent and Claydon (1983) is
published by NFER/Nelson. It consists of two equivalent forms (A
and B) and is a group-administered test suitable for children from
ages 7 to 11 years old. It tests the following skills:

- homophones
- common words
- proof-reading
- letter strings
- nonsense words
- dictionary use
- self-concept
- dictation

The test was standardized on 4,000 children in schools selected to
represent a national sample. Any test is built from the authors'
conceptual and logical analysis of the area, in this case the nature
and origin of spelling difficulties in the context of research on
dyslexia and learning difficulties. If their analysis is at fault then
the logical validity and the construct validity of the test is also at
fault and the items and diagnosis of little value. As already indicated, there are some highly contentious positions taken in this
area and in the period when this test was conducted – up to three
years prior to its publication date – the knowledge we now have
was not available. This is bound to have implications for work
with children with spelling difficulties, whose time could be
wasted having been spent on irrelevant activities.

The authors caution about the problems of children lucky-guess-
ing with the multiple-choice items and suggest that improvement
scores have to be more than double the standard error of the test,
or over seven points, to represent a significant difference.

The rationale behind the test is what gives one cause for concern
nowadays, especially in the context of diagnosis and the planning
of remediation. The manual states:

> Effective spelling relies upon the development of a number of
> closely associated skills. These are essentially visual and include
> sensitivity to the appearance of words, and knowledge of the way
> letter strings and combinations provide the characteristic pattern
> and structure of English spelling. Above all, learning to spell

requires the ability to look closely at words and the formation of clear visual images of the words in the learner's memory ... Children who perform poorly on the subtests will benefit from the work designed to develop such skills. (Vincent and Claydon, 1983, p. 3)

We now know this to be an incomplete analysis and an insufficient view of spelling as it does not take into account the prime importance of phonological abilities, in which poor spellers are invariably weak. If poor spellers were to be given only visual training it would be unlikely to improve their spelling abilities.

British Ability Scales: Spelling Test (Elliot, 1992)

This test is contained within the British Ability Scales, which are sometimes used by psychologists and other trained users. The author would like it to be available on a wider scale to trained users. The range of the test is 5.0 years to 14.5 years and within its 69 spelling items three shortened versions exist as well as the full test. Spelling ages and diagnosis of errors can be derived. What is of particular interest is the proposed diagnosis of errors. Errors are classified as non-phonetic, or phonetic. The non-phonetic errors can be regraded into 'pre-spelling', 'major non-phonetic' and 'non-phonetic order'. The phonetic errors are grouped into 'semi phonetic', 'basic phonetic' and 'plausible phonetic'. These categories, which derive from Boder's classification into dysphonetic and dyseidetic errors and Gentry's stages of spelling development, indicate the rationale behind the test. Judgements about which error group the pupil's spelling falls into can be seen to be very much a matter of opinion between non-phonetic order and semiphonetic, semi and basic and so on. The psychologist's ability to give advice based upon these inferences would be limited to references to teaching symbol–sound correspondences and basic phonics. As has already been indicated, for developmental, corrective and remedial intervention the teacher needs to discover *from the errors* made what the child does not know so that he or she can then teach it, rather than merely being able to classify the errors.

The words in the test up to item 30 are a mixture of regular and irregular two-, three- and four-letter words, chosen by frequency of use; from items 31 to 69 complex single-syllabled are mixed with two-, three- and four-syllabled words, and one five-syllabled word. There is no obvious gradient of difficulty except in relation to word length.

The methods pupils use to produce spellings given in the National Curriculum documents show the limited range of developmental strategies which are available to pupils, for example:

- asks someone
- uses dictionary
- uses another easier word instead
- writes word to see if it 'looks right'
- tries to sound word out
- tries to learn words by themselves, if so how?

Even more limiting is the categorization of errors:

- handwriting errors e.g. *b/d/p* reversals
- transposition of letters or syllables
- omissions or confusion of sounds or syllables
- reversals, e.g. *was/saw, on/no*
- mirror writing
- logical or skeletal phonic spelling e.g. *sed* for *said*
- bizarre spellings e.g. *dutwely* for *beautiful, cer* for *went*

How misspellings may be more fully assessed and interventions planned will be discussed in Chapters 3 and 4.

Interestingly enough, there are dangers in having checklists and clinical indicators such as have been described, for it has become common for LEA advisers and teachers to refuse to accept that a pupil has specific learning difficulties in reading and spelling (dyslexia) if there are no indications of bizarre spellings and reversal errors, or if there is alphabet knowledge and no confusion in reciting the days of the week and so on. Educational psychologists may show similar reservations if there is no 'ACID profile'. This may be in the presence of severe reading and spelling difficulties, e.g. reading which is two or three years below that of average peers and spelling which is five years substandard. The pupil clearly needs the specific remedial help which is given to 'dyslexics', regardless of the lack of the so-called clinical indicators, which are not to be found in every case. The most consistent indicators that teachers can have for an assessment of need are very poor reading and spelling skills in the presence of higher abilities in other areas: for instance, good oral skills, reasoning, problem-solving, artistic and design capabilities.

Some recent developments in assessment

Rack (1996) has presented evidence from 250 cases at the Dyslexia Institute that differential ability scales identified three subgroups – children with specific verbal/phonological difficulties, a distinct group with specific spatial difficulties, and a further group who have specific difficulties in non-verbal reasoning.

For some time Singleton (1990, 1994, 1996) has been working on a computer-based screening assessment which he has described as 'CoPS' – a cognitive profiling system involving ten subtests and administered to children in reception classes to identify those likely to be at risk in later stages of schooling. There are also others working in this field to produce dyslexia early screening tests (DEST, Nicolson and Fawcett, 1994).

It would be a pity if teachers' achievements in assessment and identification were overtaken by a profusion and even a confusion of technical instruments which would tell them no more than they already knew.

SUMMARY

Spelling has only lately been widely introduced into the assessment processes of schools and LEAs. Even so, the assessment may be divorced from the intervention and it is here where a much closer match is needed. The value of a system of informal and formal testing has been discussed and methods of intervention which focus on an analysis of errors have been recommended. Regular and systematic formative and summative assessments linked to classroom intervention have been proposed.

Even when good assessment processes are in place the variable definition of need and the lack of funding can constrain provision. Various definitions of dyslexia have been described to illustrate this issue. The definition of need by classroom observation and on-task analysis of literacy skills has been taken as the main theme; the way which could lead to better teaching within mainstream classes. This could then help prevent many of the difficulties which currently arise. It might make special provision less necessary.

Developmental assessment and intervention: the early stages of learning

INTRODUCTION

In the previous chapter it was proposed that a range of data on pupils' spellings, and particularly their misspellings, should be collected, using, ideally, an assessment through teaching strategy. This has also been termed performance-based assessment (PBA; Shore and Tsiamis, 1986). This chapter sets out to show how, from a close and detailed examination of an individual's work, developmental assessment and intervention can be made in the early stages of learning.

In addition, as the teacher moves round the class marking work and assisting individuals, a general pattern of errors can be noted and particular teaching points can be made and strategies practised with groups or the whole class. This maintenancing activity (Montgomery, 1989) is particularly useful for reinforcing earlier work and can be undertaken across a range of curriculum areas. Where schools have developed a whole-school policy towards spelling teaching strategies all staff can participate in the developmental and corrective techniques without requiring detailed specialist knowledge and with a modest course of appropriate in-service training.

Developmental assessment requires more than a cursory glance which takes in the misspellings whilst content is being assessed. It involves persevering in reading difficult writing and half-coded spellings from particularly needy pupils. This often requires some determination to overcome a passion to punish untidy writing and poor spelling. Once this psychological barrier can be overcome the analysis is not difficult. Addressing these problems needs to be part of in-service training and whole school policy.

The context in which the examples of work are discussed is the developmental stage theory of Frith (see pp. 16–17). It will be obvious that teachers will have many examples of a particular child's work whereas here only one or two pieces of writing can be used as illustration. However, even in a single piece of work there are usually enough spellings characteristic of that individual to begin to build up a pattern for support. To help in this pupils should be encouraged to participate in the assessment and analysis as partners and keep a record of the special pieces of work which have been developmentally assessed so that they can examine progress with the teacher, peers and parents at appropriate intervals.

A general stability of error types will be noted in work collected in the same period even though the words used may be different. In addition, some words may appear in several different spelling forms when incorrect and correct representations have been stored and one is as likely to pop up as any other.

The first section analyses errors of ordinary young spellers in accordance with logographic, alphabetic and orthographic stages. Then follow examples of writing from dyslexics and an assessment of their progress in spelling and learning needs. In the third section, a four-column analysis strategy is detailed, with a worked example. The final section compares the misspellings of dyslexics and control subjects on the Daniels and Diack spelling test to determine if the types of errors made are different and if the dyslexics' spellings really are bizarre.

This chapter is the first of six on intervention strategies. The majority of these chapters deal with developmental and corrective interventions. When pupils fall behind in spelling development to the extent of at least two years and seem to fail to make any real progress, reaching a plateau, then remedial tuition of a particular kind will be found appropriate. This is described in the final chapter. In the panel that follows, descriptions of the three types of intervention are given.

TYPES OF INTERVENTION

DEVELOPMENTAL
As pupils meet new vocabulary for reading and spelling, or often in advance of this, the teacher suggests strategies for learning the new words. The words will arise in the daily curriculum and will be dealt with by class and subject teachers on the basis of an agreed whole-school approach.

CORRECTIVE
Words which should have been learnt at an earlier stage are often present in pupils' work misspelled. These misspellings may appear

in an unsystematic fashion with different errors within the same piece of work. Relearning opportunities need to be provided to replace the old with the new correct version. Corrective strategies may be the same as developmental ones in some instances but often a cognitive strategy is required linked to a handwriting method in order for the new spelling to achieve a higher profile in the response memory. Corrective strategies should be part of every class and subject teachers' repertoire.

REMEDIAL
Pupils with very poor spelling, who have severely arrested development and have failed to acquire the alphabetic principle despite having received learning support and remedial help, will need to be given specialist remedial tuition. This can best be given by trained specialists who follow specific well tried and well documented dyslexia programmes. This tuition is best given in tutorial matched pairs in a small suitably equipped room for a minimum of two sessions per week. Someone who claims to use a mixture of methods and programmes together with his or her own brand of 'specialist' remediation is unlikely to be able to help this disabled speller and reader.

DEVELOPMENTAL ASSESSMENT AND INTERVENTION

Stage 1 : Logographic

Kate shows good development in spelling and writing skills. She writes from left to right and the letters are in their correct orientation, most of them are lower- rather than upper-case. There are indications of word and syllable knowledge appearing in the writing, for example, 'we wet' and 'we wt', with 't' and 'e' appearing between

Figure 3.1 *Kate's free writing (5 years 1 month) (half of original size) 'We went to the park and Mummy and Daddy and David we went to our grandma's'.*

other letters at frequent intervals. 'We wet' and 'we wt' could indicate beginning phonic awareness. There are no spaces to indicate
words as yet and some of the letters are drawn rather than written as
one whole unit, but each is well made and most are recognizable as
letters. Kate's teacher was not using an emergent writing approach
and not at this stage encouraging independent word knowledge, and
so there is little word knowledge apparent to the ordinary reader.

This writing should be compared with the following examples
collected from a reception class where the class teacher is using a
modified version of the emergent writing approach. She wrote
down the words for the children but they were not allowed to copy
them. Instead the children were encouraged to look carefully at
each word then turn it over and try to write it from memory. They
did of course continually cheat but knew that it was not a mortal
sin to spell incorrectly and that good representations would be
approved. The strategy also made them look more closely at the
words they were going to try to write.

There are some lower- and upper-case letters to be seen in
Figure 3.2. 'Is Bon' may represent 'Please don't'. Pencil control
appears to be shaky with some variations in pressure. These are to
some extent masked because the grain of the desk top is showing
through. Young children should have a good surface to place their

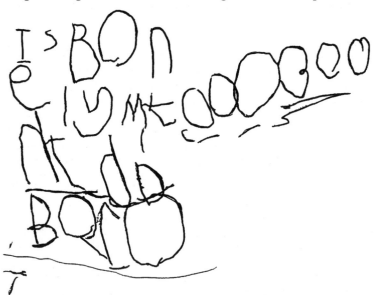

Figure 3.2 *Anthony's logographic writing (5 years 1 month) (two-thirds of original size)*
'Please don't let the children cross the road'.

Figure 3.3 *Michelle's logographic writing (5 years) (two-thirds of original size)*
'I wish to be fairies.'

writing paper on; it is important work they are doing. Alphabetic correspondences are not yet apparent although there may be a sign in 'ro' for 'road' and 'ht' in line three for 'the'. Early writing training in colouring, painting and drawing coupled with multisensory cursive writing training is needed.

Michelle (Figure 3.3) is in her first week at school. Her work shows that she lacks the alphabetic knowledge in her writing of letter forms which nearly all the other children in her class now show in their developmental writing. 'M' and 'e' are apparent and there are other letter-like shapes, e.g. 'c, u, g, O, n, a' and 'o'. It is certainly beginning to look like a Roman alphabet system but there appears to be no correspondence between symbol and sound as yet.

The above three scripts show logographic writing belonging mainly to the symbolic substage but with some clear letter forms, some capitals and some lower-case letters. Anthony's pen control is insecure and shaky, indicating a need for more fluency practice and the introduction of early cursive form. Both Anthony and Michelle could be 'at risk' and their needs might go unheeded in a busy classroom. Michelle needs to be helped to break the alphabetic code, beginning with the 'm' in her own name, then the 'i'.

She could then begin word or nonsense word making, e.g. im, mim, mimi, immi. When this is secure she could be encouraged to search for onsets and rimes with these letters and a new key sound could be introduced. Children at this stage of development in writing/spelling need to be helped to learn by using the multisensory technique SEEING, SAYING, SPELLING and WRITING. Seeing and saying only will not effect learning.

Stage 2: Alphabetic

By comparison the following examples of writing show the 'creative spelling' of five young children (aged 5) who are potentially good spellers. These are ordinary children of average ability who can be found in any classroom.

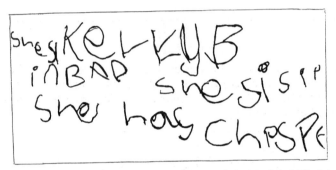

Figure 3.4 *Kelly's free writing (5 years 2 months) (half of original size) 'She is in bed. She is sick. She has chicken pox.'*

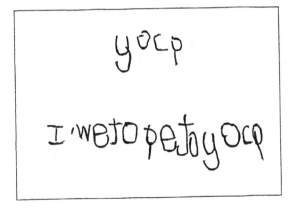

Figure 3.5 *Yacob's free writing (5 years) (two-thirds of original size) 'I went to bed. Yacob.'*

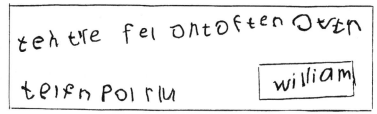

Figure 3.6 *William's free writing (5 years 2 months) (two-thirds of original size) 'The tree fell on top of the telephone pole wire.'*

wuns   a   pon   tyme   tcer   as   a
crisms   fariy

Figure 3.7 *Emma's free writing transcribed (5 years 2 months) 'Once upon a time there was a Christmas fairy.'*

Emma had a teacher who was encouraging developmental writing and who also used copy writing and tracing techniques. Emma's work was the most advanced in the class and Figure 3.7 shows her attempt at free writing.

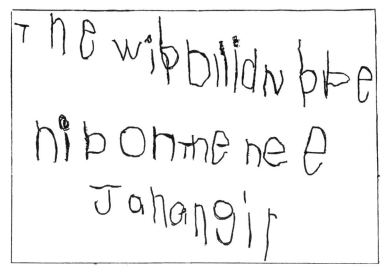

Figure 3.8 *Jahangit's free writing (5 years) (two-thirds of original size) 'The wind blew Daddy's best shirt on the tree.'*

Stage 3: Orthographic

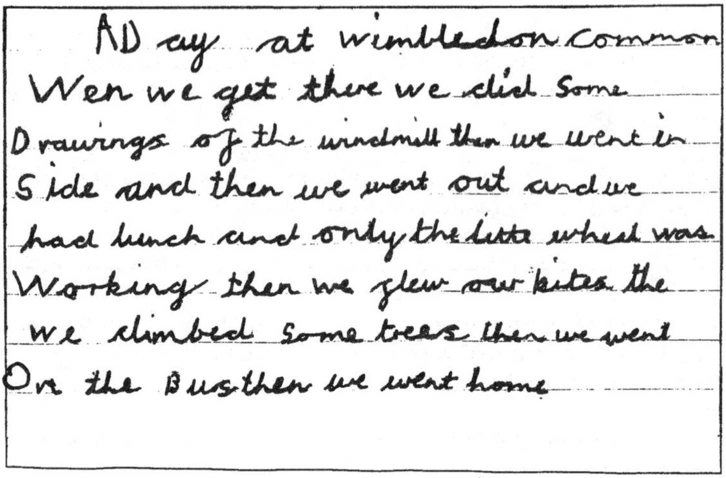

AD ay at wimbledon common
Wen we get there we did Some
Drawings of the windmill then we went in
Side and then we went out and we
had lunch and only the litte wheel was
Working then we flew our kites the
we climbed Some trees then we went
On the Busthen we went home

Figure 3.9 *Michael's free writing (6 years 8 months) (two-thirds of original size)*

Michael's writing shows fluent cursive handwriting and good spelling for his age. Cursive writing teaching has helped him overcome a mild co-ordination difficulty seen when he reverts to print and then has difficulty making some initial letters lower case size. His use of capital 'B' and 'D' suggests earlier spelling confusion.

> Giraffes are the biggst anamalls in the wald babey giraffes ant big theay are small theay ae a little bit bigger theay CAN eat the lefs off the tow the babies can't reach the levs off the tree and I wnet to sea a giraffe in the zoo it was very big it wa eating levs. I codant see him reley becos he was bending down its tadall was flicking in the hot sun was getting in my isys it was very hot and dustey there was a gate and a fense all arawd the giraffe I saw some little babey giraffes there i went to see som animalls to I saw a big elefant it was gicing some water form a steme he was gicing very much becod he was hungrey

Figure 3.10 *Emma's free writing transcribed (6 years 6 months)*

Figure 3.10 is a piece of open-ended writing. Emma was considered to be of 'low average' ability but reading satisfactorily at her age level. She was not noted for her writing ability. Her teacher complained that she would spell as she pleased and would not ask for help, as she could not be bothered. On this occasion a visit to the zoo inspired a lengthy piece of work, produced without assistance from the teacher except in the spelling of giraffe. Emma's writing shows both alphabetic and orthographic knowledge.

The spelling of *biggst* shows a typical contraction, reflecting the way the word sounds rather than its nature and origin; 'g' is doubled, however, showing some orthographic information has been acquired.

anamalls – *animalls* – as it sounds, medial 'i' as schwa sound, doubles final 'l' as in l-f-s rule responding to frequency of doubling of 'l' at the end of the words as in fall, bell, tell, etc.

wald – or (ir) combination not known, perhaps.

babey – produced from babe/y, best equivalent with money, honey.

ant – long 'ah' sound gives no trace or clue of the 'r' in pronunciation, derivation not realized so gives phonetic transcription.

theay – obtained by sounding *the*/ay, uses intrusive /uh/ or schwa sound.

ae – 'r' not detectable in pronunciation, ah-ug sound, so gives phonetic transcription of this.

lefs – uses 'f' to signify V by analogy with of? 'e' alphabetic use of name of letter to signify sound 'ea'.

tow – not clear which word this signifies from context.

babies can't reach – babies correct this time and comma for can't, interesting as is correct spelling of reach.

levs – uses 'v' here instead of 'f'.

wnet – knows each of these letters belongs in the word, unclear where the 'n' is placed since 'n' serves to nasalify vowel rather than signifies its own place. Perhaps writes it from visual recall alone and gives best fit with most of the letters in the correct position except in medial position.

sea – good phonetic equivalent, 'ea' almost as frequent as 'ee' in spellings.

wa – writing/clerical error, misses off 's', writes word correctly six times in all so does know it.

codant – good phonetic attempt, as are *-reley*, *becos*, *fense*, *to*, *elefant*, *som*.

Interesting misspellings are: *tadall* – tail pronounced 'tayall' perhaps creating confusion with the tonguing leading to the feeling of a 'd'.

arawd – around – loses nasal again – does she pronounce it correctly with the nasal? Possibly not.

gicing – getting – she is saying gething very quietly, the resultant sound recorded as closest to a 'c'?

isys – eyes. Not an uncommon misspelling produced by the

strong and quite prolonged end of the word 'i-ees'. It might also be due in part to place knowledge that there are four spaces in the word – *is* is produced first and then *ys* added for good measure on repeating the word.

steme – stream. Lack of knowledge of the three-letter blend 'str', difficult to segment it from 'st' and find the /r/, 'eme' shows knowledge of the long vowel sound denoted by final silent 'e', good phonetic equivalent.

What one can observe, given this type of analysis, is that the speller is using several different spelling strategies. She appears to use phonemic transcription as the basic skeletal structure except on the more complex nasals and three-letter blends. To these she assimilates whole-word knowledge or part-word knowledge by analogy with other known words and units, or writes straight from the visual memory for that word.

Emma was one of the average (rather fast) readers and poor spellers in her particular class and, on this basis, the teacher considered her to be a slow learner! However, she appears to be one of Read's (1986) misunderstood creative spellers. Other pupils have asked for words and used their spelling books to produce accurate spellings whereas independent, somewhat impatient Emma has not. Her writing shows that good spelling skills are developing and that she has much orthographic, phonetic and word-specific knowledge.

The analysis of Emma's writing is hypothetical; feasible alternative explanations of each misspelling have been given, except to observe the possibility that each spelling and misspelling may have been learnt, in which case they were being written straight from store. This was probably true in a few cases. A longitudinal study of Emma's work would reveal such instances. Emma herself, when asked about particular misspellings she had given, was unable to explain how she achieved them; she just did them 'out of her head'. Vincent (1983) found that it took her a number of lessons on the subject before her young poor readers and spellers could explain how they were trying to spell, so this inaccessibility to metalinguistics is not uncommon. The pattern of Emma's spelling development seems to be in the 'transitional stage' of Read (1986) that is neither fully phonological nor fully orthographic. There are indications of phonemic transcription to which is assimilated part or full orthographic structures and information. Some rule knowledge appears to be available but is implicit and not explicit. The misspellings of average or able 6-year-olds often show very few spelling errors, not because they are so much better spellers than Emma but because they keep to a restricted vocabulary. They check words about which they feel unsure in their word books, and ask teacher, helper or peer for ones they do not know. Emma's position in relation to Frith's six-step model could put her in the alphabetic stage of spelling at Stage 2b. Possibly she is fast approaching ortho-graphic level and is almost at Stage 3a whilst her average (rather fast) reading is, because of the stilted nature of the reading scheme to which she is subject, at Stage 2b. In reading, she attempts to break down words which she does not know, but these skills have not been taught and the result is somewhat odd. She cannot of course break down many words in this way for only about one in five respond to this treatment. She needs to learn syllable structure and affixing rules to be able to develop her strategies more effect-ively. In the absence of these she can only revert to rote learning, with which she seems impatient.

Other researchers have suggested similar strategies to those proposed. In helping the development of good spelling skills of young spellers, Cramer (1976) described what he calls a creative writing route. He advocated that, as soon as children have assem-bled any notions of spelling or any skills at all, they should be encouraged to use them in writing. Others have argued (Clay, 1975; Read, 1986) that a child's first literate response is to write not read. This natural tendency, according to Cramer, should be encouraged. The teacher should not worry about misspellings but supply limited but helpful information such as knowledge of sounds not yet learnt and rules if some problems persist; the rest will be learnt during reading (and writing!). He found that, in this fashion, chil-dren themselves became critical of their own performance and could see their often rapid improvement. Parents would need to have this strategy carefully explained for they are more intolerant of spelling errors than teachers, strangely seeming to expect young children's spellings to be near perfect. Cramer emphasized the need to take a positive approach to misspellings and illustrated it in the following manner by analysing the spellings in a poem by David, aged 7, written without assistance.

> *My Ded cate*
> Ones I had a cate
> He was white and yellow
> One night my father
> Came fame my grandfathers house
> Wenn father come home fame
> my grandfathers house he said
> Ruste is ded.

David made six misspellings out of a total of 18 which gives him a spelling error ratio of 0.33 (actual divided by total). Cramer argued that David's superior spelling skills were demonstrated in his correct spellings of father, grandfathers, white, night, house, said and yellow, and analyses his misspellings as common but near-miss good equivalents. The misspelling, he says, will gradually disappear with further writing practice as he becomes more familiar with orthographic conventions through reading. He counts ded for dead as a good generalization from basic knowledge for /e/ as in bed. It is the most common way of spelling that particular sound. 'Hade' for 'had' is counted as an overgeneralization of the final e rule, of which he has good knowledge for he spells 'home', 'come' and 'white' correctly. 'Wenn' for 'when' is a good phonetic equivalent when one takes into consideration that the use of double n is common, particularly in the middle of words (tunnel, funnel). His 'Ruste' for 'Rusty' indicates that he needs to learn that the /i/ sound at the end of English words is always represented by y. 'Fame' for 'from' shows lack of knowledge and sensitivity to the two letter blend /fr/ but he correctly uses /f/ and /m/ for the first and last sounds. He adds an 'e' possibly because he is aware that there are four letter-places in the word. This place knowledge is not an uncommon finding in memory span research (Wing and Baddeley, 1980). He chooses silent 'e' as that is a common ending.

If one were to suggest teaching strategies to help speed up David's spelling development, he might be taught the 'wh' words as a group, e.g. Where? Who? What? Why? When? (later Whither? Whether? and Whence?) and their formal pronunciation with aspiration which, for fun, he could listen for in different speakers' accents.

Later, not at the same time, he could be taught the closed syllable structure with short vowel sound which does not require the addition of 'e' (had, bed, pig, lot, but) and when this was absorbed, the use of final 'e' to denote the long vowel sound in the closed syllable, e.g. fade, cede, ride, mode, rude.

The sound and use of 'y' in the final position in English words would be taught and pointed out in practice games and the difficult and irregular word 'once' would be best taught by a writing route as a whole motor unit so that it becomes automatic, e.g. *once* . This could be undertaken using a simple 'say-look-cover-write-check' strategy (see SOS in Chapter 7, pp. 170–2).

David was, according to Cramer, a satisfactory speller for his age. As an example of a good speller Gentry and Richardson (1978) give the work of Lilia, aged 6. Lilia's poem is shown below. If it were, instead, the writing of a 10- or 12-year-old, one might suggest that it resembled very much what one had seen in 'dyslexic' pupils' writing.

> I am a building, I have an elavatr on me
> A lot ov pepl are on me and they work on me
> One prsn is tiping and a nothr prso is sleeping
> and that is a lot ov pepl on me.
> I see a lade cotting the gras becase she help
> the building to be open and wane I go on the elevatr
> it seas me that is the end Lilia.

The haunted house

When we were in the summer holiday's we decided to go camping. We set our camps in an open field wich was next to a derelict mantion. It had dark grey walls with a lot of holes in it. There were broken bits of stones all over the floor.

I got a fire going and cooked some bacon for our tea. Wilst the fire was still going we boiled some milk and made some coffee and then we went to bed. When everyone was asleep I got up and went to investigate the old howse. I walked through the hole that used to be the door. I thought I saw a bright figure in the corner but I looked again and it was gone. There were a lot of big sticky cobwebs. Suddenly I saw a piece of wood being thrown at me but I ran out of the house and it missed me. I ran into the tent and forgot about it and I went home the next day. The following night I had A bad nightmare and could not wake myself up. It was about the haunted mantion. I dreamt that the ghost's had captured me and were going to hang me untill I died. Just then my dog licked my face and I woke up. I was very relived after that and I haven't dream't about it since.

Figure 3.11 *Free writing of Stewart, an average speller transcribed (10 years)*

Stewart's spelling is well into orthographic stage. Some developmental help is still needed with 'wh' words; ou /ow/ diphthong; and when to use -tion, -sion and -cian.

Logographic and alphabetic spellings of dyslexic subjects

Kevin was 13½ years old when the spelling sample shown in Figure 3.13 was taken and shows his inadequate and incomplete knowledge of the English spelling system. He was otherwise of average ability but a slow reader. Both Kevin and Gina (Figure 3.12) have dyslexic difficulties. Neither had been identified as such by their schools. Both would benefit from systematic spelling teaching supported by articulation training and syllabification.

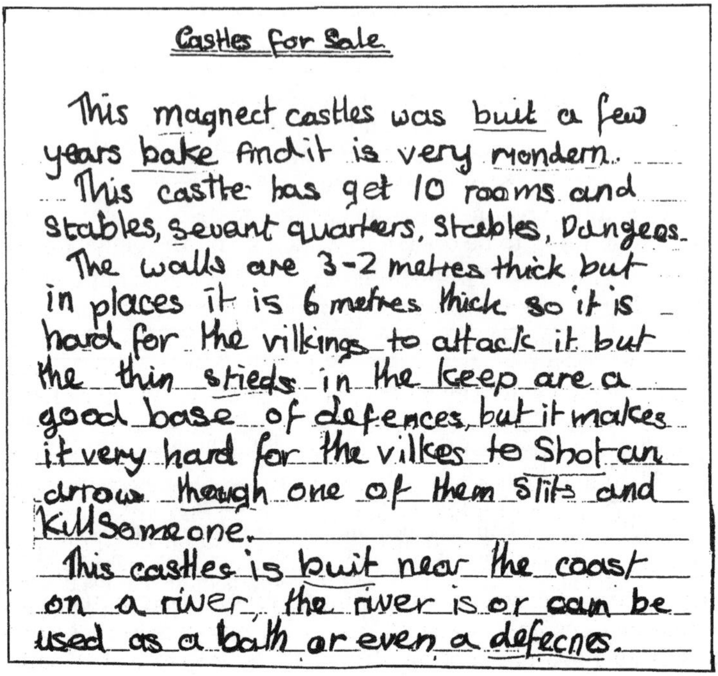

> ## Castles for Sale
>
> This magnect castles was buit a few years bake And it is very mondern.
> This castle has get 10 rooms and stables, sevant quarters, steebles, Dungeos.
> The walls are 3-2 metres thick but in places it is 6 metres thick so it is hard for the vilkings to attack it but the thin stieds in the keep are a good base of defences, but it makes it very hard for the vilkes to shot an arrow theugh one of them slits and kill someone.
> This castles is buit near the coast on a river, the river is or can be used as a bath or even a defecnes.

Figure 3.12 *Free writing by Gina, a poor speller (11 years) (two-thirds of original size)*

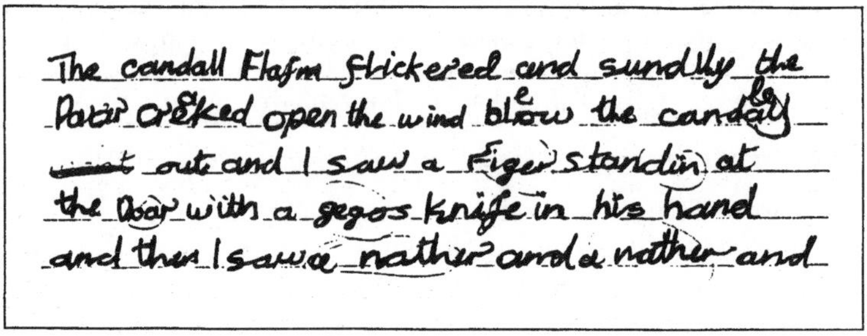

> The candall Flafm flickered and sundlly the Parir creaked open the wind blew the candall out and I saw a Figer standin at the door with a gegos knife in his hand and then I saw a nather and a nather and

Figure 3.13 *Kevin's free writing (13 years 6 months) (two-thirds of original size)*

If Gavin's spelling (Figure 3.14) is analysed developmentally it would suggest that he had a severe reading and even severer spelling problem since he was very bright. His difficulty was of the severest kind, showing that, at 10 years, he had only developed the most limited phonological encoding abilities. He had developed some symbol–sound correspondence but was spelling most phonetically. Thus 'wuns' was his phonic equivalent of the sounds in

```
'Wuns  apn  a  Time  v  sow  a
mystry  aBow  slng'
```

Figure 3.14 *Gavin's free writing transcribed (10 years)*

'once', and 'apn' shows this same level of skill. He sounded out 'ah-puh-poh-nnn', indicating that he knew the sound of 'p' and the appropriate grapheme; Gibson and Levin (1975) would suggest that this was due to orientation confusion in relation to the b, d, p, q groups of symbols. Later, he shows similar problems with 'd' and 'b' in 'about'. He overcomes the difficulty in a characteristic manner of problem spellers, by substituting capital B, about which he felt no confusion. After a pause, he wrote 'a Time' quite correctly. This could have been expected to have been written as 'a tim' in keeping with some of his other phonic representations. However, the study of 'time' in mathematics has meant that this spelling has somehow recently been learnt. It could also be suggested that he might have overcome some of his early learning problems and is beginning to acquire a store of correct new spelling. Over-training on the word, now that he does have some phonic skills, puts it into the lexicon and he is able to write it straight from the word-store at the automatic level rather than having to sound out the various parts. This lexicon may well by now contain many misspellings learnt in the past as well as more recently some of the word's correct spellings. It is these incorrect spellings which are difficult to supplant and which persist in free writing (Cotterell, 1974). Also of note is his tendency to overuse the phonic strategy which Francis (1982) found characteristic of pupils with reading and spelling problems.

Gavin's attempt at the final words illustrates this point. The spelling of 'there' proved impossible but with encouragement he eventually wrote 'v' for th. He spelt 'was' nearly correctly phonically as 'wos' but reversed the writing order. The spelling of mystry was his 'good' phonetic equivalent if one considers the following factors: he sounded out 'm' as 'muh-meh-mih' and wrote the grapheme 'm' to represent the sound 'mih'. This is characteristic of many poor spellers and often the more they try to repeat the sound the further they move from its original form (c.f. Smith's 1973 criticism). This deformation is typical of the beginning stages speller, especially when this type of sounding is reinforced by incorrect teaching, giving over-emphasis of the sound of each letter – adding the intrusive 'uh' or schwa sound after a consonant. He wrote 'st' and then 'ry' without lengthy pause, sounding 'sst' 'ree'. It is

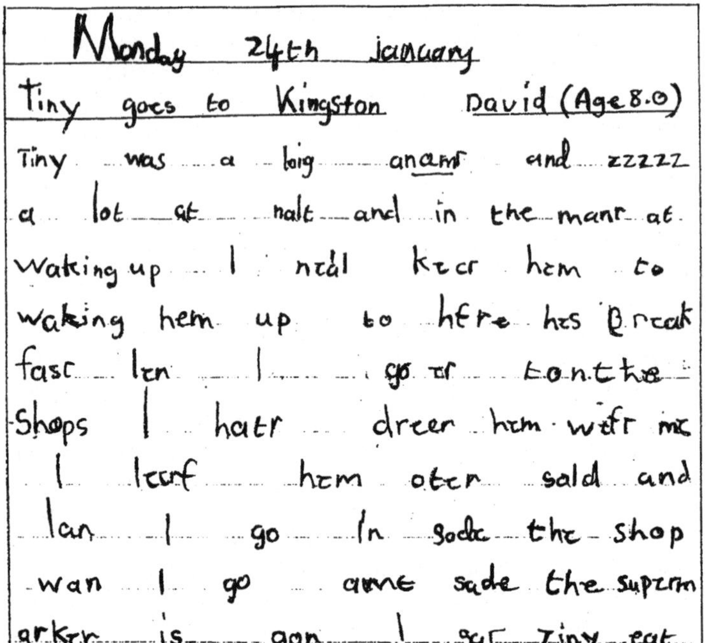
Monday 24th january
Tiny goes to Kingston David (Age 8.0)
Tiny was a big anamr and zzzzz
a lot at nalt and in the manr at
Waking up I ntal kecr hem to
waking hem up to hfre hes Break
fasc len I go tr to n the
Shops I hatr dreer hem wefr me
I leaf hem oter sald and
lan I go in sode the shop
wan I go ame sade the superm
arker is gon I sar Tiny eat
men a wem a Bisg a gisc (car) los of
lem didrer (chiern) lem I host tow
Brads a homes lat was 20000a
foot len tiny fore in to
20000 homes len I hat to eor
hem a Big drecr fast in the
mare (monin) he had a 20000
Breakfasc.

Figure 3.15 *David's free writing (8 years) (two-thirds of original size) 'Tiny goes to Kingston.'*

surprising that he knew the blend 'st', and that he noted that English orthography has a convention whereby words do not usually end with 'e' to represent the sound /ē/ but with 'y'. Just occasionally /ē/ at the end of words is represented by 'ee' as in toffee and coffee.

He has at some point learnt that 'e' can be represented by 'y' at the end of a word. As he does not pronounce the 't' in 'about' it is not surprising that he does not write it down. His last attempt at 'spelling' suggests that he does not know the blend 'sp' and he writes 's'; that the usual orientation confusions with 'p' may have intervened at this point and this made him forget its place in the word; that he does not articulate clearly enough for spelling 'sp'; it represents a typical cluster reduction phenomenon (Sterling, 1983). Perhaps, however, he did not remember the grapheme in any orientation so left it and went on to the next part of the word, which he sounded as 'lih', then adding 'ng', a sound he seemed to know the grapheme for.

When one sets this type of analysis besides that of Spache (1940) on miscues, and Wing and Baddeley (1980) in relation to their distributional analysis, it can be seen to be more complex, more equivocal, nomothetically unsophisticated but, in relation to understanding spelling errors and developing remedial programmes, more relevant than an arbitrary counting system. It is also consonant with a lexical pooling theory of spelling development. In terms of Frith's (1985) model, Gavin appears to be moving into Stage 2a alphabetic level but about four years late.

An example of a speller who has not moved much from Frith's first stage would be David, whose work is given in Figure 3.15. This uneven level of spelling development found in one individual is typical of many. It is translated as follows:

> Tiny was a big animal and slept a lot at night and in the morning at waking up I have to keep waking him up to have his breakfast. When I go to the shops I have to drag him with me. I leave him outside and then I go inside the shop. When I go outside the supermarket he's gone. I saw Tiny eat men and women, a biscuit and a car, lots of children. I came too late to stop him break into homes that was 200000 lots I see Tiny broke into to. Then I had to give him a big breakfast. In the morning he had 2 million breakfasts.

David was not receiving remedial help of any kind. He normally refused to write more than a sentence freely or from copy. His 'free sentence writing' was always the same one! This time he copied the date and title of his story and the teacher added a word or two when his intention was indecipherable. He was able to tell an adequate story but not write it so that someone else could read it, although he could 'read' it fairly well or at least reconstruct it from his text a few minutes later. His new teacher had gained his confidence and succeeded in persuading him not to worry about his spelling problem and so write down his story using his creative spelling strategies.

David's spelling would be considered typical of the 'bizarre' spelling of the dyslexic but it illustrates that what is often regarded as a medical/clinical symptom can also be interpreted as an uneven level of development of beginning spelling knowledge. After 'B' is coped with by using the capital, he can almost spell 'breakfast' (breakfasr) and gets close to 'drag' (drear), 'inside' (in sade) and 'outside' (awt sade), 'supermarket' (supermarker), 'big', and the irregular word 'was'. What is quite clear is that his knowledge of sound-to-symbol correspondence for some graphemes is incomplete and his appreciation of some of the most regular or frequent conventions and groupings is also incomplete, whilst he does have some specific word knowledge and visual notions of word length and form. He clearly has the notion of word and syllable structure, leaving spaces between words and making syllable-like structures such as 'hom'. The strategy of poor spellers in free writing is to select words, as far as possible, from the lexicon which they can spell correctly and so the problem in its weaker form may go undetected until they are confronted by new or specialist vocabulary in higher academic studies. David's writing is an extreme and late form of the problem. A remedial programme giving him mastery of the basic alphabetic and phonic structure of the language, teaching him to use the sounds in word building, could markedly accelerate his spelling accuracy when integrated with the whole word and part word knowledge which he has acquired.

A number of distinctions in relation to poor spellers have been made. Gavin and David are representative of a group of subjects who have both very severe spelling and reading retardation, whereas others have severe spelling and milder reading retardation, and some have severe spelling retardation but average or above average reading ability. David is able to segment the sound stream but not always associate the correct grapheme with the phoneme and thus is at Frith's (1982) first level of spelling development. Gavin can do both but cannot draw on knowledge of precise orthographic structures of English. Both have some word-specific knowledge or whole-word correct spellings, which they can use when appropriate.

James (7 years) (Figure 3.16)
James was unable to read any of the books in the reading scheme *One, Two, Three and Away*. During the previous six months he had been given extra private tuition of two half-hour sessions per week. This consisted of being helped to read the *Fuzz Buzz* books and engaging in copy writing. In one lesson, an attempt was made to teach him the sounds of all the five vowels with keywords (*Alpha to Omega*, Hornsby and Shear, 1976), all in the one session, with, not surprisingly, no success.

At interview James proved to be of at least average intellectual ability in conversation, and able to add and subtract tens and units, but he was unable to read any of the words on the Neale Analysis, he read no words on Schonell, he could spell no words on the Daniels and Diack test and could recognize only the common words: 'a, I, and, the' from the keywords list. He was unable to say the most popular nursery rhymes, 'Baa-baa, black sheep' or 'Jack and Jill', although he indicated that he knew them and provided some words with prompting.

When tested on his knowledge of sounds and names of the alphabet, he knew two sounds – /m/, /k/ for 'c' – and seven names: O, X, Z, S, Y, I, J (and E for 'e'). Without at least a set of useful sounds for blending to words, it is not surprising he was unable to spell any words on the test. Since he knew /m/ and could read the word 'mummy', he was asked to spell the word and write his own name again.

Figure 3.16 *James's free writing (7 years 6 months) (four-fifths of original size)*

James was unable to write more than these two words from 'inside his own head' at $7\frac{1}{2}$ years after 6 months of private 'remedial' tutorials and extra help from his class teachers. It is puzzling to find such lack of knowledge of reading and spelling skills in a child of 7 who is orally bright. It is also a cause of some surprise that the part-time tuition followed the same pattern as that of the school: copy writing for spelling, with no tuition in the most efficient means of making letter shapes and a 'look and say' approach to reading, which has already failed him.

Two years later after having spent the intervening time in a 'remedial' class with a group of ten other children, mainly slow learners, James was still unable to read or spell at a functional level and when retested on Schonell Reading Test scored 6.8 years and on the Spelling Test A scored 6.5 years. His mother had to have him privately assessed by a psychologist as the LEA refused to do so, and his full scale WISC-R score was 105 points with little discrepancy between Verbal and Performance scores. Even so she was unable to persuade the LEA to statement James and gain specialist tuition for him. She finally secured a place for him at a specialist remedial private school using the *Attack* cursive handwriting/ spelling scheme and he made some progress. He was, however, so unhappy and disturbed by being away from home that he was placed in a local private day school after only two months. His new teacher was a keen student of learning difficulties and used the Teaching Reading Through Spelling programme (see Chapter 8), with the result that at the age of 11 James's reading has improved to age level 10.5 years, with spelling 8.6 years on Daniels and Diack.

James at 7 years would appear to have been at a stage before that of David; he lacked any word-specific knowledge for spelling. He could, however, also segment the sound stream (e.g. say 'carpet' with the 'car') and had the notion of short words and long ones, saying 'Is that dog?' when shown 'cat', but had no useful phonic knowledge to give him the skeletal outline of words. He was barely into the alphabetic stage proposed by Ferreiro and Teberosky (1982) and at the threshold of Frith's symbolic Stage 1a.

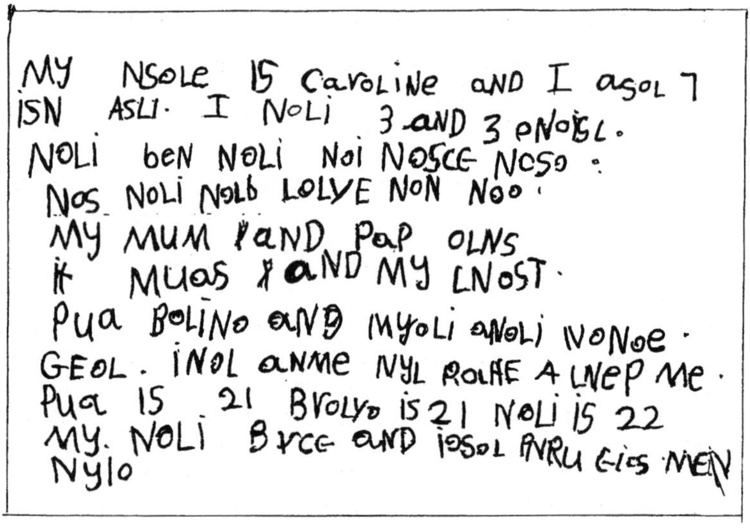

Figure 3.17 *Caroline's free writing (7 years) (half of original size)*

My name is Caroline and I am 7 years old. I have 3 brothers and 3 sisters. Some of them live at home and some of them do not. My mum and dad live at home and so do my goldfish.

Paul Breda and Mark still live at home. They are a lot older than me. Paul is 21 Breda is 21 and Mark is 22. My other brothers and sisters are a lot older than them.

Caroline (Figure 3.17) had used the letters of her own name in her account. She has no symbol-sound and little word-specific knowledge. She makes letter shapes and syllable and word clusters of letters with spaces in between. Her spelling knowledge is of the most limited kind. In-class 'remedial' support repeating earlier learning has not improved her understanding; she needs a multi-sensory APSL training programme to help break the code barrier.

James, Caroline, David and Gavin represent dyslexics who are in the early stages of spelling development and their errors are fairly easy to define. Most 'dyslexics', such as Kevin and Gina, however, do with persistence eventually learn to read and spell to some degree.

THE FOUR-COLUMN ANALYSIS STRATEGY

Making an analysis of misspellings in order to take decisions about the preparation of an intervention programme can be facilitated by following the four-column analysis strategy. The procedure:

- Collect a recent sample of open-ended writing in which no spelling support was given.
- Make a table (about a page) with four columns.
- In column 1 list all the spelling errors.
- In column 2 reorder and group spelling errors into similar-seeming groups, e.g. 'wh' words, blends. In brackets put the target correct spelling.
- In column 3 analyse the type of error, e.g. articulation, syllabification, phonic, rule errors.
- In column 4 propose a teaching intervention, e.g. teach three letter blends, teach consonant diagraphs, teach closed syllable structure.
- Calculate the *spelling error rate* by dividing the total number of misspelled words written by the total number of *different* words used. (Count extra misspellings of the same word as one error.)
- Star two interventions which will be tackled first.

Below is a worked example based on a piece of writing by Joe, 7 years 6 months, with a reading age (Schonell) of 6 years 8 months, and a spelling age (Daniels and Diack) of 5 years 9 months: a 'dyslexic'. The writing is taken from a case study by Virginia Vivian, 1993.

> I wet to a car vele in 1991 in June The 31 and I sep on the btm
> brk and I love it

I went to a caravan village in 1991 in June the 31(st) and I slept on
the bottom bunk and I loved it.

Four-column analysis

Column 1	Column 2	Column 3	Column 4
wet car vele sep btm brk love	wet (went)	Articulation awareness error.	• Check for clear articulation -nk and -nt blends. • Teach 'feel' of nasal blends.
	sep (slept)	Initial consonant blend sl-; final consonant blend -pt.	• Teach initial blend sl- . • Teach final blend -pt.
	love (loved)	Past tense suffix -d and -ed.	• Teach past tense suffixes -ed.
	car (caravan)	Check for clear articulation; syllabification error. Check consonants 'v' and 'n'.	• Teach syllabifying for spelling • Check/teach consonants 'v' and 'n'. • Teach /ă/ sound.
	btm (bottom)	Short closed syllable errors; doubling error.	• Teach CVC closed syllable structure short vowel sound only. • Teach affixing doubling rule after CVC learned.

Summary of first steps for Joe
- Teach syllabification for spelling, syllable beats.
- Only teach short vowel closed syllables CVC.
- Include /ă/ sound in the above and check knowledge of other short vowels. (Also check consonant sounds.)
- When Joe begins to demonstrate the knowledge just taught in his open-ended writing, make another four-column analysis and include new errors in the teaching programme.

Next steps
- Based upon original error list, go on to teach sl- and -pt consonant blends. If new error list contains further such errors add these to the teaching list for a future session. Do

not teach more than a pair at a time. If this proves difficult reduce to one blend at a time. Learning any new spelling blend such as sl- could take over several weeks of direct teaching to be completely absorbed. Never go too quickly, it will only confuse.

- Continue syllable structure practice with short vowel sounds and check/teach consonant v and another consonant not yet acquired.
- Continue articulation practice and use of doubling rule.
- Teach some basic linguistics, for example the doubling rule and syllable structure.

TEACHING EXAMPLE

Syllables are the basic building bricks of words. The most common and basic syllable structure is the consonant – vowel – consonant pattern:

CVC (e.g. bed, cat, dog, cut, pit)

In this syllable structure the vowel is short (short vowel sound) and the syllable is 'closed'. An open syllable pattern is:

CV (to, go, no, etc.)

Affixes: There are two groups of affixes.

prefixes – meaningful syllables added to the front of a root word, e.g. pre-, re-, ad-

suffixes – meaningful syllables added to the end of roots, e.g. -ing, -ment, -ed, -es

Roots: These are base words to which prefixes and suffixes may be added, e.g.

form – reform, forming, formed
run – rerun, running, runner
hop – hopped, hopping, hopper

Doubling rule and the short closed syllable

When a base word is a closed syllable with a short vowel sound, such as 'hop', whenever a vowel suffix is added the final consonant pattern must be doubled. For example:

hop – hopping – hopper
cvc cvcc-ing cvcc-er

Four-column analysis enables the structuring of a pattern of mis-spellings and helps in the development of an orderly pattern of intervention. In using it it is essential to realize that the patterns the teachers evolve are dependent on the theories of origins they hold. If the theory is inappropriate or not valid then the intervention can prove useless.

In the next section a range of remedial intervention strategies and programmes will be discussed. This will reveal the underlying theory and the outcome of research which tries to evaluate the relative effectiveness of strategies/programmes in remediation.

DEVELOPMENTAL ASSESSMENT AND INTERVENTION: VISUAL APPROACHES

Peters (1967, p. 79), in her studies of teaching spelling, first recommended the 'look–cover–write–check' strategy for both teaching and remediation of misspelling, and this has become one of the most popular and widespread corrective strategies. It is substantially better than instructing a pupil, particularly an older one, to write out the word correctly ten times, for we know that pupils can do this and next moment in free writing misspell it again. Perhaps if they wrote it five times with their eyes shut this would help a little to establish it as a motor programme. In either case the strategies require rote learning without any necessary understanding. She had earlier defined two main strategies for developing spelling (Peters, 1967, p. 17):

> It is clear, then, that to achieve predictable, infallible and machine-like movements in spelling, we cannot rely on the practice of reading alone to teach us how to spell .... Yet looking by itself without training in attention to word forms or training in imagery is not enough. Is the answer that we should rely on a multisensory approach involving visual, auditory, kinaesthetic and articulatory inroads? Or should we rely on looking, through careful training in the sphere of vision, in for example, attention imagery, and in the learning of probable word patterns and sequences?
>
> These two alternatives suggest the two main ways of teaching spelling ...

It is evident which was settled upon as the preferred strategy for she goes on in this and later work to recommend the *examination of common letter strings*, such as: and, sand, hand, (wand?!). It does of course have some value, for one learned element can be generalized to others in a group and cut down the memory load and the amount of learning work which has to be done. This is especially helpful where words look *and* sound the same. It is basically the onset and rime method, or the use of initial sound and then analogy with known ending parts of words, which has already been described. The identification of common letter strings, however, is based upon visual strategies and the identification of the serial probability of occurrence of these groupings, and can be overused and overemphasized so that no other strategy is taught.

In her recent work (Peters and Smith, 1993) a miscues analysis of spelling errors was advocated, based upon Gentry's (1981) theory of spelling development linked to the National Curriculum levels. The diagnostic categories used were as follows:

- Random (prephonetic)
- Phonetic (invented)
- Plausible: (a) unreadable (b) readable

According to these authors, the categories have been successfully used by teachers as the basis of a diagnostic grid into which a pupil's misspellings can be entered.

A set of dictations are provided in the form of short stories which are suitable for Years (Grades) 3 to 6 and which can be used for screening purposes for individuals or with the whole class. After the errors have been classified, strategies for spelling intervention and recovery are recommended as follows:

> The development of the productive understanding and use of words, and of words in texts, is developed by teachers capitalising on the language learning, drawing and scribed writing and as the learners develop, in the context of purposeful, meaningful writing for which the writers feel responsibility and ownership. The development of this awareness of verbal language is the same prerequisite as for the development of phonological awareness. Children also need to be shown specifically and deliberately the internal structure of words by the repeated pointing out, by the teacher, of common letter strings and visual similarities ... (Peters and Smith, 1993, p. 80)

Once the errors have been classified and any common letter strings identified, whatever grouping they fall into, the 'look–cover–write –check' strategy is applied. To this is added a tracing method (after Fernald, 1943) for beginners with rote learning of the letter strings. To support the writing, useful ideas on using scribes, word processors, drafting procedures and conferencing are presented to show how to stimulate editorial and authorial skills.

MEANINGFUL STRINGS AND LINGUISTICS: COGNITIVE APPROACHES

As English spelling is ruled by morphemics as well as phonemics (see p. 2) it seems essential that any developmental, corrective or remedial teaching must take account of both and use the strengths of each.

For example, in teaching a so-called letter string *-and*, in sand, stand, band and so on, there is a logic which suggests that the word *and* can be found and used to decode them after the initial sound has been produced. However, in the case of many other words, such as *draw*, *straw* (in which *-raw* is said to be the string) and *three*, *tree*, *reel*, *street* (in which *-ree-* is the string) there are problems which can actually hamper progress if the so-called string elements are used as the focal point for learning.

Although 'raw' in itself is a meaningful word, when it is inside 'draw' and 'straw' it is totally *un*meaningful and unrelated to the base words or roots 'draw' and 'straw'. The construction of straw and draw are better analysed by indicating the initial blends str- (a three-letter blend) and dr- (a two-letter blend) to which is added -aw, pronouned 'or' and 'au'. Dr- and str- as initial blends have the power to unlock many more words for spelling and reading than 'raw'. To teach the splitting or segmentation of the word at 'd' and 'st' is to obscure the use of the 'dr' blend in other words, such as 'drag, dry, drip' etc.

Similarly, the introduction of meaningless *-ree* as a letter string is unhelpful because it disrupts the use of initial sounds and blends in decoding and encoding. The more basic knowledge about the word is that it begins with a digraph 'th'. 'Th' is followed by 'r' which makes it into the trigraph blend 'thr', and this is followed by the very common double 'e' vowel combination 'ee'.

From the point of generalizability and the development of word attack and encoding skills 'three' can easily be spelled with knowledge of 'thr' (digraph blend) and double 'e'. 'Thre' would by analogy have a similar sound to 'the'. The word 'tree' can be addressed by the blend 'tr' and adding 'ee'; 'reel' by the initial sound 'r', double 'e' and the final sound 'l'; and 'street' by the segmentation of the initial three letter blend 'str', the addition of 'ee' and the final consonant 't'. The use of double 'e' rather than a single one is governed by a more fundamental linguistic rule which determines the basic structure of syllables. 'Stret' might be an early attempt at spelling street, after which 'street', 'strete', and even 'streat' would be legitimate variations and can indeed be seen in manuscripts from earlier centuries. The convention as in 'street' has become the accepted version and its common occurrence will help it to be learned.

The affixes pre-, de-, -ing, -ed, -ment are also sometimes taught as a string – the link between them being of course that when added to words as prefixes or suffixes they change the meaning of the words. But to teach them together in this way is not as helpful as to teach them one at a time. Each affix has a defined meaning and a consistent spelling. If the meanings and the spellings are *gradually* learnt they are a powerful help to correct spelling especially when the four affixing rules – add, double, drop, change (Cowdery, 1987) – are introduced at appropriate points.

Thus far it has been suggested that within the early developmental context of pupils' writing the teaching spelling strategies which should be employed are:

- segmentation into onset and rime
- the use of analogy with known words
- phonic segmentation and assembly skills
- morphemics
- use of linguistic knowledge and rules

At the same time as some formal teaching input about spelling knowledge is given by the class teacher this needs to be reinforced during all writing activities. In addition the teacher needs to be alert whilst moving round the class working with the pupils of the times at which individual teaching inputs can help move a pupil forward. At such times it can be judged whether a particular child is ready to make a conceptual leap and learn a new rule or structure.

ARE DYSLEXICS' SPELLINGS BIZARRE?

The question of whether or not dyslexics show a developmentally normal but retarded spelling pattern when compared with controls is an interesting one. Most teachers and researchers regard many 'dyslexic' spellings to be bizarre, but is this so? An examination of Tables 3.1a and b might help clarify thinking on these questions.

The pattern of the number of errors (Table 3.1b) is not significantly different on these fifteen words for groups of subjects controlled for spelling error, even though the dyslexics' exposure to words is likely to be greater than controls' because of their greater chronological age, a difference of 2.5 years. Only in the word 'friend' did the dyslexics seem to go for a straight phonetic strategy whereas the controls introduced letter 'i' in various medial positions more often. As a check upon these observations, the fifteen sets of misspellings were presented to sets of 120 qualified teachers who had completed special needs courses about helping pupils with specific learning difficulties and 280 student teachers in their fourth year of training, who had taken similar courses but

Table 3.1a *Which subjects are the dyslexics? Errors of dyslexics and (controls) on 15 difficult words from the Daniels and Diack Test. Groups matched for spelling age.*

Word	Number	Errors
1. so	3	sow sow sow
	(5)	(sow sow sowe soe sowh)
2. of	4	off off ov oft
	(5)	(off off ov ov ov)
3. form	4	fom from fom fom
	(2)	(fom forme)
4. seem	4	seam sean sem sean
	(7)	(seam seen sem seeme sem sheem sims)
5. who	7	hoo hoo ho hoow how ho ho
	(6)	(hoo hoe ho hoow how ho)
6. fight	8	fite fite fiter fit fite fite fite figth
	(8)	(fite fite firt fit fite fite fut fitghe)
7. great	9	grayt grayt grat grat grat grat grate grate grate
	(10)	(graet graet grate grat grat grate grate grate grate grede)
8. done	9	don doun dane dun dun dun dun dunit don
	(8)	(down dun don dune dun dun dun dun)
9. loud	9	loaed loaed loght lowd lowd loow lord lawd
	(7)	(lard lound lawd lowd lad lod lawd)
10. friend	10	frend freind frend frend frend fred frend frend frend frend
	(12)	(freind freind freind freand freind frenid frend freind frenind frend frend frend)
11. women	11	whimn wimon wimin – – wimmen whimin wimen wim wiminn wimin
	(13)	(wimon wemen wimin wimen wimin wimen wimin winim wimming wimen woner wimin wiming)
12. any	12	neary eney eny eney eney enylen eny erser eney eney ene ene
	(12)	(eany enry aney enay eney enay eney ener eney eney emey eny)
13. answer	13	answer answerwer aweser arser arser unser arser aser arnwa rser – answar arse
	(13)	(anweser answar answer ansire anrsoer answer awer asaw anrser unser ansir unser anser)
14. sure	14	shoer shoe shor shor shor sor shor sor shore shor shor shor shor shor
	(15)	(shure chore shaw shore shoe shore shour shore shore shor shore shore sor shor shore)
15. beautiful	16	beautifo bueaiful beutiful beatifal buitiful brotoful dualful buitfull – biterful birteeful boutifel buoolefle biootf burooteforl butiful
	(16)	(bauetyful beatyful beutiful beutiful buatfull (2) dutwely – – – beautiful buliefull beutiful beuitfull builfull (2))

with a more substantial theoretical component. The teachers were asked to determine which group of misspellings had been written by dyslexics and which by controls. Most of the teachers said that it was impossible for them to say which was the dyslexic group's misspellings, a few identified the dyslexic group correctly, the rest

Table 3.1b *Comparison of the number of errors made by controls and dyslexics for each of the 15 words*

	Word	Controls	Dyslexics
1	so	5	3
2	of	5	4
3	form	2	4
4	seem	7	3
5	who	6	7
6	fight	8	8
7	great	10	9
8	done	8	9
9	loud	7	9
10	friend	12	10
11	women	13	11
12	any	12	12
13	answer	13	13
14	sure	15	14
15	beautiful	16	16
	Total	137	134
	Mean	9.13	8.93

without exception but with lengthy time for study decided that the dyslexic group's misspellings were, in fact, those of controls. They pointed to a slightly larger number of 'bizarre' spellings amongst the matched controls, e.g. dutwely, fitghe, frenind, woner. It could therefore be suggested that what we are observing in dyslexics is spelling knowledge typical of that of younger normal spellers who lack precise phonological knowledge or orthographic information. Their spelling skills could be following a normal but delayed pattern. This confirms the findings of Nelson (1974) and Bradley and Bryant (1985). The misspellings of each group contain examples of Boder's (1971) 'good phonetic equivalents' (GFEs) and the so-called 'bizarre' spelling of Critchley (1970) and Miles (1983), thought to be typical only of dyslexics.

Reference to the bizarreness of misspellings occurs frequently in the descriptions of dyslexics' writing (Critchley, 1970; Pollack, 1975; Miles, 1983; Snowling, 1985). Such bizarre spellings, together with reversals, are identified as key diagnostic features, but the precise definition of 'bizarre' is seldom given. It seems to mean any misspelling which does not preserve the general sound identity of the structure of the word (according to the observer!). Examples from the Daniels and Diack test would probably be: dutwely for beautiful, rser for answer.

Table 3.2 compares the spelling performance of the same two groups of dyslexics and controls using the nursery rhyme 'Baa baa black sheep'. In this instance, the spellings that would probably be characterized as 'bizarre' are: brit (baa), shpe (sheep), eniu (any) ahed (any), hseas (yes), srer, sner, saim (sir), erein (three), dean (bags), hes (the), mnser (Master), mayn, macds (dame), ahla (who). However, arguments *against* bizarreness could be made in support of each of these except, perhaps, brit, saim and ahla. In the case of dutwely, for example, subject reverses 'b' and writes 'd', thus 'b-u-t' is equivalent to 'beauti' when sounded out with intrusive schwas 'buh-u-tih'; 'wh' as in 'who, what, where' seems reminiscent perhaps of /f/; 'h' is silent, thus 'w' inserted followed by 'e' to represent schwa /uh/ and to distinguish it from 'u' used previously as the name of the letter. The strong /l/ sound is emphasized by addition of 'y' to the end of the word and perhaps also to increase the number of letter places needed when the pupil recalls in reading that it is a long word and 'y' often comes at the end of words.

From the qualitative analysis of errors there is also an indication that this group used phonic strategies to obtain good phonetic equivalents of the words somewhat more often than did the younger pupils. This was presumably because all the dyslexics had received phonics training and were currently on a programme which used phonics as part of its approach.

When the number of dyslexics and controls were equated (Table 3.3) the dyslexics remembered slightly more words of the nursery rhyme than the controls but made more errors although they were two and a half years older. There was however no statistically

Table 3.2 *Errors (quantity and nature) of dyslexics and controls on the nursery rhyme Baa baa black sheep*

CA 10.65 yrs SA 7.44 yrs	Dyslexic N = 23		Controls N = 26	CA 7.9 yrs SA 7.85 yrs
Baa (23)	Bar Beep ba bar bar par ba bra br ba bar par bar bar par Bar Bar bar bar bar bar brit ba	Ba a (19)	Bar Ba Bar Ba Ba Bar ba ba ba Bar bar bah ba ba Bar bar bar bar barra	
Black (5)	back blak plack Blac Back	Black (2)	Blak Blacke	
Sheep (7)	She Shepp Ship chiep shep chiep –	Sheep (3)	Shpe seep seep	
have (1)	haf	have (2)	heeve hld	
you (2)	yo –	you (1)	you	
any (10)	ana ney ne eney eny ene ane eniu ane en	any (6)	eny aen enery ene eny ahed	
yes (0)		yes (3)	hseas – yers	

Table 3.2 *Continued*

CA 10.65 yrs SA 7.44 yrs	Dyslexic N = 23		Controls N = 26	CA 7.9 yrs SA 7.85 yrs
sir (6)	ser sar sar srer ser sner		sir (7)	sher ser ser – sere saim –
three (7)	theer there erein – tree 3 3		three (7)	3 3 theree there 3 3 –
bags (11)	bag bag bay bas bages bass ba bag baigs – –		bags (7)	bag bag bag bars – bages dean
full (14)	foul fule fule foul foll fall fall fall fall fuill fall ail fal foll		full (8)	fol ful fall ful fall – four fill
one (6)	1 on ome 7 1 wan		one (3)	1 Tone –
for (5)	four fo far fore four		for (3)	of – fill
the (3)	– hes hte		the (2)	– then
master (13)	marst marster marster marster morster marster murst marster marster muster mnser marster mrs		master (5)	marste marst – marster ener
and (1)	und		and (1)	–
dame (13)	darm dan daym – dam dam dam dane dan – dane dam Den		dame (9)	dam dam macds dane Dane me mayn – –
little (8)	lettle tiller littlo – litter litt litel lite		little (2)	littly –
boy (2)	day –		boy (1)	–
who (12)	have ahla how how how – how how – hoo you –		who (7)	how how ho hoe how – how
lives (9)	live live live live livees – lits live live		lives (3)	livs liv –
down (7)	dowe dwon dawn bone dawn dan dow		down (2)	dow –
lane (6)	lan lene dran lan lain lne		lane (3)	rode tane –
171	Total no. errors Bizarre = ?		109	Total no. errors Bizarre = ?

Table 3.3 *Mean words written in the nursery rhyme and spelling ratios for dyslexics and controls*

	Mean chronological age	Spelling ratio x̄ = mean score	Mean words written	Spelling age
Controls N = 23	8.04 yrs	x̄ = 0.83	30.09	7.85 yrs
Dyslexics N = 23	10.65 yrs	x̄ = 0.71	32.69	7.44 yrs

significant difference between the spelling ratios of the two groups. There is one example of a reversal in the dyslexics' scripts.

As far as can be detected, the spelling errors of dyslexics appear to be no different from those made by normal spellers of a younger age. Similar strategies seem to be used by each group and these resemble those discovered by Ferreiro (1978), Ferreiro and Teberosky (1982) and Read (1975, 1986) for normal beginning spellers.

The reports of development of normal beginning spellers' progress in emergent writing regimes are still mainly descriptive. However, Clarke (1988) found that 'children in invented spelling classrooms could decode regularly spelled words and could recognise high frequency irregular words better than those in traditional classrooms even though the same basal reading scheme and supplementary phonics programme was used by all the teachers' (p. 472). The extent to which an emergent writing approach can overcome dyslexic difficulties remains to be assessed. What can be envisaged is that it will be possible to identify difficulties at a very early stage without the aid of formal tests. Then appropriate intervention can be planned.

It would seem from these results, then, which are typical of other samples taken, that dyslexic spelling is characteristic in error patterns to those of much younger children and similar to other poor spellers who have not yet acquired the alphabetic principle. Their patterns of errors show delayed skill development. What could cause this delay and then keep them at a plateau, when they do learn to spell, at about the 8-year-old level, is at last beginning to be understood.

To use 'bizarreness' as a diagnostic clue permitting referral could exclude many severely disabled spellers and dyslexics who need help. Similarly, to refuse to make a diagnosis of dyslexia on the basis that there are no reversals to be seen is not supportable by the evidence.

SUMMARY

Spelling errors may be seen in a range of scripts from early writers to adults. The primary school period is when the vast majority move from a state of about 100 per cent error to 100 per cent correct spellings for most of the commonly used words in the vocabulary. Throughout secondary school and into adulthood extension and improvement to this basic spelling vocabularly continues. Some 20 per cent of the population will show much slower development of spelling skills and may have in addition a handwriting problem. A small number, 1 to 4 per cent, appear to have a severe difficulty in acquiring rudiments of spelling by the current methods of teaching and learning adopted in schools. These have been referred to as 'dyslexics' as distinct from other poor spellers. Some LEAs do not choose to distinguish between 'dyslexics' and other poor spellers in making special provision. Dyslexic difficulties centre upon their problems in acquiring the alphabetic principle. Scrutiny of the scripts of dyslexics and beginning 'good' spellers shows the acquisition and use of the alphabetic principle by good 5-year-old spellers but a distinct lack of its use in the 7- and 8-year-old dyslexics.

The technique of developmental assessment has been dwelt upon in some detail in order to show how the emergent writing of all poor spellers can be analysed so that intervention can be targeted at the most appropriate point. To help systematize the analysis the four-column strategy was proposed.

Developmental assessment and intervention: the later stages of learning

INTRODUCTION

Although there are many schemes which offer spelling support and intervention for the early stages there are few which are suitable or helpful for the later stages. Good spellers, when they acquire new vocabulary for GCSEs, A levels and degree studies, frequently have lapses and make errors. Many of us carry errors into adulthood even though we may have had help to correct the more glaring and common ones, such as *seperate* and *accomodate*. Once mistakes have been made they can be committed to memory and it then becomes very difficult to erase them. In fact, psychological theory and research (Skinner, 1958) shows that we cannot unlearn things. What we must do is learn to inhibit previous learning and give new items a higher profile so that they are more likely to be recalled. The results of attempts to do this can be seen particularly under examination pressure, where old mistakes from childhood pop up again; some errors appear in different spellings at different points in the script; the same word may be spelled correctly at one point and incorrectly at another; and homophones, e.g. bow and bough, appear because the wrong motor programme has been triggered.

Many such mistakes can be corrected if only the student can be encouraged to *proof-read* the work. This is the first and most basic correction strategy, to leave five minutes at the end of each paper or activity to read through and correct misspellings. Good spellers will pick up most of them and poorer spellers will find some of them. Even this is helpful and important because the more obvious mistakes, the low-level common word ones, will cause the marker concern about the candidate's level of literacy. This would certainly result in the loss of 5 per cent of marks, in accordance with Department for Education and Employment proposals for marking public examinations. Moreover as Moseley (1994) has suggested, inaccurate spelling makes markers of scripts more sensitive to other potential weaknesses in composition. This certainly fits with my personal experience of examining scripts for spelling errors and noting that poorly spelled scripts may contain an A grade content but will be given substantially less, even only a C grade or a bare pass C–, by some markers. Some colleagues even become angry and feel insulted by misspellings in scripts, regarding these as the result of carelessness and laziness, i.e. the student has not even bothered to use a dictionary.

Very poor spellers and those with severe spelling problems may be regarded as unintelligent. This is a popularly held myth. Any appeal for the need to 'raise standards' can always find unquestioning adherents to the cause. The spelling and handwriting of the young is an easy target.

On appointment panels for jobs it has been observed that some members want to bin all those applications which contain even a single misspelling and heated debates ensue about the appropriateness of such actions. What can be concluded is that there are often very rigidly held views towards spelling and handwriting which can be prejudicial to an individual's career prospects in school and beyond.

IDENTIFICATION OF HIGHER-ORDER ERRORS

There are a whole host of older pupils who, although not classified as dyslexic, have poor spelling. They conceal this whenever they can by using a range of compensatory strategies. Moseley (1989), for example, found that the 13- to 15-year-olds whose free writing he was studying

- used fewer words outside a core of 500
- used more short words
- used more regularly spelled words
- avoided common hard to spell words
- repeated words and phrases to play safe

He suggested that the constant criticism which poor spelling engendered caused a lack of self-esteem and a tendency to avoid putting pen to paper if at all possible. These findings are similar to those of Myklebust (1965, 1973) who, nearly three decades earlier, found that disabled spellers would write at least one third less than age-matched peers. They would also substitute known words for those whose spelling they knew they were unsure of. Adults report taking longer on thinking time in examinations as they try to avoid known difficult words and select/replace with a known one. In a similar effort, Gavin, in a spelling test, substituted 'box' when the teacher had read out 'parcel'. This is just an indication of his commitment and motivation to try to do what was required and to show the teacher he was not careless.

Studies of undergraduate misspellings by Van Nes (1971) showed that subjects made a small proportion of errors, in the order of 0.06–0.6 per cent. Chedru and Geschwind (1972) found higher error rates, from 1.0 to 1.1 per cent, in a control group they were comparing with confusional state patients. They classified the errors into *omissions* (clar for clear), *additions* (carefull for careful), *substitutions* (lan for van), *inversions* (on for no) and *transpositions* (librety for liberty). This is a characteristic miscues analysis set of category headings, first recorded by Spache (1940) and used by Neale (1958) and Neale *et al.* (1994) in her *Analysis of Reading Ability*. It is fairly easy to assign errors to a category. However, this seldom seems to be useful for guiding the intervention. It seems more important to *know what has been added, omitted, substituted* and so on, rather than be able to assign a category label and decide whether the words read out are positive or negative examples and then allow the subjects to read on or give the correct word.

Wing and Baddeley (1980) found an error rate of 1.5 per cent in 40 undergraduate scripts with an estimated word count of 10,000 words in total. They categorized the errors as 'slips of the pen' – correctable errors attributable to lapses or inattention on the part of the writer, which would have been amended if they had been noticed. This form of error made up 79 per cent of the corpus, of which 73 per cent had been corrected. The other category was 'convention errors' – words which were consistently misspelled and were departures from conventional spelling, requiring some remedial input. These errors made up 21 per cent of the corpus. Their study went on to investigate the slips of the pen, whereas here we are concerned with convention errors. The difference between the two kinds of error, however, is not great. The following are misspellings taken from the first 10 items on their list: intele (intellect); censorsored (censored); likly (likely); an (any); immediatly (immediately); prodi (producing); wull (will); ho (how); unabiguous (unambiguous); chose (choose).

On reading these errors it was decided to understake a collection from our own undergraduate scripts, but focus upon convention errors and not those which had been corrected.

AN ANALYSIS OF HIGHER ORDER SPELLING ERRORS

Errors were collected from a total of 55 final-year, teacher education students' examination scripts. A total of 165 errors were found overall with 162 different errors, making an error rate of 0.001 per cent in an estimated 165,000 words (an average of 3,000 words per three-hour script). This is a very low error rate indeed, which is fortunate seeing that the students are intending to become teachers. Examples of their errors were: arguement (S), agressive (P), auspecies (B), allert (P), adaption (Syll), appart (P), advise (N/V), advantagous (S), accomodated (B/Sh), bothe (L/rule), deficits (B) encreased (P), liasing (B), opperate (P), payed (S), psycologists (R). It was possible to analyse the errors into convention types with a fair degree of accuracy (bracketed in code). A list of all the error types found is shown in Table 4.1.

Table 4.1 *Error types found in the error corpus*

Key	Error type	Total	Key	Error Type	Total
S	Suffixing error	43	H	Homophones	5
B	Base word errors	36	L	Long vowel error	4
P	Prefixing error	26	Ph	Phonetic confusion	3
R	Root errors	19	Sh	Short vowel errors	2
Syll	Syllabification error	9	AA	Articulation awareness	0
Slip	Slip of the pen	7	N/V	Noun-verb confusion	0

It can be seen from this analysis that the bulk of the errors of these advanced spellers centre upon affixing – the addition of prefixes and suffixes – and thereafter upon base words and roots. It would therefore not be unreasonable to base corrective intervention on strategies directed to these areas. When their errors are compared with those made by younger subjects they can be seen to be more advanced, they are mainly *linguistic* rather than alphabetic and phonic. Following on from this analysis, other students' written work was examined and when errors were noted that particular student was helped to correct the error and a range of strategies began to be clarified.

Evidence in support of this approach comes from Henry, President of the Orton Society, who stated in her paper to the Orton Society Conference (1995) that the root words hold the key to reading, spelling and understanding. She recommended teaching older learners syllable patterns, affixes, Anglo-Saxon, Latin and Greek roots.

INTERVENTION STRATEGIES

Moseley (1994) reported successful interventions with his 13- to 15-year-old poor spellers, in which spelling ages increased by 19 months in 5, an average of 3.7 per month in comparison with controls who received a 'look–cover–write–check' strategy and whose scores remained the same. The best results were obtained by the teacher who gave daily tests to monitor the learning.

The successful intervention strategies were (Moseley, 1994, p. 469):

- say the word to suit the spelling
- trace and say
- sky write
- visualize the word and count the letters
- use mnemonics
- use spelling pattern and some rules
- focus on the tricky parts
- say the alphabet names
- make rhyming word

If we examine these strategies four of them can be seen to be rote learning methods (trace and say, sky write, mnemonics and visualize the word) and, as such, potentially limited for remedial work. Radaker (1963) found that visualization training strategies did help improve the spelling of his experimental groups over controls. His subjects had to imagine the word they were learning set in glossy black letters on a white background or cinema screen. If the image was unstable they had to imagine pasting the letters in place or fixing them as large metallic letters with holes at the bottom and top to 'nail' them in place. However, these were pupils aged from $8\frac{1}{2}$ to $10\frac{1}{2}$ years. It is difficult to imagine unwilling learners in some secondary schools wanting to be seen imaging, tracing, saying or sky writing.

Developing a mnemonic takes time and effort and then itself has to be remembered. If many were needed (as is likely) then this could prove a uselessly confusing strategy. Giving a person a ready-made mnemonic is merely giving him or her something else to rote learn. Rhymes might only work with some pupils if they were crude but perhaps here he is suggesting analogy strategy. However, there are strategies on this list which could prove useful, especially for one-off items.

Another cognitive approach is to be found in *The ACE Spelling Dictionary* (Moseley and Nicol, 1988). The title stands for Aurally Coded English. To use it the reader has to do two things: pick out the first strong clear vowel sound and decide on what the first letter in the word is. Herein lie the problems for dyslexics: they can seldom do either of these tasks before they have been on a specialist teaching programme. They would simply find the task confusing. Even when they have developed some spelling knowledge they would still find it difficult, for they have to syllabify the word correctly and then find it in a long list of other similar words. As an aid to spelling for the average individual with developing skills and for the poorer student speller it would make a useful spellchecker, and as such should be available in a wide range of classrooms.

LINGUISTIC AND COGNITIVE INTERVENTION STRATEGIES

Leong (1995) defined linguistic awareness as phonological or phonemic awareness *plus* morphemic awareness. Most of us pick this up incidentally during reading and writing but poor spellers and dyslexics need to be taught it directly. Even good spellers' spelling may be enhanced by having aspects of morphemics brought to conscious awareness by explicit teaching.

Linguistics teaching had not been a feature of the English curriculum of many of the undergraduates who took part in the studies described below. Therefore it was not surprising that many of them did not know the basic long and short vowel structure of words and the effect on this of adding affixes. Many were also unfamiliar with the less common prefixes and suffixes which were now needed in their lexicon. Most of them, however, did know the so-called 'magic e rule', in which the silent 'e' at the end of a syllable lengthens the preceding vowel, e.g. lake, cede, like, rote, lute. (With younger children it is sometimes more helpful to explain that the silent 'e' makes the vowel 'say its name', separating the teaching of short closed syllables given early on from the long vowel sound, which if taught too close together can confuse some children, particularly potentially poor spellers.)

With older and adult spellers it is possible to examine the corpus of errors that they make and then, targeting those most amenable to improvement, teach relevant linguistic structures and rules. It is advisable not to teach more than two such structures/rules at a single session, as otherwise even reasonably competent spellers can become confused.

Strategies which good spellers use

The developmental needs of student and adult spellers are seldom addressed. They are beyond the need for phonics teaching and often the only advice they are given is to look up the word in a dictionary or to rote learn the correct spelling. However, good spellers do use a range of strategies to help them learn new spellings and tend to stick to well-tried ones when sometimes another strategy would be more effective. A collection of the misspellings of adult spellers was made. The errors they produced were found to be governed by rules of which they had no experience or knowledge. Sometimes there were no rules to correct a particular error. So an investigation was set up to discover the strategies which good spellers used to spell unknown difficult words. These would confirm or supplement those which some spellers already used. The technique for investigation was intended not only to extract the maximum number of strategies from the widest group, but also to serve as a teaching strategy and help subjects learn those strategies they were not using or of which they were unaware.

In the trial period 900 teachers and 800 undergraduate teachers were given a *misspelled spelling* test (below). The purpose of this was to get subjects to reflect upon their analysis strategies as they were trying to give the correct spellings and then report on them.

ass-ee-9
brag-ar-doh-chio
virr-mill-aeon
rare-ee-figh
im-pahst-err
row-cocoa
lick-we-fye
sack-ree-lidge-ious
pav-ill-eon
ack-omme-oh-dait
se-pehr-ate
dessy-kate

The subjects were asked to say the word to themselves and write the correct spelling down. At the same time they were to make a mental note of how they had arrived at their particular spelling.

In the feedback sessions most subjects explained that either they thought they knew the word and wrote it down *or* they wrote it down and then inspected it to see if it *looked right*. This is a proof-reading strategy. If the word looked wrong they tried an alternative spelling, or even several spellings, and chose the best fit. Some subjects reported that both spellings looked right and so they had guessed which was correct. Some found that the one which they had chosen because it looked right was in fact wrong, which caused some consternation.

A small proportion of the group (about 10–20 per cent for each word) offered, on reflection, different strategies from this. Subjects sometimes had no strategies for some words and several for others. By a process of judicious questioning the following twelve strategies were elicited. It was surprising that the same group of strategies was evoked on each occasion and appeared to be constant.

As the focus was upon *cognitive* and linguistic strategies, rote strategies were not included in the final list. They were noted, however, and included *mnemonics, visualizing, rote memory routines* – such as *singing* and *rhyming* ('MI – SSI – SSI – PPI' was given as an illustration of this strategy).

TWELVE PLUS ONE COGNITIVE STRATEGIES FOR CORRECTING MISSPELLINGS

In the correction phase the subjects were asked to draw a ring round the region of error, that is, round the individual letter or letters which were incorrect or omitted. Two most appropriate strategies were then selected from the following list to correct the misspelling.

1. Articulation. The misspelt word is clearly and precisely articulated for spelling: 'chimley' corrected to 'chimney'; 'skelington' to 'skeleton'; and 'braggadocio' clearly enunciated. The point where the stress comes in the word should be noted – helpful for words such as: vermilion, harass, embarrass, refer.

2. Over-articulation. The word is enunciated with emphasis on all the syllables, particularly the one normally *not* sounded. For example: parli(a)ment, gover(n)ment, Wed(n/e)sday, sep(a)rate.

3. Cue articulation. The word is pronounced incorrectly to point up the area of difficulty and cue the correct spelling, e.g. necessary spoken as 'neckessary' to remember the (here mispronounced hard) 'c' before the double 's', Wed(nes)day for 'We'n'sday', pavilion, vermil-ion.

4. Syllabification. It is easier to spell a word when it is broken down into short syllable units and spelled syllable by syllable. Good spellers unconsciously do this. Poor spellers, however, need to be taught this syllable segmentation skill. If necessary syllables should be counted and the 'beats' clapped. Leaving out syllables is sometimes termed a 'concatenation error' or a 'contraction error'. Clear articulation and syllabification used together can do much to support and improve spelling, preventing the contractions of polysyllabled words which are frequent in dyslexic spelling as well as in the poor spelling of others, e.g. misdeanour – mis/de/mean/our; criticed – crit/i/cise/d; accodated – ac/com/mod/ate/d.

It should be noted that in the syllabification strategy an attempt has been made to reflect linguistic rules and structures which will support the later learning of these. After treating syllables as beats is established, the short closed syllable structure should be introduced and recognition of the short vowel sound practised for spelling and reading.

5. Phonics. Phonics refers to assigning a grapheme (written unit) to a phoneme (sound unit). For most words in the English language there is not a direct symbol-to-sound correspondence. It only occurs in 'regular' words, such as bed, bred, bled, sat, set, sit, pin, trap, bend, blend, plan. These are relatively few. For the rest orthographic rules have to be applied to 'capture' spellings in their correct forms, e.g. late, lute, separate (effect of silent 'e'). Note, however, that although the phonic strategy is of limited usefulness, when a poor speller begins to crack the alphabetic code and to apply sound-to-symbol correspondence this should be celebrated, for it produces a basic skeletal framework of a word to work on, e.g. mastr, mstry, nite. And for words such as 'rococo' a simple phonic strategy actually works.

6. Linguistic rules. A few well chosen rules can help unravel a range of spelling problems. (It is also important for the idea to be conveyed that there will always be a few exceptions to a rule. Sometimes there is a story behind this, or a story can be made, which helps the exceptions be remembered.) The silent 'e' rule has a wide use. The l-f-s rule is helpful: at the end of a one syllable word which has a single short vowel sound the letters l, f and s have to be doubled, e.g. tell, sell, pill; off, stiff, cuff; toss, loss, less, miss, and so on. Words which end in a single 's' have the sound /z/ or they denote a plural. There are of course some exceptions to this rule: pal, nil, if, of /v/, bus, gas, plus, this, thus, us, yes. There are the four main affixing rules, and eight suffixing rules overall, as well as plural rules, rules about accent and stress, and so on. The most useful and accessible source for all of these is *The Spelling Notebook*, written for pupils and teachers by Lucy L. Cowdery (1987).

7. Stress and other orthographic conventions. When stress occurs on the second syllable of a word doubling must occur, e.g. referral, embarrass, deterrent, ebullient, occurrence. The base word's pronunciation can give guidance here, e.g. refer, deter, occur – where the stress is clearly on the second syllable.

Scribal 'o' has the sound /uh/ and is used to spell the /uh/

sound before 'm', 'n' and 'v' as in some, son, won, love, above and London.

8. Family. This notion is often helpful in recalling silent letters and correct representation of the schwa or /uh/ sound in some words: e.g. Canada – Canadian; telephone – telepathic, television, telescope where meaning and origin clues can also be used for 'tele'; bomb, bombing, bombardment, bombardier; signal, sign, signing, significant and so on. These are examples of real families of words. (Words which have common letter strings and no other relation can hardly be called families.)

9. Analogy. This is the comparison with the spelling of similar words or parts of words which are already known and correctly learned. So-called letter strings may have a role here. Students should learn to say, for instance, in the case of 'braggadocio', 'It is like braggart'. This helps spell part of the word about which there may be doubt (whether to double the 'g'). In the case of 'hazard', 'It is like maze' (only one 'z').

10. Meaning. 'Separate' is commonly incorrectly spelled as sep(e)rate. Quite often subjects know exactly where the problem lies, but when they need to write the word cannot remember whether 'a' or 'e' in the middle is correct. Looking up its meaning in a dictionary can dispel this error quite easily for it will be found that to sep*a*rate means to divide, to *part*, cut a*part*, or even *pare*.

11. Origin. Often a word's roots in another language can provide the framework for correct recall, e.g. sensation is often misspelled as sen(c)ation and sense as sen(c)e. The origin *sens* (= feeling) in both French and Latin can help to put the word and the rest of the family – sensible, sensibility – right.

The word opportunity is often misspelled as opp(ur)tunity or opp(er)tunity. When the origin of this is found in *port* or harbour, 'an effective or timely opening', this revelation prevents recurrence of the error.

12. Funnies. When it is not possible to use any of the foregoing, something funny, or even rude, can be used to aid the memory. This strategy can be brought into play. For instance, to spell necessary correctly one subject used 'knickers' to remind her and another used 'cess pit'.

Simultaneous Oral Spelling: SOS (a rote learning strategy). Finally, when the misspelt word has been corrected by having at least two strategies applied to it, for safety's sake it needs to be written down to check that it can be recalled at will. The recommended strategy for this is SOS, which has been shown to be a better aid to recall than 'look–cover–write–check'. (The full format for SOS can be found in Chapter 7, at pp. 170–2.) One important factor in SOS is that the word should be written as far as possible in one continuous writing movement, i.e. in cursive writing. If it is a long word then the pauses should be at the base word then the syllable boundaries, e.g. opport/unity, so that the writer writes or flows through the region of error, unless this is actually at the boundary, when the pattern should reflect another meaningful division, e.g. re/ferral.

As the above strategies were made explicit, so some of the teachers and undergraduates reported beginning to apply them more widely, using them on their own spellings and with their pupils. However, it is not easy to persuade people to switch to new and different strategies when they have preferred and fixed ones, no matter how limited the latter may be. What was important was to encourage them to teach strategies to young learners, who, having become familiar with them early, would retain some flexibility. A number of teachers did undertake a programme of introduction of the 'Twelve plus one strategies' with evident success, and the next section of the chapter summarizes one of the more controlled of these studies.

Case studies of a group of a dozen students in higher education were also made. They had been referred for support with spelling or had referred themselves. In a 30-minute to one-hour tutorial their individual learning needs were assessed and a list of misspellings made which they needed to correct. Two spellings per student were addressed, using the cognitive process protocol, and the student went away to practise them and to address the next misspelling on the list. Tutor and student met for a few minutes over coffee in the refectory, when the student reported on the spellings learnt, the strategies employed and spelled the word aloud correctly. After about six such sessions the students felt able to continue the project on their own. Their examination papers before and after the intervention were compared for spelling errors and in the majority no errors at all were recorded afterwards and in the rest they were significantly fewer, with no lower-level ones.

Klein and Millar, in their book *Unscrambling Spelling* (1990), come closest to this approach in their analysis of errors. They identified the following types: spelt like it sounded, rule not known, letters out of order, mixed up sounds, missed out or added bits. In order to improve spelling they advised the following range of strategies: 'look–cover–write–check'; chunk words for reinforcing visual aspects; teach word-building, i.e. roots, prefixes and suffixes; find rules from spelling patterns and lists; proof-reading; dictations; discuss spellings; and teach cursive writing. They provide seventeen resource sheets to illustrate their various proposals, which they had developed in particular for their further education students but which can be widely used.

Klein and Millar's strategies can in part help adult dyslexics. The misspellings of the adult dyslexic below would respond in part to word-building approaches. There is, however, a lower order and more fundamental set of strategies which he requires, which were evolved using the misspelled spelling test. For example, clear and accurate articulation for spelling, syllabification and phonics.

REAR FLor L/R (rear floor)
PEDDER RUBDER (pedal rubber)
BUSHER Top STAIRG COM (bushes, top steering column)
WASH NOT WORKING P L (washer not working)
DIS pad (disc pad)
STNING BOX ARM (steering box arm)
L/H STOP LAMP

As can be noted, the orthographic knowledge of this 40-year-old is minimal. The errors are alphabetic, phonic, syllabic, articulatory and linguistic. The script was mainly in capitals, the letters poorly formed. The spelling is akin to that which might be produced by much younger spellers required to use the same vocabulary. The strategies taught need to be packaged to meet the developmental needs of the speller. The impact of stress and higher-order linguistic rules, for example, are not appropriate to correcting lower-order errors. The simplest possible interventions should be selected at first, but over time and with progress the full range need to be taught.

USING COGNITIVE PROCESS STRATEGIES WITH YOUNG MISSPELLERS

A teacher, Heather Parrant, who had attended the in-service programme on dealing with spelling problems, decided to test the strategies in an experiment.

The experimental subjects were a mixed class group of 11-year-olds in an ordinary middle school. There were 21 pupils, 8 of whom were identified as having specific special needs in relation to reading and spelling problems. A parallel class of 23 pupils was used as a control group. The classes were larger, 26 and 27 pupils respectively, but absence prevented full data being collected on these other subjects. At the outset of the test period the subjects were given a dictation of 100 words drawn from their current favourite book, *Charlie and the Chocolate Factory* by Roald Dahl.

Over the period of the next six weeks during normal curriculum activities the teacher offered cognitive strategies for correcting any misspellings in the following manner.

Since any misspelling was usually confined to a specific and predictable location in a word, e.g. at the 'schwa' point or the syllable/prefix boundary, a *critical features* (Farnham-Diggory, 1978) identification strategy was used to draw attention to it. This simply meant *a ring was drawn round the error letter or the omission area*:

e.g. accom◯odation and practiⓢe

All attention was then directed to correcting this error item rather than attending to any part of the word already known. The pupils were taught how to *remediate only two* of their misspellings at any one sitting, no more. On each occasion they were shown two remedial strategies for the word and were asked to remediate another of their errors using these strategies, and to report back. They were then asked orally to spell the words correctly. They were praised for the amount of the word they correctly spelled. Although the pupils found that even with this exercise they might still misspell the word in story writing, whenever they came to it they had warning bells or signs that this was one of their 'specials'. They would misspell it and then correct it, using their special strategy. As they used the word more often, they could begin to correct it before writing it down for they were cued to attend carefully and avoid the old error. Eventually, they found that words frequently used were spelled easily and correctly without pause as the old motor programme was substituted by the 'higher profile' new one. In some cases, practice in writing the word in full cursive was a good means of overriding old writing habits.

The control group did not receive the cognitive strategies but were given the usual practice of 'look–cover–write–check' for their errors.

The same dictations were given pre- and post-training and although, not surprisingly, the total number of errors of each group fell on the post-training test, the difference between the totals for both groups was significantly different on the post-training test. The control group's pre- and post-training scores were not significantly different, whereas the experimental group's scores of 273 errors falling to 162 were highly statistically significant.

The control group's pattern of errors on the 'post' test showed a highly variable pattern of improvements and deteriorations; the experimental group error scores all diminished markedly, except for one subject who made one error on each and one who made no errors on the pre-training test and one on the post-training test. A change in attitude was reported by the experimental group pupils from a learned helplessness or neutrality to positive interest and self-esteem through finding a way through to improving their own spelling. Within the class the special needs group's spelling also improved but less significantly. They would still write 'SED' for *said*, phonetic transcription, *CKUP* for *cup*, a standard spelling in the wrong position, 'rodot' for *robot* and were not surprised to see reversals.

The evidence of these studies was that when cognitive intervention strategies developed from the responses to the special spelling test were applied with the adult dyslexics their spelling error rates decreased. The general groups of students introduced to the techniques reported diminishing error rates/improved spelling.

The corrective/developmental cognitive spelling strategies used with a class group of 11-year-old pupils were found to improve their spelling development markedly. Similar reports were received from teachers using the techniques with primary and secondary pupils, but who were not taking part in the testing sessions. The analysis of errors has enabled a set of remedial strategies to be developed which *non-specialist* teachers may effectively use with both good and poor spellers as corrective and developmental interventions. The 12+1 cognitive strategies are now offered as a basis for whole school policies on spelling in in-service development training.

COGNITIVE PROCESS THEORY APPLIED

Correcting misspellings is additionally problematic, for it is not possible to unlearn something (Skinner, 1958), it can only be suppressed. Thus any corrective or remedial strategy must help suppress the misspelling and give the correct version a higher profile so that it is more likely to be evoked or retrieved during writing. For this reason spellers were told to draw a ring round the region of error for spellers usually get most of the word correct and there is therefore no point on focusing on this. A *critical features* analysis (Gibson and Levin, 1975; Farnham-Diggory, 1978) was the approach adopted and the correction strategies were all targeted to this area in order to give it a high profile. Students reported that this was indeed successful for when they were writing and came to one of their problem words they would be cued to halt and go back and proof-read or would halt, use their cognitive strategies and then speed on. After a while they found that the correct spelling was absorbed into their word memory (lexicon) and would come

out automatically when required. Only under stress did they occasionally regress.

From this feedback, the experiments and case study interventions, a protocol was drawn up for making cognitive interventions.
Of particular importance in relation to schools was the purchasing
of a good dictionary for class reference, for many school dictionaries do not have in them all the five necessary elements, i.e. correct
spelling, meaning, pronunciation, derivation, base word and roots.

Cognitive process protocol for correcting misspellings: recommended procedure

- pupil tries to identify misspellings by proof-reading
- teacher also proof-reads pupil's writing for errors
- pupil lists misspellings
- pupil looks up words in dictionary
- pupil draws ring round area of error
- teacher helps select two words for intervention
- two words looked up in good dictionary for meaning and origin
- teacher discusses with pupil *two* strategies for dealing with the
  area of error of one misspelling (word one) using cognitive
  process strategies
- pupil tries to write the correct spelling three times using SOS
- pupil tries to develop two strategies using the cognitive process
  strategies already suggested by the teacher for word two and
  tries to think up a 'funny' in addition for word one
- teacher teaches a cognitive process strategy on a regular basis to
  the class as a whole and encourages its use in writing
- pupil reports on self-developed correction strategies for word
  two and spells word orally to teacher as a check

Two new words are selected … and so on.

It would appear from a number of researches (Goswami, 1992;
Lennox and Siegal, 1994) that children will use any method to spell
and that logographic and alphabetic strategies operate in parallel
rather than sequentially (unless of course the teaching method
stamps out the other strategies). What is becoming increasingly
apparent is that the researches are moving towards an interactive
approach 'where different sources of knowledge constantly inter-
act and are brought to bear on the spelling process' (Brown and
Ellis, 1994, p. 7). Longitudinal studies by Ellis (1994) on spelling
confirmed the importance of spelling to the development of
reading. This is an important step forward, which all teachers
should recognize. It should help dispel the idea that teaching

spelling dampens creativity. It can instead release creative output by skilling or reskilling learners so that they can indeed write what they think.

Dyslexics' abilities in reading and spelling non-words using grapheme–phoneme information always remain poor despite improvements in their literacy skills. This has led researchers to conclude that this is because they have a disordered system. What computational models have shown (Brown and Loosemore, 1994; Rumelhart and McClelland, 1986) is that when there is a similar restricted input to the computational model this also results in a difficulty and slowness in spelling non-words.

According to Treiman (1994), spelling errors and errors in phonological knowledge reflect inadequate knowledge rather than sound-to-spelling translation problems. This is important for it means that if we directly teach the dyslexic or poor spellers what they do not know then they will improve their spelling and spelling strategies.

Cognitive processes are particularly concerned with *metacognitive events*. According to Kolb (1984), it is not enough for the learner to be actively engaged in learning; the learning occurs not in the doing but in the reflection and conceptualization that takes place during and after the event. Thus the speller must be actively and reflectively engaged in correcting the misspelling. Flavell (1979) found that such metacognition was a highly important contribution to higher order learning and contributed to intelligence.

SUMMARY

A developmental analysis of good spellers' errors showed that these usually involved linguistic inaccuracies, such as affixing the words' roots when the roots come from different languages. Thus the errors frequently occurred at syllable boundaries and in relation to unstressed vowels in syllables, the schwa sound. A number of cognitive process strategies, including the use of linguistics, were developed. These proved to be successful in helping undergraduates correct and improve their spelling. When they were used as corrective and developmental strategies with class groups of younger spellers, spelling of both good and poor spellers improved. Similar reports were received from a wide range of teachers who used the techniques in class settings but without control groups. With younger spellers and poorer spellers in secondary schools a preponderance of lower-level strategies such as articulation, phonics, rules, syllabification and analogy needed to be used.

Cognitive process strategies elicit metacognitive activity and help learners hold learning conversations with themselves (Thomas and Harri-Augstein, 1985). This enables them to gain insight into the reasons for their errors and enables them to correct them. The technique gives the error region a temporary high profile so that the learner can in advance of writing pause and select the correct spelling and this eventually over-rides and replaces the incorrect version, enabling it to be suppressed. The strategies offer an opportunity for some creative problem-solving so that the learner gains ownership of the problem and the means for remediation. Teachers who have no knowledge of specialist remedial strategies can easily acquire this cognitive approach to developmental and corrective spellling and build their linguistic knowledge in the process so that they can tackle most of the typical misspellings seen in pupils' written work. Schools can develop whole school policies based upon this approach and so build communities of spellers in which peer tutoring and counselling can provide the supportive framework for creative exploration and problem solving.

5

General remedial strategies: abilities training

INTRODUCTION

In education generally, the results of linguistic analyses of children's narrative and expressive writing are beginning to influence teaching theory and teaching strategy, as exemplied in recent texts by Clay (1979, 1989), Perera (1984) and Read (1986). The work of Goodman (1969) and Smith (1973, 1978) however still seems to be the most influential in theoretical terms within the reading field. Least progress appears to have been made in the field of remedial education, now 'support for learning'. On the one hand there are programmes which can, through their structured and sequential analysis of the spelling task, offer a coherent framework to spelling error analysis. These schemes were first developed five or even six decades ago and have been redeveloped and steadily improved ever since. They appear to be thoroughly consonant with the latest models of reading and spelling which refer to phonological processing deficits, but their theoretical basis is often absent or references are made to the older theories of visual perceptual processing. On the other hand, there are well-established remedial practices and programmes whose theories are found to be equivocal or even wrong but the programmes are still in use. In addition to these are schemes which teachers like to use and which are well promoted but which may lack any theory or research to substantiate them. Teachers claim to use only strategies known to work, but strategies which work for the majority and have already failed the few cannot be expected to work simply by being repeated or given more individual attention and time.

TEACHING FAILURE AS OPPOSED TO LEARNING FAILURE?

It has been suggested that, in the general teaching of reading and spelling, a significant amount of learning under the most popular system of teaching in England takes place incidentally with the learner actively operating on the environment of words to develop basic and then higher order reading and spelling skills. It does seem, however, that this approach is not satisfactory for all, especially those who have specific learning difficulties and those with general spelling problems. Where there is any failure to learn or a learning deficit, such a pupil is seriously disadvantaged because so much in schools, despite the advent of computer-assisted learning and word processing, depends upon spelling and writing skills. In these circumstances the teacher cannot, it seems, provide the necessary support strategies or alternative routes to learning if he or she does not have the necessary theoretical and practical knowledge of literacy skills, the diagnostic skills to identify weaknesses and the remedial or developmental techniques to help overcome the problems. If identification of at risk children could occur within the first year or so of schooling, it might be possible to train reception class teachers in the appropriate skills for overcoming the pupils' difficulties before specific remedial intervention on the spelling problem becomes necessary. A more eclectic approach to the teaching of reading in these early stages might reduce the failure rate from 4 per cent to 1.5 per cent as in Scottish schools (SED, 1978). The extreme position in relation to this form of argument is that, perhaps, 'dyslexia' could be viewed as pedagogical rather than learning failure. Perhaps, too, the gender differences among referrals of approximately 4:1, or even 5:1, in the studies underpinning this text may arise from differences in approaches to learning by boys and girls, and attitudes to boys and girls.

EARLY VERSUS LATE REFERRAL

The issue of early versus later referral has been discussed frequently in learning difficulties forums. Suffice to say that may specialist remediators seem to believe that the earlier they can identify the pupils' problems, the better and the more effective they can make their remediation. However, there seems to be a marked resistance at the administration level to refer any pupil before the age of 7 to 8 years for specialist help, particularly where this help involves withdrawal support. Clearly there are financial considerations at work. Early referral can mean that some pupils are included in the group whose difficulties would be overcome gradually without support. By increasing the hurdles and the size of the decrement formula only the most severe cases are allowed to

register in the system. It could be argued that by this stage –
dealing with them at 8 and, even, 11 years – the provision has
become very costly and time-consuming and, probably, decreas-
ingly effective. So many more financial resources have to be
absorbed in administration, case conferences, expert involvement
from other teams who are recording, statementing and reviewing,
than in the tuition of the pupil.

Research by Schiffman and Clemmens (1966) showed that the
earlier the remedial intervention is made the more likely the
problem is to be resolved (see Table 5.1). No similar surveys have
taken place in this country because it is difficult to obtain research
funding for such studies. What is needed is a comprehensive long-
term comparative study of clearly defined remedial interventions.

However, Ridehalgh (1997), analysing progress made by cohorts
of pupils in four remedial centres using different programmes,
found that referrals after the age of 12 years made little or no
progress. The reasons for this were not simple and resulted from an
interaction between type of programme, tutor skill and experience,
pupil motivation and the number of sessions of remediation per
week – two being a necessary minimum.

Table 5.1 *The percentage effectiveness of remedial intervention at particular ages*

Age at which 2-year remediation programme began	Percentage improvement after remediation for 2 years
7 years	85%
8 years	75%
9 years	42%
10 years	16%
11 years	10%
12 years	8%

Source: Schiffman and Clemmens, 1966

The Learning Difficulties Research Project's small-scale studies
show that *appropriate* intervention, and this is a most important
word, can lead at 7 years (Year 2) to fewer children being shown as
in need of additional support. There are several conditions,
however, which need to be 'appropriate' and a system is required
to back this up by providing in-service training and updating:

- identification in first few weeks of schooling;
- class teacher trained in the appropriate identification and intervention strategies (as detailed in Chapter 8);
- classroom helpers/support tutored by teacher with specific tasks
  and objectives to fulfil;

- local support for Learning Network;
- peripatetic support consultants and team;
- local centre linked to national training network for in-service updating.

TYPES OF LEARNING SUPPORT

The role of teachers responsible for children with special educational needs has become complex over the last decade. At one time a school might have a remedial department at secondary stage, with a full-time head and several part-timers to help with assessment and teaching pupils withdrawn from the mainstream or, in primary schools, ex-teacher parents coming in for a few hours to do 'remedial' work in the classroom. Now there has been a strong move to provide support within classrooms, which may comprise: planning only, planning and teaching with the teacher, teaching key skills areas instead of the teacher, team teaching, and working alongside the pupil to help with literacy skills. This approach was strengthened by the emphasis put upon it in the Fish Report (Fish, 1985). Some LEAs closed their specialist centres and schools closed their 'remedial' departments.

In a range of small-scale studies in which teachers examined the relative effectiveness of the remedial withdrawal versus the integrated support approach where they had the opportunity to do both, the results, usually in the form of sets of case analyses, showed that withdrawal for tutorial work singly or in pairs was essential to give the 'dyslexics' the necessary quiet and detailed teaching to bring them to functional literacy. These sessions needed to occur, at a minimum, for two half-hour periods per week. The direct teaching input in the integrated setting could not be sustained because of the subject-content of the lesson from the class teacher and the distracting effect of the 'tutorial' on other learners. In the early years simply having another teacher supporting the reading of a group of children was found to be particularly helpful, but it was insufficiently focused when general support was provided for the needs of the potential dyslexic. In certain classrooms the methods used by the teachers were found to be antagonistic to the needs of the learner with specific difficulties and this caused even greater problems. The learning support teacher currently has many other roles in addition to the one just described. Under the new provisions for pupils with special needs (DfEE, 1994), it would appear that there will be little time to work with pupils. Instead SENCOs will become administrators assessing, recording and reviewing pupils' progress, and interviewing parents termly. The setting up of this continuous round of procedures and interviews will consume most of their available time. Who will work with the pupils? However skilled class teachers and subject teachers become they currently do not have the necessary knowledge and skills for us to be able to hand over the specialist interventions to them.

SKILLS VERSUS ABILITIES TRAINING

In the remedial field itself there are, according to Stephens (1976), two distinct approaches which can be observed. These are abilities versus skills training methods and programmes. In the abilities training approach, assumptions are made as to the underlying deficits contributing to reading and spelling difficulty and then an attempt is made to remediate these deficits. After this, it is assumed that the normal reading and spelling skills will establish themselves and then develop. The theories which seem to have given rise to this approach are the visual perceptual and visuo-motor problems theory of Bender (1957) upon which the Frostig and Horne (1964) remedial programme is based. Snippets of this programme have found their way into the practices of most of the generalist remediators. The sequencing deficit theory of Bakker (1972) has also given rise to sequencing training activities and practices linked to visual and auditory tasks, and both types of abilities training have been adapted and promoted on a wide scale through lectures and books by Tansley (1967, 1971) and in the Aston Index and Portfolio (Newton and Thomson, 1976). These training materials were extremely popular and are still used as early reading activities for normal readers.

The intersensory integration theory of Birch (1962) has seemed to have a more limited appeal and less promotion, although such ideas permeate the multisensory programmes of earlier decades and are, of course, implicit in some of Frostig's perceptuo-motor activities. They may now perhaps be traced through the work of Fernald (1943) through to Hickey (1977) and Cowdery *et al*. (1984). Here one is not arguing for a direct causal link between a theory and a remedial programme, or a success in remediation giving rise to a theory although, in some instances, this has been the case as with Frostig basing her programme on Bender's (1957) theory. Instead, theories evolve in the research field and many years later become accepted wisdom in the applied field to justify seemingly successful practices which have been developed, because they accord with individuals' implicit theory about dyslexia or because they appear to confirm prima-facie evidence. Word blindness (Hinshelwood, 1917), an inability to read despite being able to see, is an example of this. This theory was endorsed by the establishment of the Word Blind Institute in 1964. The theory of visual perceptual difficulties and visual memory deficiencies became the more sophisticated field version of this. It would seem an irrefutable logic to the non-expert observer that reading problems in the presence of good intelligence and good eyesight result from visual perceptual problems. Similarly, reversals of letters and words in reading and spelling would appear to arise from an inability to perceive and preserve the sequential order of written material but symptoms or indicators can become dignified as causes. In this field there is no shortage of theory or research to justify notions and confirm practices of all kinds.

Researchers, too, in the past may have operated in a similar fashion and taken symptoms as key indicants for a particular theory which they have then systematically researched and found evidence to support. Dyslexia has been notable for such paradigms. Snow (1973) argued that prevailing paradigms are not always subjectable to inspection and analysis, and actually control the way in which research – and we can add remedial practice – is designed and executed, and define the results which may be obtained. What is interesting is that there was a massive change in paradigm in the research field from visual to verbal processing difficulties, particularly with reference to phonological deficits, in the late 1970s, but that in the educational and remedial fields there have only recently been the beginnings of a corresponding change. Perhaps this is the expected time-lag for the influence of one field to be brought to bear upon another.

In the abilities training approach, if the underlying theory is wrong then the training can never be effective. Even when it is correct the remediation is one place removed from the problem. In the skills approach a reading and spelling deficit due to some unknown cause or causes is observed and a remedial intervention is applied directly to the problem. Thus, if the pupil is found not to know sounds of the letters, then he or she is taught these sounds and perhaps how to use them to build simple words. There are also unsatisfactory versions of this approach where pupils with spelling problems who know the sounds and names of letters are still retaught basic phonics and not more advanced strategies for word-building and linguistic structures. The theory may be implicit or only half developed, for example phonics is all that is needed to help with spelling.

ABILITIES TRAINING PROGRAMMES AND MATERIALS

The development test of visual perception (Frostig, 1963) and the Frostig and Horne (1964) visual perceptual training programme

This test and training materials were based upon several years of observation of children who were referred to Frostig's School of Educational Therapy because of learning difficulties. The children had, in the main, been diagnosed as having minimal brain damage and most, according to the standardization manual, were found to have visual or auditory perceptual disturbances as measured by such tests as the Bender–Gestalt (1957), Goodenough Draw-a-Man test (1942), and the Wepman Tests of Auditory Discrimination (1958) and tests of aphasia. This makes Frostig's target group different from the dyslexic group already defined.

Frostig's researchers reported that disturbances in visual perception were by far the most frequent symptoms and seemed to contribute to the learning difficulties. Thus it was that Frostig attempted to construct a test to explore further the development of visual perception, postulating five key areas based upon clinical observations and research.

Frostig concluded that children who had difficulty in writing seemed to have poor eye–hand co-ordination, children who could not recognize words often seemed to have disturbances in figure ground perception. Other children were unable to recognize a letter or word when it was written in different sizes or colours, or when it was printed in upper case and they were used to seeing it in lower case. She hypothesized that these pupils had poor form constancy. The pupils producing mirror writing were said to have difficulty in perceiving position in space; and those showing reversals in a word, difficulties in analysing spatial relationships. She noted that, in this last group, many could neither read nor spell longer words, and that many of those children with evident disabilities in visual perception had difficulty in paying sustained attention and/or showed behavioural deviations. The test Frostig devised sampled abilities in these five areas and it was recognized that these were not the sum total of the problem areas but were the most important and seemed to develop relatively independent of each other.

Sub-tests I and V tested motor skills, and II and IV required visual perceptual recognition (see Figure 5.1). The subsequent standardization studies showed clear evidence of age progression from 3 to $7\frac{1}{2}$ years but with little development thereafter. The 1961 standardization was based upon the responses of 2,100

a. *Visuo-perceptual training*

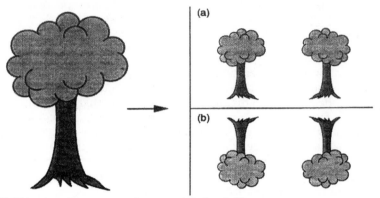

Child has to point to correct shapes on right-hand side.

b. *Visual sequencing*

Child selects and places counters or shapes in the correct sequence.

c. *Visuo-motor training*

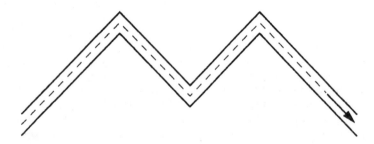

Child draws between the lines.

Figure 5.1 *Examples of visuo-perceptual visual sequencing and visuo-motor training materials*

children with over 100 subjects in each six-month age span.

Validity studies showed (a correlation with classroom adjustment of $r = 0.44$) that there was a tendency for teachers to report behaviour problems and adjustment problems in the pupils with visual perceptual difficulties. There were correlations of +0.5 and +0.5 between the test and reading performance in two further samples, again significant but very low. Sprague (1963) found 40 (36 per cent) of 111 first grade children had perceptual quotients of 90 or less on the Frostig test. Subsequent studies showed that, having identified children with low perceptual quotients, remedial training programmes offered were effective in increasing scores on the Frostig tests but these studies did not include indications of any transfer to reading, spelling or writing, although studies are reported showing correlations between visual perceptual ability and reading achievement (namely, +0.4 and +0.5 or 16 to 25 per cent).

The Frostig tests and training programmes became popular in remediating the underlying difficulties in pupils with reading and spelling problems, and a number of studies reported their use but their findings seemed equivocal. When all the variables were held constant, however, there was no transfer from training on the Frostig materials, abilities training, to reading according to Smith and Marx (1972). Later studies showed that the reason for lack of transfer was evidenced in the materials themselves for, in a perceptual training task which affords transfer, the training materials must be a sub-population of the group to which transfer is required (Attneave and Arnoult, 1956). Thus training for word-reading must be based upon the sub-population of words. This is the principle of 'ecological validity' in perceptual training and found support in pre-reading teaching (Montgomery, 1977, 1979). Since the drawing aspects do not relate to letters or words the transfer to writing can also be viewed as marginal.

The Frostig materials would seem more suitable for use with perceptuo-motor impaired pupils with minimal cerebral dysfunction, for whom they were originally developed, and not for those whose primary difficulty is in reading and spelling with no neurological impairment. It is often the case that children presenting with developmental dyslexia have additional difficulties in perceptuo-motor areas. In the circumstances it would seem that skills training rather than abilities training could still be the most effective procedure.

Auditory perception and modality training (Wepman, 1958; Johnson and Myklebust, 1967)

In 1958 Wepman developed his Auditory Discrimination Test (ADT) in which forty pairs of similar words are presented to children aged from 4 years upwards. The individual children have to listen carefully to each spoken pair and simply say 'same' or 'different' as appropriate, the tester having checked on practice sets that they understand the meaning of the task by using, for example, gate – gate.

Certain pronunciations are different in American English and need to be noted during the practice run for the tester. Wepman (1958) went on to propose the Modality Training Concept that children with learning difficulties should receive compensatory training through their stronger modality and remedial training in the weaker modality, and thereby turned attention of remediators and researchers from visual to the auditory modality. There are, however, numerous difficulties associated with Wepman's test. Snowling (1985) suggested that preliminary findings showed that speech-disordered children often passed such auditory discrimination tests but that their difficulties were more likely to be revealed in more complex non-word items of the same type, e.g. *bikut – bituk*, *besket – bekset*. Such items revealed underfunctioning in children within the 11-year age group with persistent speech problems. This is an interesting phenomenon for, if they can hear the differences between single-syllabled items, they should surely be able to hear the difference between polysyllabic ones. Is the difference perhaps in the way they decide to process and make their judgements? Perhaps the children sub-vocalize more of the complex items to help in their judgemental processes as an *aide-mémoire* (Vellutino, 1979) and this, because of their speech problems, leads to deficient judgements of 'auditory' pairs. They are perhaps using different or intermediary stimulus pairs. Perhaps some older children may also, or instead, use a spelling knowledge strategy to aid their judgements. If their spelling skills are deficient, this could again lead to error from reversals or transpositions in medial positions in words, which are commonly found in dyslexics' spellings. It might then be assumed the child has disordered perception when, in fact, she or he does not. Snowling (1985) pointed out that the errors noted are on place change (g/k), high frequency sounds (f/s) and cluster sequences (sk/ks). Each type of error could be accounted for in terms of production error rather than perception. It has been demonstrated by audiometricians that discrimination of certain speech sounds, particularly in running speech, becomes impossible to most listeners after about the age of 6 and certainly by adulthood (Wisby, 1984). The judgements are made then according to context. For example, if one explains that one's holiday was spent in Harris, the listener who does not lipread may say 'Ah, Paris'.

On the basis of her earlier research, Bradley (1980) produced what she called an Auditory Organization Test. Children in preschool years were asked to do the 'odd one out' task, as in: lot, pot, cot, hat or bud, bun, bus, rug. Their performance on this task was found to be predictive of reading and spelling performance at 8 years. On the same test, a speech-disordered 15-year-old with severe phonological difficulties in reading and spelling (Stackhouse, 1982) performed less well than the level of a 5-year-old. It would be interesting to determine the extent to which pre-schoolers and the 15-year-old could approximate the spelling of these words using Read's (1986) creative spelling technique. What is being suggested is that the proposed phonological difficulties could be closely related to spelling difficulties.

As the research emphasis on visual training receded, it was replaced by more emphasis upon auditory discrimination training and, in 1972, Johnson and Myklebust proposed a two-factor theory of dyslexia in which they suggested that some subjects had visual perceptual difficulties whereas others had auditory perceptual problems. A few subjects had both problems. The authors proposed a direct relationship between reading achievement and auditory discrimination, and suggested that the ability to discriminate sound parts of words was at least as important as IQ in beginning readers. They explained that, when children can say whether or not words in a spoken pair are the same or different as in the Wepman (1958) Auditory Discrimination Test (ADT), when they can match a spoken word to a picture, hear phonemes in words spoken in serial order in which they occur and then blend these phonemes to say the word, or tell whether a particular phoneme occurs at the beginning, middle or end of a spoken word, then they will rapidly and easily progress in reading. Some of these tasks such as blending and segmentation are phonological rather than auditory discrimination tasks. Although specific named programmes dealing only with auditory perceptual training have not been produced, many schemes incorporating training in these areas have been set up and become widely used.

It is Wepman's (1958) research using ADT which is most often quoted in support of auditory discrimination and its close relationship with reading, but this test, so widely accepted at face value, has the same problems as that of Frostig and Horne (1964); its apparent lack of empirically established validity and questionable theoretical or logical validity. The critical cut-off point of 34 used by Wepman for 'adequate' as opposed to 'inadequate' discrimination skills was seemingly totally arbitrary and not researched, and casts doubt on those researches which also used it without question.

Di Carlo (1965) concluded, for example, that the information which Wepman presented under 'validity' suggested a relationship between auditory discrimination and intelligence, hearing, speaking and reading, but did not necessarily support the validity of the test. Researches other than Wepman's, which found support for 'ear training', in fact contained results which showed that, on one occasion, ear training was least effective and on other occasions no more effective than visual training or a mixture of both (Groff, 1975).

Closely related to the auditory perceptual aspects in the remediation area is the subject of phonics training. Phonics programmes usually incorporate some 'auditory perceptual' training tasks in their early stages, under 'listening' skills, before moving on to auditory sequencing and blending.

Intersensory integration tests and training methods (Birch, 1962)

The intersensory integration hypothesis was developed by Birch to account for the origin of dyslexics' problems. He proposed that dyslexias arose out of difficulties in the transfer of information from one modality to the other, for example, in the transfer from visual graphemic information to verbal phonemic output and vice versa. This, he suggested, would be corrected by intersensory integration remedial training.

The techniques involve pupils being shown, for example, patterns of dots for a few seconds and then being required to tap with the right hand for all the dots seen at the top and the bottom and with the left hand for all those dots in the middle, in order from top to bottom, for example:

• • • •	The letter 'E' is shown in dots
•	thus and then the subject taps:
• • •	
•	4 taps with right hand
•	6 taps with left hand
• • • •	4 taps with right hand

Responses can be made orally or motorically and vice versa by pointing to patterns heard or felt. Koppitz (1977) developed the Visual Aural Digit Span (VADS) test on this type of principle. She presented random digits aurally and visually for oral and written recall. In a replication of this work it was found that VADS scores correlated highly with reading and spelling ages rather than chronological age or IQ.

It was found that the dyslexic subjects did appear to have difficulties with 'intersensory integration' tasks but it was impossible to ascribe the difficulties to any one problem for they appeared not to be able always to remember the sequences or patterns and often confused their right and left hand when tapping or confused the naming of left and right. In the task as set it was not possible to distinguish cross-modal confusions from memory and orientation confusions.

The remedial effects of intersensory training programmes have been seriously thrown into doubt by studies such as those of Bryant (1975) which showed that deficiencies in the research results invalidated most of the findings that had accumulated, for they had not controlled for intra-modal judgements before investigating cross-modal transfer. Of particular significance is the second point made by Bryant (1975): learning to read does not require that the individual perceives natural or universal equivalence (p. 210), but neither does it necessitate the learning of quite arbitrary cross-modal associations. These are qualitatively different processes. Many of the other studies of the integration hypothesis have involved additional memory factors (Koppitz, 1971, 1977, 1981). When these and intra-modal factors had been controlled for according to Vellutino *et al.* (1975), then no differences were found between poor and normal readers on non-verbal intersensory learning tasks (Bryant, 1975, p. 209). The groups differed on tasks involving verbal components. They argued that this deficit was more likely to be a dysfunction associated with the co-ordination problems in relation to visual, verbal and motoric functions in spelling.

When intersensory integration finds an application in multisensory skills training, more support from remediators and research findings for its use emerge. This will be examined in a later section.

Sequencing deficits and sequential order training (Bakker, 1972 and Tansley, 1971)

Bakker's proposed sequential order deficit underlying dyslexia has achieved little backing from other researchers in the experimental field, but there has been a great deal of support amongst educational psychologists and remedial practitioners at least in their diagnostic reports and from some neurologists (Kappers, 1990). Amongst teachers on special needs courses the most popular diagnostic category was that dyslexics suffered from difficulties in the sequential ordering of material as evidenced by these types of mistakes in their spelling and reading, by their lack of knowledge of the order of the alphabet, days of the week, and months of the year, and by their inability to repeat polysyllabic words. The

Bangor Dyslexia Test (Miles, 1983) identified these as key indicants in its diagnostic profile. In the educational psychologists' reports investigated these statements and inferences also appeared, together with additional comments derived from digit span tests and order errors observed on visual sequential ordering tests. This prima-facie evidence has had a powerful influence such that most general schemes for pre-reading and remedial training involve sequential ordering tasks in both visual and auditory modalities. Where these tasks involve pictures and symbols and not words or sub-populations of words such as letters in words, the training materials would not observe the principle of Ecological Validity and no transfer to reading and spelling could therefore be expected. In addition, it is suggested that order errors seen in pupils' misspellings are more attributable to the visual approach used in spelling rather than a sequential order difficulty.

Tallal (1994) has also found evidence that dyslexics cannot process verbal input at the same rate as control subjects and suggests this as a cause of their problems. It is possible that it may be a cause or a result of their problems. If dyslexics have not established the verbal codes necessary for processing verbal input then it may well slow down their processing capacity. In learning symbol–sound associations for onsets slow processing may be a less important factor than is supposed, especially when this is accompanied by direct teaching of initial sounds by teachers. Even in these settings dyslexics have failed to acquire the alphabetic principle. In learning to spell the learner tends to articulate slowly and the processing speed may not be relevant. Johnson and Myklebust's (1967) case studies showed that words dictated at normal speeds were misspelled by dyslexics, whereas if they were spoken slowly and syllable by syllable the words could be spelled correctly. This could indicate a practice and lack of familiarity problem.

OTHER DEVELOPMENTS IN THE VISUAL MOTOR, VISUAL PERCEPTUAL, AND SEQUENCING FIELDS

Random eye movement problems (Pavlidis, 1981, 1986)

The interest in visual correlates with spelling problems and dyslexia has shifted in recent years, towards optometric considerations and remediation, with Pavlidis's (1981) theory and research on random eye movement problems. During normal reading the eyes move along the line of print from left to right in quick jerks known as saccades. Reading only occurs in the pauses or fixations. Fixations occur 90 per cent of the time and movement 10 per cent.

A typical 9-year-old can be expected to make about five fixations per line of print.

Regression is when the eyes move back to examine a word which has not been recognized. If too many regressions occur then this suggests that the text is too difficult for the reading age of that individual. As reading skill develops so the span of recognition and comprehension slightly increases. Most average and above average readers have satisfactory and systematic eye movements which improve as their reading skills improve. Pavlidis, however, took a different view. He found that the dyslexics referred to his clinics demonstrated random eye movements from an early age and he regarded this as being the origin, rather than the result, of their difficulties. After a two-year study of 400 children aged from 8 to 18 he found that dyslexics displayed irregular eye movements which differed significantly and consistently from those of normal readers.

Pavlidis developed a computerized test for random eye movements in which his subjects were required to follow the patterns of moving lights. By means of this test it was proposed to identify potential dyslexics and so be able to institute eye movement training. There were, however, a range of criticisms levelled at the studies which prevented the system being widely adopted. Rayner (1986) found it difficult to replicate Pavlidis's research and suggested that the results were more to do with the selective group referred to Pavlidis's clinic and that the REMs (random eye movements) were most likely to be the results of reading difficulties rather than the cause. The wide-range screening of pre-schoolers with and without REMs and the long-term follow up of their cases would be very costly and further investigation in this country would thereby be prohibited, but the research is continuing in America and the controversy continues.

The electronystagmograph and the opthalmograph both provide methods for analysing ocular movements. When the eye movements of 50 dyslexics and matched controls were recorded during reading it was found that when the material was above frustration level the eye movements became more synchronous and regular. When in a subsequent experiment the frustration words were taught in advance of the reading material, within minutes the graphs showed definite improvement. These findings showed that the degree of comprehension produces the type of ocular movement rather than that ocular motility determines the degree of comprehension (Pirozzolo and Raynor, 1980). Attempts at remediation involving training in rhythmic eye movements with fixations would therefore be unlikely to transfer directly to reading or spelling.

Fixed referent eye (Stein and Fowler, 1981, 1985)

Unstable, crossed or mixed dominance have been popular theories since Orton (1943) proposed his original theory. When applied specifically to the visual area according to Evans (1993) the controversial nature of the area results from the fact that the various tests of ocular dominance are measuring different things. There are three categories of dominance – sighting, sensory and motor – and within each category different tests are unlikely to show that one eye is consistently dominant in the same person. Evans (1993, p. 26) therefore regards the concept as archaic and inaccurate and concludes that most authorities now agree that atypical sighting dominance is not a significant factor in dyslexia.

The theory has been revived in a new form by Stein and Fowler (1981, 1985) as problems resulting from the lack of a fixed referent eye (FRE). They used the Dunlop test (1974) for identifying the eye which controlled binocular functions rather than use tests which were monocular and therefore likely to be poor predictors. Their subjects were required to report which eye saw the marker move when each was presented with a picture of a house with a tree. One tree was larger than the other and as the pictures in the viewer were moved further apart fusion was lost. The eye which saw the picture jump was denoted the non-dominant eye. The researchers found that dyslexics had significantly poorer convergence of images and stereopsis together with mixed laterality than controls.

Since 1980 Stein and Fowler have been studying the FRE phenomenon. They regard cross-dominance as unimportant but lack of FRE in reading as crucial in causing visual dyslexia for it is known that during reading only one eye does the work and the information from the other non-dominant eye is suppressed. Lack of FRE would mean that information was not consistently locating in the reading hemisphere and would result in an unstable perception of print. In 1985 Stein and Fowler published a key study in which they reported that two-thirds of their dyslexic sample had an unstable FRE. However, most other researchers have failed to replicate Stein and Fowler's findings.

Bishop (1989), reviewing theory and research, concluded that many good readers as well as some dyslexics in the Dunlop test, including nearly one-quarter of Stein and Fowler's controls, had unfixed referent eyes. She also reanalysed their studies of remediation by monocular occlusion (covering one eye during reading and writing activities for several months) and found no evidence of improved reading scores.

Spelling might not be so affected especially if it is acquired other than through reading practice. Not infrequently apparent unfixed referent eye may be noted in the classroom. Pupils may report only being able to read with one eye shut and their reading ability with one eye shut supports this. Some children may lay their heads on their arms so closing one eye and then happily write their work, until the teacher makes them 'sit up properly' and their ability to write reasonably deteriorates.

Occluding one eye, usually the left, is said to help establish fixed referent eye, now called ocular stability. Whether this has any special influence on reading or spelling remains equivocal but it might help in visual tracking tasks.

Irlen Syndrome (Irlen, 1983, 1988)

In the 1970s, Moira McKenzie first drew my attention to some rare cases she had met of children who could not read if words were printed on a white page but suddenly became able to read when the words were printed over colour, particularly on red or green, despite the fact that the adult by comparison found the text now difficult to read. There have also been occasional references to this condition in early texts on dyslexia.

The Irlen Syndrome was first reported in 1983 at the American Psychological Association convention when it was named the 'scotopic sensitivity syndrome'. The report consisted of the results of observations and self-reports of 37 learning disabled students, aged 18 to 49 years, after wearing tinted lenses for one month. Reading periods lengthened from 15 minutes to two hours before frustration set in and one subject increased his rate of reading from 63 to 117 words per minute. Standard statistical treatment and experimental controls were not instituted. Irlen and Lass (1989) reported that 50 per cent of dyslexics in their studies had a visual perceptual dysfunction which could be treated with tinted lenses. Irlen Institutes have been established in a number of countries including the UK and offer diagnosis and treatment.

The Irlen Syndrome symptoms were reported by P. Clayton, Director of the Irlen Institute in London (1988) as follows:

- photophobia – inability to tolerate glare and bright lights, problems with white on black with shapes becoming distorted, headaches;
- visual image problems – letters blurring, moving, distorting, becoming darker or lighter, swirling, flashing or flickering;
- depth perception problems not only in reading;
- eye strain – blinking, squinting and poor concentration;

- focusing problems – difficulties in keeping words in focus, eyes become tired and sore easily, span of focus reduced.

This range of symptoms is not present in all cases but pupils complaining of swirling unfocused words should have their symptoms checked to see if placing a tinted overlay of a particular colour can improve the reading response. It has become noticeable since television broadcasts about the lenses that pupils may sometimes express their difficulties as 'swirling moving words' even when testing reveals no other indications. It can become a useful explanatory device, helpfully shifting the locus of feelings of blame and shame to a seeming medical condition.

The Irlen treatment consists of tests with a small range of overlays. If one of these proves to be helpful after a period of use then tinted lenses are made up. These are rather expensive. Specialist teachers in the dyslexia field have reported successfully using tinted overlays bought at stationers. Although it is worth checking all children who have reading and spelling difficulties for evidence of the Irlen Syndrome, some will be found for whom the use of tinted overlays is merely a placebo, no reading recovery is noted and the pupil voluntarily ceases to use them. In the large majority of poor readers and spellers there seems to be no evidence at all for the syndrome and the research findings to date appear equivocal.

Otitis media (glue ear)

Glue ear is a condition of the middle ear in which fluid collects and damps the sound transmission capabilities. Approximately 10 per cent of all children suffer from it in their early years. Glue ear results in partial deafness but the degree of hearing loss varies and can remain undetected. The condition may come and go or become chronic. In the former case antibiotics usually help to clear it up but if the condition does not clear up in six to eight weeks surgical treatment may become necessary. This usually involves the insertion of a grommet to assist in draining the fluid. Grommets are naturally pushed out by the healing of the ear drum in six to eight weeks and are then removed in the outpatients department of a hospital.

The results of glue ear can be mild to severe hearing loss. The problem is made worse in the busy classroom. If the child is sitting at the back of the room only parts of words or segments of the teacher's speech may be heard making much of what is said unintelligible and often impossible to follow. These pupils have to find out from peers what is going on and can lose key information, such as basic sounds and concepts crucial to learning to read and spell. It was suggested by Wisby (1984) that this condition was a significant one in the development of certain types of dyslexic difficulties.

Some common types of errors which might be observed in the glue ear condition are:

- confusions with 'p', 'b' and 'm' which all look the same on the lips when they cannot be heard;
- omission of 'k' and 'g' which cannot be seen on the lips;
- omission of unstressed syllables, endings and 'schwa' sounds (ə) and -ed, -es;
- omission of high frequency sounds – 'p' and 'f'.

General failure to understand and follow instructions may also be observed, particularly when there is a figure–ground problem – picking out an instruction against ambient noise.

Routine testing for visual and hearing difficulties should precede any decision about remedial intervention.

SUMMARY

For over 100 years perceptual theories have been prominent explanations for difficulties in reading. As spelling was assumed to be 'caught' during reading it was assumed that training in perceptual abilities and sequencing would have a direct transfer to reading then spelling. However, there is little evidence to support this viewpoint. Within a range of studies of dyslexia 8 to 15 per cent of subjects are found to have some perceptual difficulties; it is unlikely that they cause literacy difficulties but are associated with them. Theories and practices of remediation revolving around auditory perceptual difficulties are most frequently linked to phonics training programmes, which will be discussed in the next chapter.

Children with specific learning difficulties in reading and spelling are part of a larger group comprising those with learning disabilities. Many of these children have other types of learning difficulties, such as problems in maintaining attentional set (ADHD) or hyperactivity, overactivity, distractibility, impulsivity, handwriting difficulties and clumsiness. For such children perceptuo-motor training, tracking and co-ordination activities undoubtably can have benefits and there are a range of materials available to assist with these training activities. The subject of handwriting training and remediation, depending on when and how it is taught, can have a direct and beneficial effect in the developmental or the remedial programme; details of how are provided in Chapter 8.

6

General remedial strategies: skills training, 'sound' methods

INTRODUCTION

The term 'remedial' offers an assumption that an intervention will be successful and bring spelling up to, or back up to, grade level consistent with age and/or ability. However, an analysis of 500 case histories of dyslexics as a background to this book showed that the subjects had not been brought up even to the grade level by the age of 12 years although they had already been offered extra help with reading in infant school, 'remedial' support in class and withdrawal teaching in a small group in junior school. Their reading and spelling scores were still more than two years below their grade level.

The methods offered followed a seemingly logical pattern from extra help of the same kind at first; then a different reading scheme usually emphasizing phonics, remedial teaching of sounds for blending and use in reading and spelling in withdrawal groups or on an individual basis; and, finally, the use of a remedial scheme such as *Spelling Made Easy* (Brand, 1993) or *Alpha to Omega* (Hornsby and Shear, 1985). At 12 years they were four time failures. These interventions had not appeared to make any significant difference, a result which Tansley and Pankhurst (1981) and Ysseldyke (1987) in their surveys of remedial teaching had reported. Of course there are many reasons why these approaches might have failed and there was no record of those who had benefited and were screened out of the programmes. There were in addition to those who had entered the specialist centres each year an equal number, if not more, on the waiting lists. Turner (1990) reporting on a decline of approximately seven months over a five-year period in reading standards, in eight LEAs, blamed this on a lack of direct phonics teaching and 'real books' approaches. However, the HMI report (DfE, 1990b) found that 95 per cent of classes used graded reading schemes and a survey by Child

Education (1991) found that only 6 per cent of schools were involved in a real books policy and 89 per cent were using a structured programme of phonics teaching. Wray (1991) in fact proposed that the argument by Turner could be turned on its head and it could be that it was precisely because schools were using these graded and structured programmes that there was a decline in standards. The decline could also be attributed to factors quite outside the schools – demographic changes, fewer books in homes, video games rather than stories and so on.

Many teachers giving learning support may have had no additional training in this field other than the occasional in-service training days or short course. It is only relatively recently that the BDA and the Dyslexia Institute have certified approved courses of training for dyslexia and a few institutions of higher education and the Hornsby and Helen Arkell Centres also run their own courses. Training courses, however, do not all teach the same principles and practices and there has been a dearth of research funding to evaluate their different methods. A £3 million Reading Recovery (Clay, 1979, 1989) pilot project was funded by the DfEE in a number of LEAs in England and Wales. A high degree of success was claimed by Wright and Prance (1991) but Dombey (1994), in a critical review, suggested the limitations in the methodology permitted no such conclusions. Any method which offers training in structured reading teaching and assessment and time to pursue it with individuals and small groups is likely to be beneficial to pupils. The Chief Inspector's summary report of an OFSTED (Office for Standards in Education) survey of London literacy stated that at 7 years one-third of children were significantly behind with reading and one in five could not read due to poor standards of class teaching and assessment (C. Woodhouse, Chief Inspector for Schools, speaking on the Radio 4 *Today* programme, 1996, about a report on reading standards in three London boroughs). In the smaller print, which did not capture the headlines, it was also reported that at 11 years most of them had caught up. The survey results had, according to A. Sofer (in a response to the Chief Inspector's comments on reading standards in the *Times Educational Supplement*, June 1996), been weighted by half the children in one LEA having English as a second language, with which they were only just beginning to get to grips. Special funding for learning English plus 'Reading Recovery' had contributed in a major way to the change at age 11. Politics now intervenes between results and their reporting. The 'politics' of literacy teaching itself seems to have made spelling the poor relation or, perhaps, the opposition. To speak about it can bring censure in some circles. What are needed are properly funded joint programmes of research and practice in reading *and* spelling and, for a change, in spelling alone.

A remedy, perhaps, is to plug the gaps which exist because a pupil has missed critical amounts of schooling or was 'absent in class', day-dreaming or preoccupied by his or her own concerns, suffering intermittent 'glue ear', and so on. Any interventions, corrective or remedial, should begin with an assessment of what the pupil knows and what is known about the pupil's learning experiences. The best source is often the pupils themselves at interview (Cowdery *et al.*, 1983). Developmental and corrective strategies such as have already been described may be all that is required by a range of learners who have slipped behind in progress or who have gaps in their knowledge. When distinct areas of omission or problems hampering progress are found, so-called *general remedial strategies* may need to be applied – if only to be able to gain some withdrawal time so that the pupil can be concentrated upon and he or she can also have time to focus and reflect upon spelling skills. This intervention should not duplicate a technique that has been tried but has not worked. Conventional practice has been to start intervention programmes by reteaching phonics and basic sounds to symbol correspondence to help the pupils develop alphabetic knowledge and word attack skills. There are however few research studies which have been undertaken to evaluate the results in controlled experiments.

Gittelman and Feingold (1983) claimed to have undertaken a carefully controlled experiment with subjects randomly assigned to treatment groups. Their remediation involved 'intensive' phonics training which they suggested directly transferred in a limited manner to the spelling but was not so good for reading. Their remediation training also included intersensory integration training in reading, whole-word recognition training and all perceptual motor training techniques – a classic example of 'hedging bets', i.e. include anything under remediation which might conceivably work. Although the phonics work did not show much transfer to reading, reading skills did improve in a limited way. This was surprising since four types of treatment were given to it. It can only be presumed that they were not effective as remedial strategies. Perhaps if the pupils had been taught to generalize or practise using their phonics knowledge in reading and writing more transfer might have been observed.

Pupils on remedial programmes often appear to make good progress in the remedial setting but their class teachers may see no difference in classwork. There are several reasons for this; in particular, what takes place in the remedial setting needs to be reinforced and supported in the classroom if it is to be significant in the pupil's eyes. The phonics teaching may be narrow and only transfer to similar items found in the early levels of spelling tests. Inappropriate phonics teaching strategies may result in the pupil being 'over-phonicked'. An example of this is from Thomas, aged $7\frac{1}{2}$ years:

I w l t fg w my cat d b iw vy

I s b in m gdn

Translated as: 'I would like to forget when my cat died because I was very sad it is buried in my garden'.

A helpful approach here would be to go over the text with Thomas to get him to articulate it slowly and clearly to see if he can feel and identify more of the consonants. A series of redrafts undertaken jointly and one on his own could reveal more knowledge. At another session he could write it again from memory to see what had been retained and then the single closed syllable structure could be introduced – CVC. One word could then be addressed, e.g. 'sad', and he could learn to generalize this knowledge to other words with the same rhyme – dad, pad, mad. Thomas should be the one to try to generate the words rather than be assisted. At first he will find this difficult and need a lot of support.

Now Thomas has cracked the alphabetic code and has some whole-word knowledge such as 'cat' and 'in' he could be taught 'my' as a whole-word writing unit and the scaffold 'gdn' shows the potential for progress if more linguistics teaching is built in. Without the developmental linguistics input Thomas will find it hard to make enough progress to become a competent reader and writer. This illustrates the limited scope of a purely phonics scheme. It is a necessary but not a sufficient part of remediation.

If Thomas were a slower learner, a pupil with general learning difficulties in memory, language and thinking, he would find it extremely difficult to move on. He would need an approach to literacy learning which was built into all curriculum activities (Montgomery, 1990). Withdrawal for short sessions would not enable him to grasp the essentials.

In this chapter a range of remedial interventions will be outlined under the heading '"Sound" methods'. Each intervention should take place in the class and be within the class teacher's repertoire, and can become part of the whole-school approach. An essential prerequisite is that each proposed intervention should be the subject of analysis and assessment, and that the terms of this should be determined at the outset. There is little point in proceeding with something which is not working or repeating something which has already failed with a particular pupil.

DIFFERENTIAL ANALYSIS AND ASSESSMENT

Assessment and monitoring of corrective and remedial input is an important contribution to improving standards in literacy teaching. Differential analysis requires more than recording test results and noting progress in written work. As a minimum the children's increase in age over the remediation period must be taken into account. After six months' tuition twice weekly a pupil may have improved in spelling by four months on a test. This actually means that he or she has slipped backwards by two months. If retested on the same test even though the test rule, not to reuse within six months, has been adhered to there can be a familiarity effect building. A difference of one correct spelling may give an increase in spelling age score of two to four months. Most research on efficacy is calculated on the basis of group data which can show big improvements or, most often in this field, no improvement. Keeping accurate records will enable teachers to review the effectiveness of their own and others' interventions and enable them to differentiate between methods and find *which* is working for a particular pupil and *who* is making it work. From here it is a shorter step to find out *why* it is working and who else might benefit.

In the following example 30 pupils of average age 8 years 10 months, all in Years 4 and 5, who had been assessed as children with learning difficulties were given a weekly session of one hour in-class support for learning to help with their reading and writing in the curriculum. Each was also given half an hour of individual teaching each week using phonic and other worksheets. When they were tested after a six month period there was an average loss in reading age of 8.6 months. In reality one subject made no gain but no loss, thus keeping up with his increasing age; one subject made 20 months progress above the six months increase in age; five subjects made an average gain of three months over chronological age; and 23 subjects made a loss of 12.74 months. They were losing skills.

In relation to spelling in the group of subjects overall there was a loss of 0.04 months or no observable gain over chronological age;

they were now keeping pace. Twelve subjects made 7.6 months progress over their increased age; five subjects made 14.6 months progress, a ratio of more than two to one; 14 subjects lost 6.6 months in progress – in other words they stayed where they were when they entered the programme.

It can be seen that the phonics programme was helping substantially just over half the pupils in spelling but except for one pupil it was not transferring to reading. This could be owing to teaching method or other skills may be needed by the pupils. What is of great importance here is a reappraisal of the withdrawal and in-class support teaching content and strategies in consultation with the class teacher so that those slipping back can have their needs met. One pupil has jumped ahead in both reading and spelling and thus the input was just what he needed. After this general analysis of progress a profile of what each pupil has actually learned should be evident from his or her individual results on the pre- and post-tests and portfolios of work. At this point direct feedback from the pupils is helpful for it is important to know if they 'feel' they are making progress and what their thoughts on the process have been.

'SOUND' METHODS

Preventative phonics

Research has shown that phonics teaching should be introduced for word decoding from the very first reading and spelling sessions in school. It is important not to wait until a sight vocabulary is built as phonics should be used from the outset to support word learning. Here the *developmental intervention* during writing and the *onset and rime* strategies during reading and spelling, as previously described, should be used. These will help prevent the learner trying to tackle all words letter by letter as though they were phonically regular.

Letterland was first devised by Lynn Wendon (1984) and was originally known as the Pictogram System. Letterland is a secret place lying invisibly inside the written word. Clever Cat, Eddy Elephant and Wicked Water Witch live there. Each letter shape is a pictogram in which picture clues have to be fused to give its shape. Stories have been developed which explain the behaviour of each letter and how it reacts with other letters. There are two teaching programmes: 'First Steps in Letterland' and 'Big Strides in Letterland'. Included in them is work on language, phonics, whole-word recognition, reading development, writing and spelling. Storytelling, drama role-play and singing are integral to the scheme. Although correct letter formation is taught from the outset it is presented in print script form. This is satisfactory for reading but not for writing.

The scheme has a great appeal for children in nursery and reception classes but will not be appreciated by older learners, for whom remedial phonics approaches are needed.

Remedial phonics

There is a vast array of teaching schemes which include phonics teaching, and also a range of schemes which are specifically phonics based and can be used for remedial work. However, some of the schemes and some of the methods do not actually enable the learners to learn the skills they need. Thus any scheme needs to be carefully assessed for its validity. One of the most useful resources for teaching phonics and listing phonic resources was written by teachers and edited by Hinson and Smith (1993). It is a National Association for Special Educational Needs (NASEN) publication. In explaining their philosophy in the book the editors state:

> As already discussed, not every child will need to be taught phonics. Nevertheless, the majority will benefit from help at some point in learning to read. The actual teaching of phonics should not therefore be introduced too early. However, do not lose sight of the fact that much valuable pre-school preparation for learning to read will have been going on at home from the time children are very young ...
>
> The acquisition of phonics is essentially an oral skill which depends for its success upon well developed auditory discrimination ... (Hinson and Smith, 1993, p. 11)

Whilst the information contained in the rest of this book is factual and highly valuable this extract can be regarded as inappropriate to children with spelling difficulties. If Hinson and Smith mean that phonic drills and systematic phonics teaching for the majority is unnecessary then this is one thing, but all children need to acquire knowledge of initial word sounds as they meet print. Their phonic knowledge needs to be very carefully monitored and direct teaching input given at the first signs that they are faltering. This will mean that as well as general class teaching of alphabet sound knowledge there should be individually tailored inputs on a need-to-use basis. It also has to be recognized that in many homes there are no pre-reading activities. Phonics as essentially an oral skill depending for its success upon auditory discrimination must be examined further; it does not seem to be quite as simple as this. Dyslexics and other poor spellers who have not developed sound

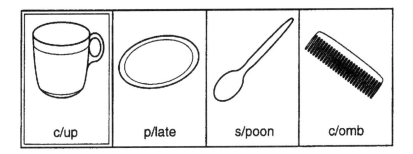

'Which one begins with the same sound as the one in the box?
Listen! Cup, plate, spoon, comb?'

Figure 6.1 *A phoneme segmentation task*

to symbol correspondence rarely seem to have any auditory discrimination difficulties. If they are offered a 'sweet or sweep' they instantly know which to choose. What a wide body of research has shown is that they do have problems associated with *phoneme segmentation*, very often mistakenly called 'auditory discrimination' activities (see example in Figure 6.1).

A child with ordinary hearing and memory has to compare /k/ in c/up with 'p' or 'pl', 's' or 'sp' and /k/ in comb. Although sound frequencies in syllables are shingled on top of each other (Liberman *et al.*, 1967) and cannot be separated out by the human ear, initial sounds are clearly decipherable as onsets, extra bursts of energy fractionally in advance of the rest of the buzz of sound frequencies. Children who cannot process fast sounds (Tallal, 1994) would be at a distinct disadvantage if left to their own devices in early learning. Direct teaching of these key features is essential. If the learner could hear the sounds perfectly well, but when articulating words slowly for spelling could not make use of the articulatory feel of the initial sound and split it off from the rest of the word, then this could also be a severe handicap. The phoneme is said to be an 'abstract perceptual unit' (Ehri, 1979) and has to be linked to an arbitrary and abstract visual system. For a 5-year-old abstractions are somewhat difficult to deal with and having a concrete articulatory pattern for at least 20 letters of the alphabet, the consonants, can prove a great help. When they are using these cues it is known as *scaffold spelling*, for example: btm – bottom, ckpx – chicken pox, bd – bed, gdn – garden, mstr – master, and so on. This spelling is not quite phonetic, phonological or phonic, hence the term 'scaffold'.

In phonics teaching there are a number of problems which need to be avoided if confusions are not to reign.

Avoid intrusive schwa

This is the 'uh' sound. Most teachers know about this but class-room helpers must be trained to avoid it or they can wreck any programme:

Phonics teaching in the open air, 10 June, Maldon Quay
Year One pupils with clipboards and questionnaires at the ready were writing. A Learning Support Assistant worked with a group of three children presumably with learning difficulties. She said, 'No you spell it like this: RUH – OH – PUH – EH – rope'.

To another pupil she then turned and said, 'Yes it starts with LUH, LUH – IH – NUH – EH – line'.

This brand of crazy phonics with intrusive schwa and overempha-sized consonants was delivered in a loud important tone. The children were quiet and subdued and seemed, not surprisingly, mystified by the task of spelling.

Avoid unsupervised worksheets and completion activities

This is inherent in many schemes. For example, a text might say – 'This is an apple. Look at the picture. Say the word apple. What sound does it start with? Here are some words with the "a" sound in them. See if you can read them: *an, and, am, fat, man, cat, Pat*. They all have the *a* sound in them. They all belong to the same family' (Tansley, 1971, Book 1, pp. 2–3).

Exercise: Find the *a* family words and write them in your book:
1. am and little cat fat
2. Pat gas has him had

It could be argued that in the brief introduction the pupil may not have time to establish the phoneme–grapheme link. If so, the subsequent exercise is little more than searching for a particular shape and then copying the configuration that it is in. When this occurs, and the letter is later presented out of context, the pupils will be found not to have learned the sound for they can do the task entirely visually. If there is a teaching input the relationship can still be lost in the labour of copying all the other letters although the exercise is completed accurately in the book.

Exercise Two: Draw a picture of a fat man with his hat and bag.

There is no significant association of phoneme and grapheme here and it can be considered to be a way of spending the pupil's time whilst the teacher deals with others in the group. It is therefore essential that remedial phonics teaching takes place singly or in pairs so that teaching and pupil time is not wasted. There should be at least two sessions per week if there is to be any treatment effect (Gittelman and Feingold, 1983; Ridehalgh, 1997). It can be inferred that the methods used in books full of colouring and worksheet completion activities *may* elicit phonics responses but do not teach them. Children who do have phonic skills may spend endless hours filling in worksheets; this does not mean that they do not enjoy them. It is very satisfying to children to show how clever they are at completing worksheets; correctly and means that they can chat happily at the same time – an exercise in wrist movements using different coloured pencils.

Avoid irrational orders for the introduction of phonics

Orders of introduction may be based on the order of the alphabet, hypothesized ease of construction in writing and day-to-day need – serendipity, vowels first, following what a scheme provides without question, and so on. It is recommended that the order of introduction of phonics for direct teaching is based upon frequency of use in writing. Thus the first five letters should be:

i t p n s

This order will be found in the remedial schemes of Hickey (1977) and Cowdery *et al.* (1984). The subsequent recommended order based upon frequency of occurrence and level of difficulty can be found in the *Teaching Reading Through Spelling Book C, The Early Stages* (pp. 49–53) remedial scheme by Prince-Bruce *et al.* (1985).

The suggested order, based upon their teaching experience of what pupils need and can best cope with if skills are being built upon, is as follows:

i t p n –nt s sp– sn– a –sp st– l pl– sl– d spl– f –ll –ff –ss –nd h –kt fl– –ft g
gl– –ng –ing o –st m –mp sm– r dr– fr– gr– y pr– e tr– spr– str– u c cr– cl–
sc– scr– –ct k sk– –sk –lk –nk –ck b bl br j w sw– tw– dw– qu– v squ– x z

At any point after i t p n s, a particular letter or blend can be introduced if the pupil especially needs to learn it but then a return to the order is advisable.

Some of the main concepts are introduced with the letter names and sounds at the following points:

> At i – the short vowel sound, t and p consonants – non-voiced, –nt consonant blends, s, plural s and second sound of s /z/, d voicing, l–f–s rule, –ng and –ing suffixing and short vowel pattern, r name and sound differences, y as a consonant at the beginning of words, rules associated with c and k in words.

Further rules and combinations such as consonant digraphs and silent 'e' are introduced in *Books D1 and D2, The Later Stages* (Prince-Bruce, 1986) and all levels include a wide variety of games and exercises for reinforcing the teaching points. Phonics and linguistics are introduced in a structured and sequential order with regard to the hierarchy of skills that pupils need to develop. This is a very different order of introduction from traditional schemes where there is more clumping together of things which *appear* to go together but which may prove too difficult for the pupil with learning difficulties, for example: 'easy' consonants t n r m d s p b f, or in another scheme c a o d g, and yet another t n s g d m l f b r c h w p. They may appear easy to the teacher but there are a number of problems associated with learning these sounds and their graphemes, especially without interpolating blending, syllable structure and frequency of use.

Avoid teaching sounds without using them

As soon as two sounds have been learnt they should immediately be used to show the pupils how words can be built for spelling and used in word attack and word search in reading, for example: it ti tit, and then, it tit pit tip ip ti. It is important that real and nonsense words are made up and spelled to dictation. After this, with the use of joining words such as 'the', sentences can be constructed, for example: Tip it in the pit.

Avoid teaching phonic errors

Many programmes contain conceptual errors. Digraphs are called blends, blends are split, diphthongs are called vowel digraphs, and so on. A list of the correct meanings of each of these terms should be compiled and translated into words which pupils can understand as this vocabulary is gradually introduced to them. In addition, schemes should be evaluated to check for these errors and, where necessary, discarded. Key example concepts are:

- *Consonant digraph*: a combination of two consonants making one sound which is different from either of them – ch, sh, ph, wh, and th (voiced and unvoiced).
- *Vowel digraph*: this is a combination of two vowels in one syllable but there is only one resulting sound. One of the vowels will retain one of its own sounds. 'When two vowels go walking the first one does the talking and it usually says its own name' – raid, bean.
- *Diphthong*: this is a blend of two vowels in one syllable in which neither retains its own sound. A completely new sound is formed. There are only four vowel diphthongs in English and these are: oi (oil), oy (boy), ou (out), ow (cow). It is notable that two of these contain 'y' and 'w' acting as vowels and that ow can also be a digraph as in 'snow'.

Avoid teaching all aspects of phonics and then some linguistics

The vocabulary of linguistics includes phonics aspects and needs to be built in as the teaching progresses. Linguistic strategies arising from this should be taught as soon as they can help a pupil unravel a spelling problem. For example: consonants; voicing; vowels – both short and long sound versions; diacritical speech marks such as the breve indicating a short vowel sound and the macron denoting a long one; syllables; syllable structure; affixes – prefixes and suffixes and their meanings; Anglo-Saxon, Latin, Greek and French roots; rarer origins such as Hindi and Erdu.

Avoid rote training on rules

Rules can be an aid to good spelling but the pupils need to be ready for them and this means they need to be able to understand the basis of the rule, not just learn to chant it as in: 'i before e except after c'. The latter is better taught as a problem-solving activity first, to generate 'c' words using the dictionary if necessary and to examine their spellings to see if there is a principle which governs them, for example as in can, cat, cut, cycle, cede, cop, cook, clean, cram, cream, cup, cuss, cull, cell, cello, etc.

In summary, remedial phonics needs a much more careful teaching plan. It is not appropriate to use the same order as in developmental phonics and great care needs to be taken that the pupil securely knows a particular sound before moving on to the next sound. If the pupil appears to know the sound one day and forgets the next, that sound has not been securely learnt. It is far better to spend five sessions ensuring that one sound is learnt than that five sounds, particularly vowel sounds, should be presented one per session and none of them be learnt. In the latter case all that has happened is that the teaching programme has been completed without regard to the pupil's learning need – the learning agenda.

Computer-assisted learning and skill software packages

The majority of current software programs are designed to produce phonic drills. Some of them only teach one aspect, for example:

- *An Eye for Spelling*: patterns (ESM)
- *Animated Alphabet*: initial letters (Sherston Software)
- *Magic 'e'*: rule (Sherston Software)
- *Short vowels* (Sherston Software)

Other programs address a range of skills and care has to be taken that the speed of introduction is not too fast for remediating spelling. Similarly a great deal of time can be taken using software when a particular set of skills has already been acquired, so careful monitoring is necessary. As corrective input these programs can be useful. Programs addressing a range of skills include:

- *First Phonics*: EMU
- *Let's Learn Phonics*: Starnet Ltd
- *Readwell*: Daco Software
- *Word Attack Strategies*: Folio Publications

In addition to teaching software there are also a range of spellcheckers and dictionaries available which can find a word and its meaning from partial clues. All of these should be regarded as aids to discovering spelling, not a substitute for it. The advantage of such software is that it can help separate out the secretarial skills from the composition and development of ideas, giving a chance for the latter to have free rein. Printing out the text and proof-reading before using the spellchecker can help identify areas of spelling difficulty which the pupil, with the teacher's help, can then address. Here the pupils are taking some initiative and responsibility for their own learning.

It is particularly noticeable that a number of software programs have in-built errors in what they regard as blends, digraphs, diphthongs and so on, for example: *Starspell Plus* does not distinguish vowel digraphs from diphthongs, and groups double consonants, consonant digraphs and blends together.

A number of teachers and researchers have designed their own remedial programs. Nicholson and Fawcett (1994) report on a multimedia program for Apple Macintosh which they devised and used with 10–12-year-old dyslexics. The pupils had to learn 20 spellings, ten with a mnemonic approach they called *Selfspell* and the other ten with a mastery learning whole-word approach, *Spellmaster*. In each there was an overlearning strategy which they said was 'generally considered to be one of the most effective for dyslexic children' (Nicholson and Fawcett, 1994, p. 519). Both programs proved effective in remediating the 20 errors with *Spellmaster* showing more improvement on the immediate post-test. Performance on the elapsed test however gave equivalent results for both tests. On the whole the dyslexics found the mnemonics-making method in *Selfspell* more attractive. This is not surprising for it has some appeal to the intellect and the dyslexics selected for such programs are usually well above average intelligence.

What is of note is that both programs are mainly based upon rote learning and the strategies lack the power of generalization to new and different words. Once the novelty effects of the experimental conditions and the extra attention have worn off it could be quite a chore to have to make a mnemonic for every new word encountered, and this in itself could create memory overload and confusion.

In a review of using computers to teach spelling to dyslexics Wise and Olson (1994) concluded that children can improve their spelling and thereby enhance their reading with computers. The programs should, they concluded, teach typing skills and involve handwriting if they are to be effective; they should not teach too many items at a time and 'should offer good support from a knowledgeable adult or from the program itself' (Wise and Olson, 1994, p. 498). In their studies in Colorado they found that students were more stimulated to work harder and study words longer when there was speech feedback on their own attempts. They found that computer programs can be motivating, easily individualized, provide as much checking and repetition as the student needs (and without impatience and criticism) and can, with speech, repeatedly dictate items to be spelled. With the synthetic speech programs they can hear their errors as well as the words to be spelled. Most importantly the studies showed only small gains if there were no teachers or tutors present offering support.

Phonological awareness training (PAT)

Wilson (1994), an educational psychologist, describes the background to a PAT project as based upon research on phonological skills and phonological awareness. She refers to the work of Rack *et al.* (1992), Bradley and Bryant (1985), Goswami and Bryant (1990) and Goswami (1994) in particular. She describes traditional phonics programmes as the progressing from letter sound relationships to CVC words and then moving on to blends and so on and stated: 'This route now appears to work entirely against the course of the development of phonological skills' (Wilson, 1994, p. 5).

On the basis of work with case study 'A' who was 10 years old and at the end of Year Five, Wilson devised a system of phonological training. She reports that A had already received a great deal of 'specialist' teaching and had worked on word families without success. This time he was to spend not more than ten minutes each day during the summer holiday generating words which shared the same rime. She provided him with the onsets and a selection of common rimes giving examples of how to word build using them. If necessary his mother was simply to remind him of what a specific rime said. Two months later he was tested with words using the rimes, some familiar and some new ones. He could read them all and spell those with the training rimes.

Wilson then piloted the system with colleagues in schools and found that all the children benefited, not all to the same extent as A. The teachers used it with other children and a test project was set up of 48 children aged 8–12 years old. They all had reading difficulties (spelling not mentioned) as identified by the schools. After a psychological assessment 24 children followed the PAT programme over a 20-week period and the other 24 followed a programme arranged by the schools. They were all then reassessed by the psychologists before the names of those in each programme were revealed.

Of the two matched groups the PAT group were found to have made significantly more progress in reading *and* spelling than the others. Wilson does not recommend this particular strategy for use with children below the age of 7 years because the basis of the intervention is through making and finding analogies, which younger children, unless highly able, would find difficult. It is essentially a spelling learning strategy different from using onset and rime in beginning reading and spelling. Wilson suggests that younger children might find the strategy confusing and recommends other forms of phonological awareness training. The PAT programme has been implemented in primary and secondary schools in Buckinghamshire.

There are now two PAT programmes, and a third in development.

They are not designed to replace reading schemes but are used to supplement and underpin them. There are five placement sheets and placement is based upon the pupil's ability to read the words on the reading lists in them. If longer than 60 seconds is taken to read a particular list then placement begins at the next level down. the programme only deals with regularly spelled words at both levels and there are 25 photocopiable worksheets and 25 related reading lists and dictation sheets. The procedure is to spend 10–15 minutes a day, five days per week on the programme. The first three days are spent on worksheets. These are headed by the whole alphabet and underneath there are four columns each beginning with a different rime. Pupils are given a new worksheet each day but only if their score on the previous sheet is more than 14 correct out of 20. On the fourth day the pupil does reading and ten spellings and on the fifth day five sentence dictations are given; there is a special format for the latter as well. It is important that the procedures laid down are carefully followed and this includes supervision of the worksheets and 'slicing' or cutting the task to half a worksheet for those with the severest difficulties. According to Thomas (1996), 'the children enjoy the worksheets and find them exciting and challenging although teachers looking at them at first think they look dull and uninteresting … one cannot fail to notice the excitement as the children begin to improve' (p. 17). One of Thomas's referrals reported to her teacher, 'I am doing very well now because I have this special programme which really makes me spell better and has helped my reading. I find that I say words automatically without the struggle I used to have' (*ibid.*, p. 18). This pupil had made progress in reading age from 7.9 to 10.1 years in 12 weeks on the programme.

Phonetics to support learning

Children who are having difficulties in learning to spell often have to engage in a self-help approach when it comes to phonics, and their errors can be misinterpreted. This can create problems in a teaching programme and time can be wasted on the wrong kind of input. A knowledge of some aspects of phonetics can be helpful to remedial teaching. Phonetics is a system of 46 symbols which represent the separate speech sounds that are made in the English language. The speech sounds are described by how they are made – plosive, fricative, nasal and lateral in relation to the key articulators – for example the movement of the tongue, alveolar ridge, nasal cavity, velum (the position of the soft palate and where it directs the air), vocal cords (whether they vibrate or not), and the shape of the lips.

The consonant /m/ is made with lips closed and voicing, /n/ is made with the tongue contacting the alveolar ridge and /ng/ is velar. 'M' and 'n' are frequently confused, and helping the pupil articulate and identify the *feel* of these consonants can help spelling. When /n/ is followed by 'd' or 't' in the final blends –nd and –nt the result is that the preceding vowel is nasalified and the pupil can easily fail to detect this and so makes spelling errors as follows:

fed for fend, bed for bend, wet for went, set for sent

Pupils may make reversals in spelling such as 'was' for 'saw' and 'on' for 'no'. If they were to prepare the mouth or articulate the initial sound, the onset, subvocally they could not then write 'was' for 'saw' and 'on' for 'no' because their formation is quite different. They may also omit final consonants such as 'd' and 't' even when trying to articulate clearly for spelling. Strategies for articulation training should be accompanied by teaching about word meanings and origins together with the affix –ed and final –t and –d.

Another common error is in b and d confusions. As these are characteristic of many poor spellers' scripts their appearance or reappearance can be misinterpreted. If, when they are noted, multi-sensory retraining is given again to correct the error a lot of time can be fruitlessly spent when the pupil actually thinks that the football ticket 'Abmits' one and has a similar notion about 'abvantage'. Teaching the prefixes 'ad' and 'ab' along with the meanings which they convey will be a more appropriate strategy.

Some knowledge of *assimilation* can also be helpful for it is then possible to identify spelling error patterns which at first might seem to indicate articulation difficulties such as 'hoe' for 'hole' and 'showder' for 'shoulder' or dialect transcription such as 'grand' for 'ground' and 'woeter' for 'water' from 'bab boys', 'fak cat', and 'tem men'. *Elisions* may also be directly transcribed such as 'tem pence', and 'dome be' for 'don't be'.

A book entitled *Simple Phonetics for Teachers*, by Smith and Bloor (1985), is a useful sourcebook for these problems and enables more specifically targeted help to be given to a pupil with severe language problems whom they describe thus:

> Even though the child's auditory acuity may be adequate, he [*sic*] may have poor auditory perception and discrimination skills. He may be unable to remember sounds long enough to reproduce them accurately and he will therefore mispronounce consonants and poly-syllabic words. He may confuse the sounds of back vowels – (hot) and (eh) and the front vowels – (pit) and (red) or (bat) and (but). He may not be able to discriminate between voiced and voiceless

Figure 6.2 *The i.t.a. alphabet*

sounds. He will not hear devoicing, aspiration and vowel shortening clues. He is difficult to teach to read and often learns to read through writing. (Smith and Bloor, 1985, p. 2)

(A pupil with such a problem may be able to hear devoicing and so on but may not be able to detect the feel of these clues in the mouth. Articulation training can be a support here.)

Phonetic alphabet systems

The initial teaching alphabet (i.t.a., Figure 6.2) (Pitman, 1961) was introduced as a phonemic system of 44 symbols representing all the speech sounds of English. There was only one correct sound response to each symbol and there was a graded introduction based upon frequencies. It had direct phoneme–grapheme correspondence, but a considerable number of new graphemes had to be invented and it was these which adults trained in the 26 letters of the Roman alphabet found difficult to accept. In the i.t.a. system transfer to traditional orthography was achieved towards the end of the second year where difficulties ensued only for the minority (Downing and Thackray, 1970). This system was once quite a popular scheme but now is used in only one school because parents and governors find the script too different to accept and there is a lack of up-to-date reading material being published. Cashdan and Pumfrey (1969) reported that i.t.a. can be used successfully with either a phonic or a meaning emphasis approach and can lead to much earlier writing and reading. Few children failed to learn in this system but those who did often experienced difficulties in other systems. Mostly they began to show these difficulties at transfer. They were able however to read and spell in a relatively decipherable manner, whereas dyslexics often fail even to do this.

The Phonic Handbook (Lloyd, 1992) was a modification or adaptation of the i.t.a. approach. Sue Lloyd had had extensive experience in the teaching of reading using the 'look and say' system with i.t.a. and then a system in which all the 44 sounds of the initial teaching alphabet were learned before starting the reading books. In the sounds first method, at the end of the second year the children were reading as well as they used to at the end of the third year. Before the change in method the average score on Young's Reading Test was 102. Afterwards it was between 110 and 116 and the reading itself was more fluent. Lloyd also reported that the pupils' independent writing was far better although it was not always in conventional spelling at first but the teachers could read what the children had written.

In her phonics teaching system, what Lloyd has done is instead of using i.t.a. symbols for the 18 sounds which do not correspond to single letters of the alphabet, she has used the 'digraphs' which most closely matched them. In taking this simple but ingenious step traditional orthography can be made to carry all the benefits of i.t.a.

The 42 sounds can be learned as part of the same basic system which is simpler for children than a two-tiered system consisting of monographs followed by digraphs. This means that children can write any words they wish just by using this logical sound bank. A multisensory approach is used to help the sound and the grapheme connect, and includes saying and sounding; the ears, eyes, larynx, body and finger muscles are all drawn into the action.

The handbook, in ring-bound format, is in two parts: the first is made up of seven short chapters on methodology and the second contains 12 sections of photocopiable materials for instruction, exercises and games. The manual describes auditory skills training, the order of introduction of the symbols, and tracing and copying exercises. Finally, more advanced spelling skills and rules are dealt with. Teachers who have used the scheme in general remedial settings have been very enthusiastic about it. Once again some controlled studies in its use as a developmental and a remedial programme would be helpful.

Spelling Made Easy: a structured remedial scheme (Brand, 1993)

Spelling Made Easy is a scheme of worksheets and stories devised by Violet Brand and first published in 1987 by Egon. It is now in its fourteenth impression and is very popular with teachers and especially with pupils who love the Fat Sam stories. Brand established the Watford Dyslexia Centre and promoted the understanding and teaching of dyslexic children with her own strategies and schemes over a number of years. She has been awarded the MBE in recognition of her work.

Spelling Made Easy is presented as a multisensory structured spelling scheme suitable for children from 6 years of age through to university students. The central principle is that *word families* should be the basis of our teaching of spelling at every level.

There is an *Introductory Book: Fat Sam*; then *Level 1: Sam and the Train; Level 2: The Adventures of Augustus*; and *Level 3: Making and Taking Notes from Text*. There are copy masters for each of the above books and a *Teachers Book on Remedial Spelling* giving the rationale and details of how to use the materials. The order of introduction of the key aspects of the scheme is as follows:

- basic vowel sounds not in alphabetical order – teach 'a' then 'o' because those with speech problems often have difficulty hearing the difference between 'a' and 'e';
- common words needed early on;
- common principles:
  - doubling of vowels (ee)
  - combinations of vowel and a consonant (ar)
  - combination of two consonants (sh)
  - effect of silent e on a vowel (cake);
- combination of two vowels (ai);
- grouping of two or more letters to produce one sound (–igh, –air);
- ir ur er.

General recommendations to the teacher are that spellers should be taught to listen to the voice and feel the shape of the mouth when making sounds. Only one word family should be introduced per week irrespective of age group. When learning basic words the pupil should be shown how to finger trace over the letters saying the *whole word* (not sounding it out). The children are given copies of the word and trace over it saying the word six times. The cards are then turned over and the word is then written *without* looking. The card is then turned back and the spelling checked. If it is correct the pupil hands in the card, if not he or she must repeat the exercise – keep practising. This method of whole-word tracing is based upon that of Fernald (1943) and the phonogram approach based upon the Spalding and Spalding (1967) method, both acknowledged in the text. The order of introduction of the phonic aspects of the scheme are as follows:

$$a \; o \; i \; e \; u \; ck \; ee \; oo \; ar \; or \; sh \; ch$$
$$th \; a–e \; i–e \; o–e \; u–e \; ai \; oa \; ir \; ou$$
$$ea \; /ē/ \; ing \; ur \; aw \; oi \; er \; all \; y \; /e/$$
$$ea \; /ĕ/ \; ow \; igh \; a(/ar/, /a/) \; o \; /u/ \; y \; /i/ \; ow$$

Some details of the worksheets will serve to illustrate the fundamental approach to the scheme.

Introductory Level: Fat Sam

The aims of the worksheets are set out as follows:

- Word families are identified not only for spelling but also in reading processes.
- Word chunks are speedily recognized in tracking print.
- Information carried in print is understood, remembered and used.

- Recently acquired word families can be recalled when required.
- Literacy knowledge can be used in proof-reading.

There are said to be 'thinking activities which will hopefully form useful *automatic habits* for the future'. Thinking activities and automatic habits are however mutually exclusive activities and thus this interpretation would seem to be somewhat contradictory.

The first little story in the *Introductory Level* is about *Sad Gran* and is typical of the humorous story, and one can see why children find the tales so attractive:

Gran is sad
The bad cat sat on her hat
It is flat.

The worksheet activities which accompany this story are arranged as six activities:

1. Choose a colour. Draw a line under the words in the 'a' family.
2. Can you draw a picture of Sad Gran?
3. Can you draw a picture of the bad cat and the flat hat?
4. Can you write about the hat?

There are then six line drawings of objects and six words:

tap, jar, bag, flag, bat, hand

5. Write the words under the pictures.
6. What is wrong? (with the following sentence)

The man has the flag the bag and the tap in his bat.

On each of the subsequent pages there is a similar format as each new word family is introduced. On page 21, question 6 asks 'What is wrong?' with the following: a b e f c d h g i.

Levels 1 and 2

These workbooks follow the same format with stories and follow-up activities as in the introductory book. At each level the text becomes more complex and the tasks more difficult. Level 1 begins with a six-line story about Grandad's van. The exercises which follow set the pattern for the rest in the book:

1. Draw a line under words in the 'a' family – 'was' and 'gave' look the same but sound different ...
2. Can you write 4 words ending in –amp?
3. Can you write 4 words ending in –and?

4. What's wrong? A jumbled sentence is given – the man had cramp...
5. Make your own comic – finish the story in pictures and write a sentence under each picture. (There are two pictures of grandad's van in sequential boxes and two empty boxes to draw in.)

At *Level 2* a set of similar but more advanced worksheets are provided; again a range of activities are suggested, for example, 'Here is the news' presents text from which stories have to be extended, followed by facts, spellings and elements such as o words, and jumbled sentences.

Level 3 helps students write text and take notes from text. A page of detailed and informative text is presented concerning a range of subjects such as Wales, Ireland, temperature, the Thames, oboe and saxophone, and then pupils have to engage with the text to develop a range of study skills. Aspects of spelling are still included:

- Look for familiar word families or families within new words.
- Decide on the tricky part of a spelling. Look (and think about it) then cover, write and check. Cover again, write and check.

The list of spellings was supplied by Watford Grammar School from those found difficult by girls entering the school. Recently this strategy has been changed to 'say–look–cover–write–check'. *Level 3* is intended for pupils in their final year of primary school but the worksheets can be selected and adapted for use with other pupils and adult students.

The scheme is easy to use and enjoyed by pupils, but there are some reservations about its use with severe dyslexics. It is possible for a pupil such as Omar who is 8 years old and who can neither read nor write to become quickly confused at the Sad Gran stage. He can choose a colour and draw a line under words with 'a' in them once he has been shown an 'a' word. He then *matches* all the words with 'a' from visual representation. His picture of Gran, the cat and the hat look vaguely similar but the instructions have to be read to him several times. He cannot write about the hat. He randomly matches words tap, jar, bag, etc. with the picture and he cannot read the final sentence to discover what is wrong with it. When it is read to him he still does not know the answer.

All the extraneous drawing of pictures and colouring, for pupils such as Omar, distracts from the central problem of learning the sound–symbol correspondence for 'a' and then writing it. Writing 'i' in a reasonable size and form and learning its sound (using the

TRTS method) actually took Omar several weeks of lessons and six months to understand the basic code with i t p n s and to write simple sentences.

Spelling Made Easy emphasizes multisensory whole-word tracing and making analogies by identifying 'word families'. The notion of 'word families' contained in the books is not so widely shared; the approach has more in common with letter strings or clusters approaches in which any parts which look the same and appear together regularly are called strings, clusters or families. It is however helpful for pupils to learn the vowel /a/, the blend '–nd' and the commonly used word *and*, and then learn that this word, letter string or cluster is helpful in encoding words with similar sound patterns by analogy:

and, hand, sand, grand, brand

For the severe cases presentation of vowels in context (in words and sentences), even though at weekly intervals, can lead to confusion. Learning to build words from two sounds as they are learnt is quite a monumental task for dyslexics and frequently underestimated by teachers. So often the devisers of schemes are so highly skilled and so responsive to an individual pupil's needs that they can use any scheme effectively and quickly invent new activities of a finer graded kind to meet those needs. Schemes at their best are not interactive and need skilled interpretation.

Egon Publishers provide a set of supplementary workbooks presenting colouring and drawing activities associated with individual letters and their sounds in simple words but pupils like Omar can complete these workbooks without having learnt the basic sounds and so they need to be used with care. Learning support assistants are particularly fond of schemes which include worksheets. At the end of their support session the evidence of a completed worksheet helps them to justify their role and gives satisfaction.

ARROW learning (Lane, 1978)

ARROW (aural, read, respond, oral, written) was a technique first developed by Lane in 1978 and 1980 during his MEd studies with pupils in a Somerset middle school. The pupils were normally hearing and hearing-impaired children with various language/ learning disabilities. He had noticed gains in the ability of the pupils to recall facts as an incidental benefit of the ARROW technique.

ARROW requires pupils to listen through special equipment to a taped or 'live' voice, copy it by speaking, then listen to their own recording (the echo). During the echo process the pupil may undertake other learning tasks – reading, dictation, auditory discrimination, and so on. In later trials by Lane and Chinn (1986) with dyslexics they noted that pupils using the ARROW self-voice learning technique made the greatest use of silent mouthing (subvocalizing) as they practised the facts. They compared their methods and found those with a large self-voice content gave the greatest gains. The tutor-voice method gave the lowest gains and the 'write and say' method was also low on gains.

The recommended approach is that pupils should operate the equipment in practice sessions of 10–15 minutes per day. Improvements can be expected within five weeks. Positive effects were still seen after two years in the experimental group.

The system is claimed to be a multisensory teaching–learning approach. Training can be given by parents, welfare assistants, teachers and the pupils themselves. The recommended frequency is now 15 minutes per day in three to five sessions per week, preferably with the ARROW two-track recorder (available from the Cambridge System Limited, Buckden, Huntingdon) which does not erase any pre-recorded material and includes a headset and boom microphone.

When using the ARROW method for reading and/or spelling pupils use at least one or all of the components. The *self-voice* is the key to the approach. The components are as follows:

- *Aural*: the pupil listens to speech on the headset from single words to complex sentences (live or taped).
- *Read*: whilst listening to the voice the pupils refer to written material, a non-reader looks at visual support material.
- *Respond*: then the pupil usually responds by imitating the words on tape (or live).
- *Oral*: the pupils repeat the utterances (by the teacher) and listen to their own recorded speech on replay. (They often elect to turn off the teacher voice at this point.)
- *Written*: when their own voices are being replayed the pupils may be asked to write down what they have heard. Non-readers can be asked to rearrange visual support material.

The manual details ways in which pre-readers can be helped, structured reading schemes can be used, sight vocabulary practised, reading for meaning undertaken, curriculum subject reading incorporated, and spelling, listening and memory skills improved.

With regard to spelling, two approaches are described. The bottom-up approach involves pre-recorded material which can be used with pupils at various levels of spelling development and includes a set of software:

- *Level I* (Sounds). book and tapes. There are three sections.
  Section 1 – auditory/visual training on initial sounds
  Section 2 – all short vowels
  Section 3 – consonant blends linked to short vowels
- *Level II* (Keywords). This also in three sections involving frequently used words.
  Section 1 – keywords in isolation
  Section 2 – keywords presented in phrases and sentences
  Section 3 – keywords presented within passages
- *Level III* (Word families). This introduces pupils to visual and phonic patterns presented as word families with nearly 300 examples of letter/sound combinations.

The ARROW system is flexible in that it can be adapted to a top-down strategy in which the child's own spelling error lists can be included as well as curriculum-based spellings. The words are given in their 'look and say' form followed by the naming of each letter. Repetition is required and corrective procedures should be introduced where there are difficulties in learning particular words.

A number of attempts have been made to provide empirically tested research results using ARROW, more than with many other schemes. The main *self-voice* appears to have had a number of facilitating advantages:

- motivating endless repetition;
- increased attention to self-voice inputs;
- increased sub-vocalization.

Each of these can contribute to learning to spell. Whether similar results can be achieved with standard tape recorders as claimed by some remediators has yet to be demonstrated.

SUMMARY AND CONCLUSIONS

In this chapter a range of general remedial strategies and schemes have been reviewed. An indication of their value has been given in relation to their use in the general classroom and in the withdrawal setting.

It has been suggested that all primary school teachers should have a knowledge of these techniques for developmental, preventative and first stage remedial work. Secondary school and college

teachers all need to have some basic training in corrective strategies, especially those related to the core vocabulary of their
disciplines. Teachers need to be able to identify spelling and handwriting problems, and not harass the pupils about them but obtain
specialist support and advice.

The main types of remedial intervention were described in
approaches which involved the teaching and learning of sounds.
After a careful assessment of the pupil's learning needs the most
appropriate technique should be selected and implemented.
However, monitoring and evaluation are crucial to the successful
outcome and after a predetermined period without any significant
advancement for the pupil the programme and the assessment
must be reviewed and, if necessary, amended or changed.

Sound-based schemes have their limitations in that they deal in
the main with the lower levels of spelling acquisition such as
phoneme awareness and phonics. Those schemes which include
syllable knowledge do so in a rather limiting framework. A sound-
based scheme, although essential, is not sufficient for meeting the
needs for good spelling development of poor spellers or dyslexics.

General remedial strategies: skills training, writing and other methods

INTRODUCTION

Handwriting is a recent acquisition for the human race, especially in alphabetic scripts, and it requires an additional set of skills to perform as well as being able to spell. Despite the widespread use of word processors and e-mail a considerable amount of hand writing still takes place in the form of note-taking, list-making and for general communication purposes. A study of handwriting quickly reveals that it is almost entirely a *motor skill* but is conceptually driven, for it is possible to write one's name and address with one's eyes shut and people who cannot see can learn to use it as a communciation system.

Handwriting has two purposes which can overlap – *calligraphy* and *communication*. Calligraphy as a term is derived from Greek and means 'beautiful writing'. Beautiful writing is a pleasure to see in ancient illuminated manuscripts and on displays and certificates when italic (Figure 7.1) is conventionally used.

Italic is frequently taught as a form of lettering in art classes and some people have absorbed this into their general hand-writing style. It was originally designed in Renaissance Italy to speed up writing and copying large amounts of text. It is a compressed slanting style based on an elliptical *O* with contrasting thick and thin

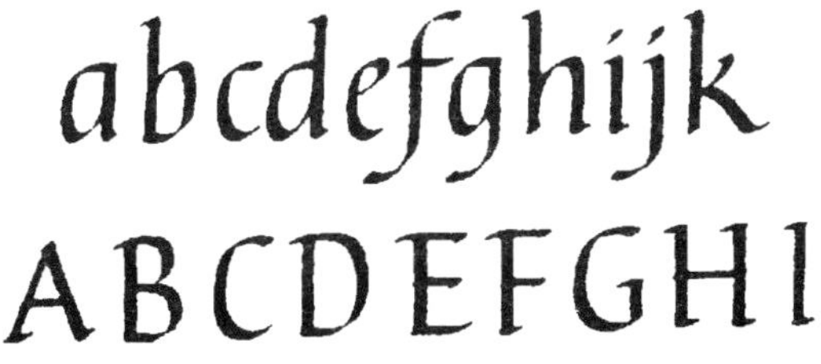

Figure 7.1 *Italic-style handwriting*

strokes and simple serifs. It may well have speeded up writing 400 years ago but today we have developed even faster forms. The slanting O does have merit in that it is quicker and easier to make in a fluid form than an upright round O. The thick and thin strokes are an accomplishment which many with poor pen control, and especially beginners, would find beyond their powers. However, there have been schools which after the infant stage have adopted italic as the school's formal handwriting style. It is important to warn against this, as this section of the chapter will set out to show. Calligraphy should be regarded only as an art form and left as such because it is difficult and time-consuming to form.

Handwriting for learning and recording in school has one basic purpose, and that is communication. What is required is for the pupil to learn a *'fast running hand'*. Herein lies the problem. Ten per cent or more of pupils have a mild handwriting co-ordination difficulty (Gubbay, 1975; Lazslo, 1987; Alston, 1993). They have difficulty in learning to form letters correctly and in producing a neat style on a page. Teachers are very concerned that pupils develop and use neat writing and some can pressurize pupils unmercifully to do so. Such pupils, whenever they can, try to avoid any written task and some even become disruptive when they are required to sit down and write. 'Now write it down' can bring forth a chorus of groans from older pupils. Avoidance and difficulties with writing tasks can have a serious effect on spelling development through consistent lack of practice and use.

Neatness may be so great a concern that it is obtained at the expense of content and studies have shown that neat writers, more often girls, tend to be awarded higher marks in some classrooms. Pressure focuses upon the production of a neat print script which is patterned upon a simple style found in infant texts, which was introduced by Edward Johnstone to a group of London teachers in 1913. It was based upon an early form of church writing which he had simplified as more suitable for use with infants (Jarman, 1979). This *print script* was of a simple 'ball and stick' construction and it became so popular that throughout England and Wales it replaced the earlier joined 'civil service hand' or *cursive*.

Ball and stick print (Figure 7.2) is still the main form introduced in reception classes. At the age of about 8 years the pupils, usually on entering junior school, are then introduced to joining. Rubin and Henderson (1982) found that 12 per cent of pupils were considered by their teachers to have serious handwriting difficulties. In a survey carried out with third year junior school pupils in Cheshire, Alston and Taylor (1993) found that, according to assessments made by five experienced remedial teachers, just over 20 per cent of pupils were

a b c d e A B C D E

Figure 7.2 *Ball and stick print*

not writing well enough for the needs of the secondary school curriculum. In urban schools they found this figure rose to 40 per cent. Incorporated in their handwriting checklist there are also some spelling items. Sassoon's (1989a and b) research showed that, in her study of 100 15-year-olds, 40 per cent of girls and 25 per cent of boys had actually said that writing was painful for them. The Assessment of Performance Unit (APU, 1991) surveyed 2,000 pupils at 11 and 15 years and found that 20 per cent of boys and 10 per cent of girls said they hated writing. Twice this number, 60 per cent, said they avoided writing whenever possible. No doubt they then became candidates for disruption. If we could improve their writing skills we might improve discipline in schools.

Scripts of undergraduate students, the successes of the school system, also demonstrated a noticeable range of handwriting difficulties and many students failed to produce a fast running hand in their final examinations. Their writing was a poorly formed, rounded hand based upon half-print and half-joined script (Figure 7.3). Unjoined and rounded script takes fractionally longer to form and thus in

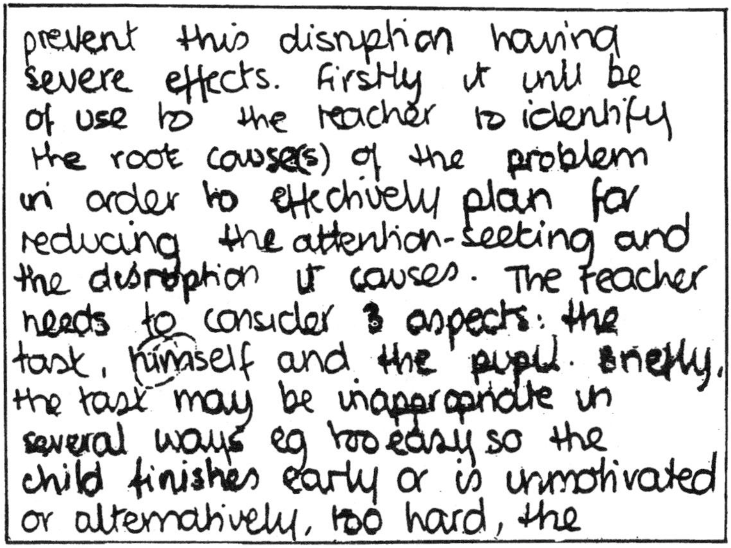

> prevent this disruption having severe effects. Firstly it will be of use to the teacher to identify the root cause(s) of the problem in order to effectively plan for reducing the attention-seeking and the disruption it causes. The teacher needs to consider 3 aspects: the task, himself and the pupil. Briefly, the task may be inappropriate in several ways eg too easy so the child finishes early or is unmotivated or alternatively, too hard, the

Figure 7.3 *An example of an undergraduate semi-print script (two-thirds of original size)*

examinations these writers could write less and so their arguments would be shorter and supporting statements more limited than those with a fluent script. Italic also takes longer to produce and over a period of years it was noticeable that slower writing could contribute to lowering the class of a degree when there were timed periods of writing. Stainthorp (1990) found 20 per cent of her BEd students were unable to produce a fluent cursive script and half of them could not join letters at all.

Pupils and students who use a print script often prefer to do so because they feel that it looks neater especially in the early stages. Occasionally, parents encountered in our remedial programmes refuse to permit their children to learn cursive. For a number of years it has been clear that the teaching of a remedial cursive was beneficial to the pupils. Cursive was an important factor in overcoming incorrect motor habits and it had an appeal because it was 'more grown up'. It became apparent that many classroom teachers would not permit pupils to use the remedial hand in work in the classroom. This was a considerable handicap to the pupils who were at last learning to write and spell but using a cursive system. It was also distressing for them and their remedial teachers and so we jointly ran in-service training courses on learning difficulties in order to try to change these perceptions. Students in training and those in in-service courses undertook research projects investigating ways of achieving policy change and the relative effectiveness of cursive over print learning in reception and with remedial pupils. As a result 16 schools in the LEA introduced cursive writing teaching in reception class (Morse, 1991). Two years later at 7 years the vast majority of pupils had achievements at Level 3 in the National Curriculum writing area.

National Curriculum handwriting target

Level	Statements of attainment Pupils should be able to:
1	begin to form letters with some control over the size, shape and orientation of letters or lines of writing.
2	a) produce legible upper and lower case letters in one style and use them consistently (i.e. not randomly mixed within words) b) produce letters that are recognizably formed and properly orientated and that have clear ascenders and descenders where necessary (e.g. b and d, p and q).
3	a) begin to produce clear and legible joined-up writing b) produce more fluent joined-up writing in independent work.

> Note: Pupils may be exempted from this target if they need to use a non-sighted form of writing such as braille or if they have such a degree of physical disability that the attainment target is unattainable.

The statements of attainment at Levels 1 to 3 are as specified by Order and published in a statutory document entitled *English in the National Curriculum* (1989).

PREVENTATIVE MEASURES: DEVELOPMENTAL
TECHNIQUES

Although young children in reception classes throughout England and Wales learn the print script, in the rest of the world they learn cursive. In the early part of this century our great grandparents also learned cursive and so the argument that it is too difficult for infants really does not stand up. Attitudes to the introduction of cursive in reception classes can bring forth very strongly held views (Montgomery, 1990) even though the teachers are unable to cite any evidence in support of these views. A similar attitude exists towards the use of lines for writing in reception class. Burnhill *et al.* (1975) found that use of lines helped the learner with placing and letter construction and made a significant and positive contribution to improving the overall appearance of the writing (Figure 7.4). Others hold that lines are too difficult for infants to

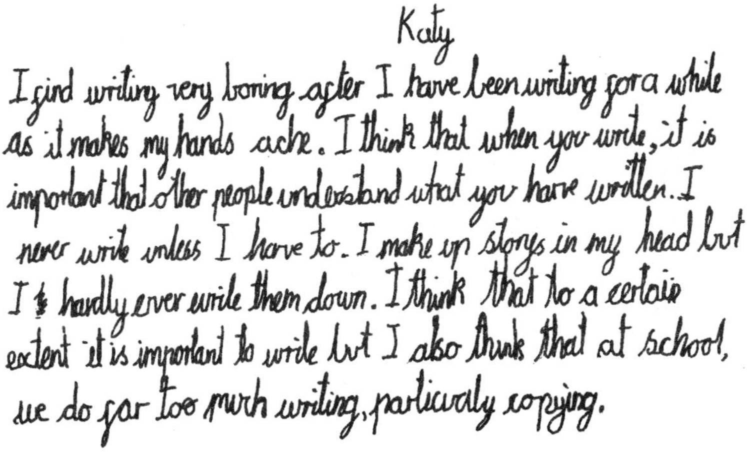

Figure 7.4 *Katy's writing (7 years) (two-thirds of original size)*

place their letters upon, but early writing is more difficult to do well without them – and it does not hamper their creativity.

In the remedial setting, lines and cursive are essential. Wedell (1973) insisted that children with co-ordination difficulties must learn to use a continuous writing movement. Dysgraphics such as these have difficulties, once they find where to make contact with the paper, in making the required shape and the precise size and length. As soon as they lift the pen from the paper in print script and make the next letter the directional, orientational and locational problems begin all over again. The effort involved becomes greater, the pen is seized more tightly, the knuckles go white and the whole body tenses, and there is a further loss of fluency. To aid focus and concentration and stop contra-lateral movements the edge of the desk may be held and the tongue stuck out. It can take half an hour of formidable effort to produce a neat sentence.

Early's (1976) research advocates the exclusive use of cursive from the beginning, because it was found that the major advantage of cursive lay in the fact that each word consists of one continuous line where all the elements flow together. This means that the child experiences more readily the total form or shape of a given word as he or she monitors the kinaesthetic feedback from the writing movements. Now there is a considerable body of evidence being collected and published in *The Handwriting Review*, a journal edited by Alston and Taylor, which is lending support to the movement of change from print to cursive in early writing, known as the *developmental preventative approach to writing*, and there are some materials to support this (Morse, 1988). Cripps (1988, 1989) has also produced a joined handwriting training scheme, *A Hand for Spelling*, with a series of developmental workbooks. He has based his work on the research of Peters (1967, 1985) in adopting a visual emphasis and a rote training approach to letter strings. In his view: 'Spelling is a visual skill. Good spellers look carefully at words and it is through this visual familiarity that they learn the probability of certain letters occurring together' (Cripps, 1988, p. 1).

Cripps stresses the development of kinaesthetic imagery needed for free-flowing handwriting and he claimed that these skills are brought together in his booklets. Although the letters have small ligatures to encourage joining they are initially formed as print script from the top of the letters. For potentially good writers and spellers this is not going to pose too much of a problem but it does make difficulties for the pupil with spelling and co-ordination difficulties for the reasons already presented. Nevertheless Cripps's evaluation studies (Cripps and Cox, 1990) have shown marked improvement in spelling and writing in the trained groups.

home   home

come   come

hope   hope

Figure 7.5 *Examples of joined writing (1)*

Even greater difficulties can be caused by schemes in existence which claim to teach joined writing but which offer examples such as those in Figure 7.5. Joining bits of words and not others without using lead-in strokes is disadvantageous to children with learning difficulties, for example: 'three trees on the street' and 'how do you do' (as Figure 7.6 shows).

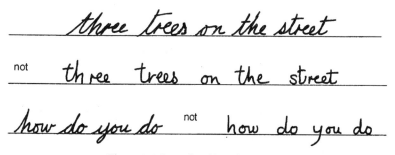

Figure 7.6 *Examples of joined writing (2)*

Multisensory word training

This is the most common method of handwriting training for spelling. If, as part of the remedial strategy, the 100 most common words used in early writing and reading are worked on as whole units, this can prove helpful. Each new word to be learned has to be taught as a whole writing unit with a continuous line as far as possible through the first and second syllables at least. In order that the pupil always knows where to begin the word it should be taught as always starting on the line and an ovoid shape to the body of the letter should be encouraged for the reasons already given.

Table 7.1 *One hundred most common words*

a	and	he	in	is	it	of
that	the	to	was			

all	be	have	on	they		
are	but	him	one	we		
as	for	his	said	with		
at	had	not	so	you		

about	down	made	other	up		
after	first	make	our	want		
back	from	me	out	well		
been	get	more	over	went		
before	go	much	right	were		
big	has	must	see	what		
by	her	my	she	when		
call	here	new	some	where		
came	if	no	their	which		
can	into	now	then	who		
come	just	off	then	will		
could	like	old	there	your		
did	little	only	this			
do	look	or	two			

From Table 7.1 the first words in cursive script thus become those shown in Figure 7.7a.

All new single syllabled words should be taught as continuous writing units and practice given for similar groups (Figure 7.7b).

Where there are base words plus their affixes these should be taught separately and then fused or linked together to encourage word-building (Figure 7.7c).

Writing patterns of similar groups of words can be practised to develop rhythm and flow (Figure 7.7d).

At the same time as whole words are being learnt the correct formation of the individual letters can be taught, each starting from the line (full flowing cursive), and the alphabet sequence can be reinforced (Figure 7.7e).

The most succinct form of cursive needs to be presented. Too many overhead loops tend to make the writing look more confusing but individual style should be allowed to be infused. Marion Richardson (1935), famous for her recommended style of writing, produced copy books in a joined style halfway between italic and copperplate (Figure 7.8b). This style was recommended for infants from the start. The principle was 'start as you mean to go on'. This message was lost and teachers modified the ball and stick form to a continuous flow through an individual letter. This has now given way to a form 'with ligatures' (Figure 7.9) as a nod in the direction of cursive to assist later joining, but it is insufficient.

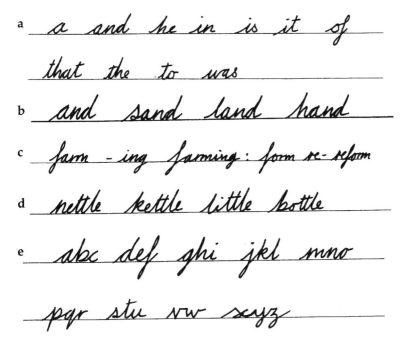

Figure 7.7 *Cursive writing progression*

The hours spent by infants in copying 'news' can lead to the errors shown in Figure 7.10 when not closely supervised. These can still be seen in the copy writing of older dyslexics such as James (Figure 7.11). What they do is *draw their letters* and in so doing may attend to all the wrong cues.

Morse (1988) gives the following reasons, based on her extensive experience of remedial writing teaching, for teaching cursive writing (Figure 7.12):

- aids left to right movements through each word across the page;
- word is treated as a unit;
- eliminates reversals and inversions of b and d and n and u;
- more efficient use of movement because of cursive's flow;
- smoother flow reinforces tactile learning;
- no need to change or relearn shapes later;
- gives spaces between words;
- automatically gives spaces between letters;
- facilitates earlier development of a personal style;
- gives potential for speeding up.

a b c d e f g h i j k l m n o p

q r s t u v w x y z

Figure 7.8a *Print script*

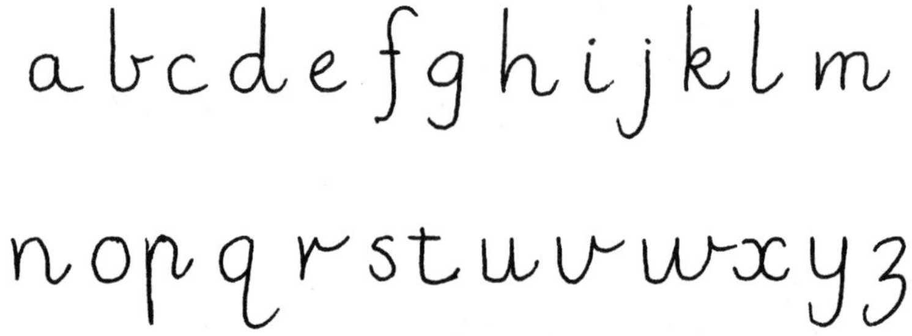

a b c d e f g h i j k l m

n o p q r s t u v w x y ʒ

Figure 7.8b *Marion Richardson's 'writing' (1935)*

a b c d e f g h i j k l m n o p

q r s t u v w x y z

Figure 7.8c *Christopher Jarman's 'monoline' model (1979)*

Alice (Figure 7.13) has been taught infant print but now an attempt
has been made to teach her cursive. She has been taught how to
make each letter but not how to link them as words and syllables.
Her writing remains a ligatured print. Some pupils refuse to use
joining as they feel it makes their work look untidy.

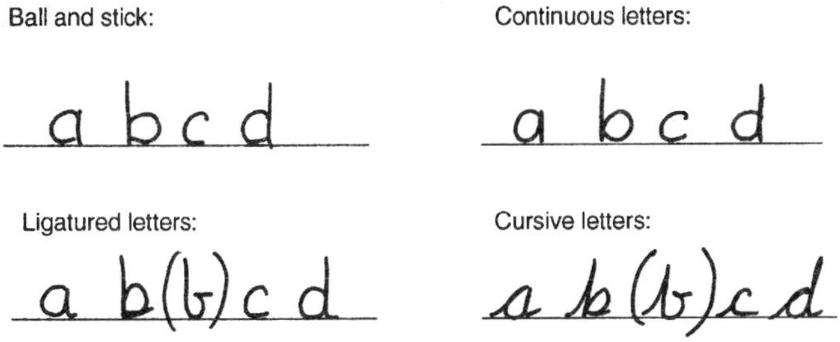

Ball and stick:

Continuous letters:

Ligatured letters:

Cursive letters:

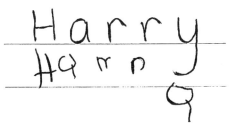

Figure 7.9 *Four letter forms*

Figure 7.10 *Harry's 'drawing' of his name (4 years) (half of original size)*

Figure 7.11 *James's copy writing/drawing (7 years) (half of original size)*

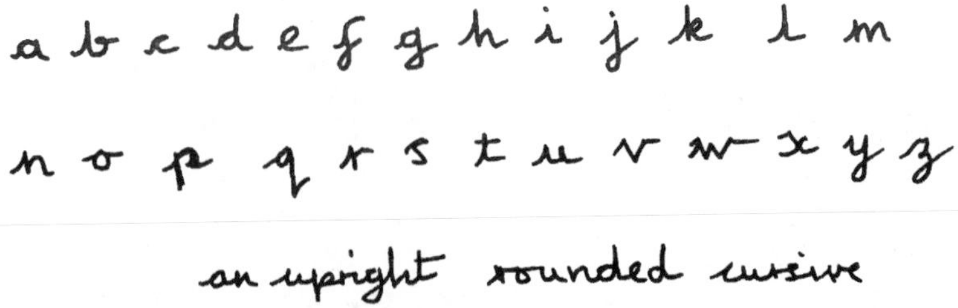

a b c d e f g h i j k l m
n o p q r s t u v w x y z

an upright rounded cursive

Figure 7.12a *Kingston 'cursive' based upon Palmer style*

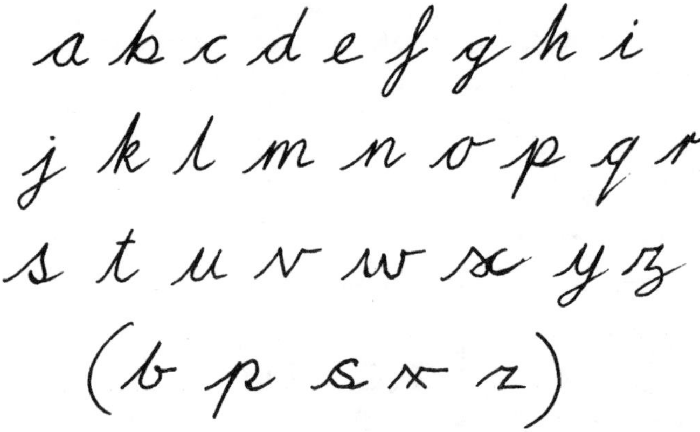

a b c d e f g h i
j k l m n o p q r
s t u v w x y z
(b p s x z)

Figure 7.12b *Ovoid cursive*

Cursive 'look–cover–write–check'

In a study with matched groups of 24 experimental and control groups who were all remedial readers, spellers and writers Vincent (1983) found that there was a highly significant improvement in the writing and spelling of the experimental group who were given cursive writing training in 'look–cover–write–check', whilst controls were given print script training. Bueckhardt (1988) confirmed this in a similar study and, equally important, found that the class teachers' attitudes became more favourable to the pupils because of their neater writing. Teachers tend to think that untidy writing is a reflection of carelessness and the unwillingness of the pupil to work for them. This is not reinforcing for the teacher and a negative attitude is engendered. Nothing could be further from the truth; the pupils, if observed closely, will be found to try and try and only lose heart and motivation when continually criti-

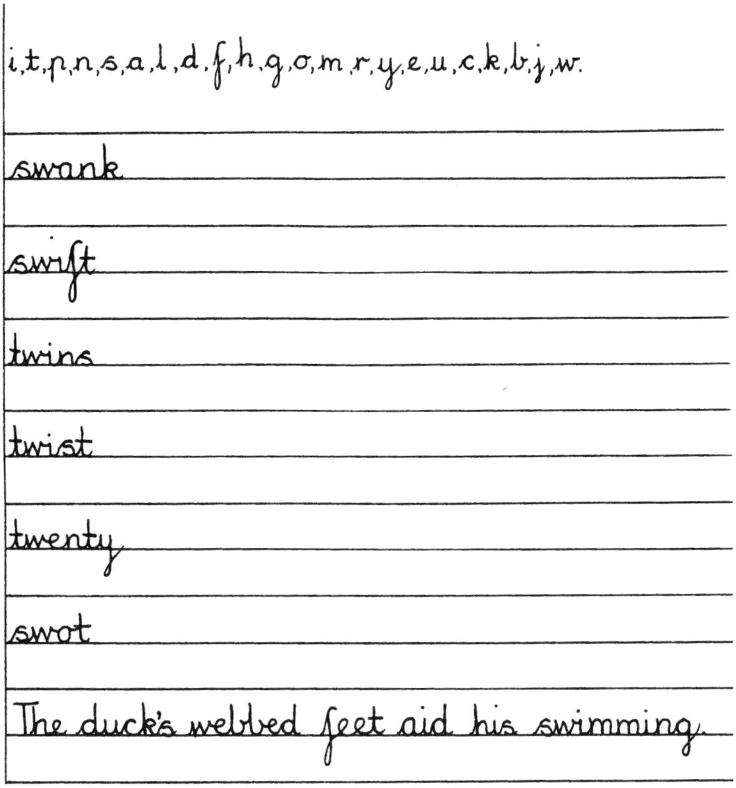

Figure 7.12c *Kingston cursive (two-thirds of original size)*
Source: Morse, 1988. Copyright P. Morse. Used with permission.

cized for untidy writing. This is the point when emotional and behavioural difficulties can ensue.

Phonogram cursive writing training

Spalding and Spalding (1967), in *The Writing Road to Reading*, describe a system of teaching 70 phonograms through cursive writing training which, once learnt, would enable the pupil to read any of the early reading texts. They claimed success for their method in teaching both reading and spelling. The phonograms begin with initial letter sounds, blends and digraphs and progress to –ing, –igh, and –tion, for example. They reported that with

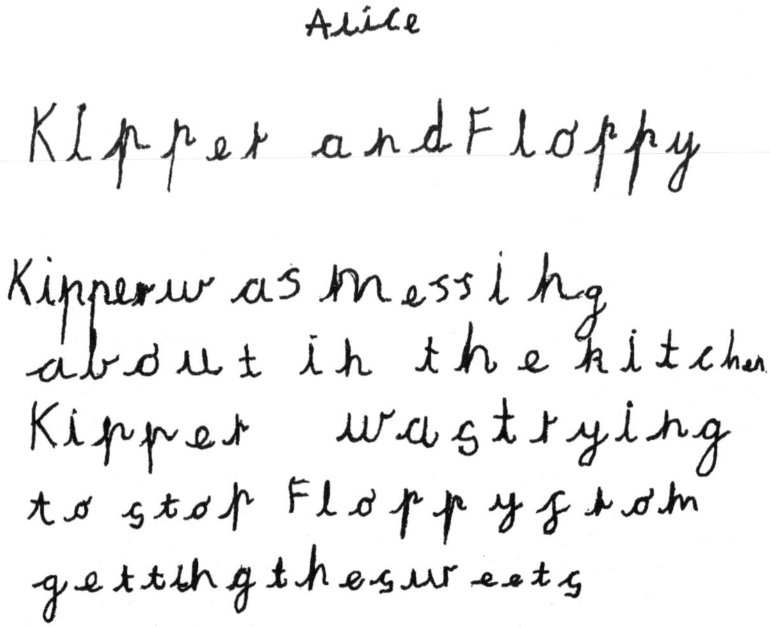

Alice

KIpper andFloppy

Kipperw as messihg
about ih the kitchen.
Kipper wastrying
to stop Floppyfrom
gettihgthesweets

Figure 7.13 *Alice's ligatured print (two-thirds of original size)*

daily tuition, it took about six months by their cursive writing system to learn all 70 phonograms but that both reading and writing involving the phonograms could be practised from the earliest stages.

Guidelines for teaching handwriting to overcome learning difficulties

- Teach the basic letter shapes as a single fluid motor movement.
- Do not permit copy writing or tracing.
- Teach the letters singly but encourage joining immediately.
- Teach the letters in use order with the sounds and names, not in alphabetical order or shape families.
- Use lined paper.
- Start each letter on the line with a lead-in stroke.
- Teach base words and affixes as one writing unit wherever possible.

Position for writing

This is an aspect of writing teaching which is often overlooked. The position which the pupil adopts for writing can be quite revealing and can induce difficulties. It is important to ensure that the pupil's writing posture is relaxed and controlled. If the furniture is an inappropriate size and style this can place particular stress upon pupils with co-ordination difficulties and is likely to occur where the pupils are growing rapidly or have to use furniture more suitable for older, bigger pupils. The pupil should hold the pen in the standard triangular grip shown in Figure 7.14.

Any difference in the standard grip should be investigated. Younger pupils can be helped by being given a plastic grip to put round the pen or given moulding substances which can take on an individual pupil's corrected finger pattern and be left to harden. A range of grips may be used by pupils in their efforts to gain better control of their pens.

The distance of the fingers from the pen tip should not be too far or too near, but left-handers need to keep a longer distance from the point so that they can see their writing as they pull the pen towards the mid-line. The elbow of the writing arm should be 'locked' to permit the pen to glide smoothly in an arc across the page (Figure 7.15). This means that the paper for right-handed pupils should be slightly sloped away from the mid-line. The paper for the left-handers should have a marked slope in the opposite direction. It is most unwise to make pupils write with their paper square on to the table's edge. The pupil should place the non-writing hand on the paper to keep it in place.

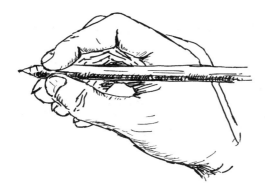

Figure 7.14 *Standard handwriting grip*

The writing arc   Left-handers   Right-handers

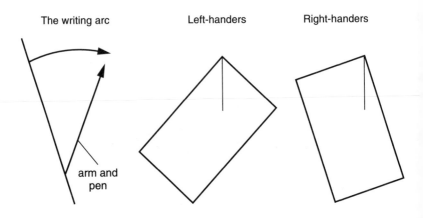

arm and
pen

Figure 7.15 *Positions for writing*

Teaching left-handed pupils

To be left-handed has not always been considered acceptable and, even today, some left-handers suffer from living in a right-orientated world. In previous centuries left-handedness has been connected with possession and satanism. However, it was not until children went to school that pressures began to be placed upon them to change from being left- to right-handed. In the earlier decades of the twentieth century children often were forced to write with their right hands and for some this proved to be both distressing and difficult, allegedly resulting in some children developing stuttering, nervous habits and emotional difficulties. Since the origin of left-handedness is understood a little better now some of these children's difficulties can be comprehended.

Annett (1983) proposed that there was a genetic right shift factor responsible in the human brain for making the right hand the dominant or lead hand in skilled manipulative tasks. In about 10 per cent of the population, however, no shift gene was carried and handedness could settle at random in either hemisphere. If it settled in the left, usually also dominant for language, then the person would become right-handed. By chance it could be expected that about 50 per cent of this no shift factor group could expect to be left-handed and 50 per cent right-handed. In small numbers of cases the left hemisphere might have suffered injury at birth, or was not able to take on the handedness role, and the person would be obliged to become dextrous with the other hand. Thus it is possible to find true left-handers and left-handers, and true right-handers and right-handers.

Where there has been an enforced shift either way it is said to be recognizable in that the person tends to write with the palm of the hand almost facing upwards and curled round the pen. Trying to improve the grip towards the more traditional palm-down posture could well prove fruitless and lead to a deterioration in the subject's writing.

Figure 7.16 *Left-handed pen grip*

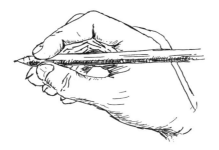

Figure 7.17 *Right-handed pen grip*

Modern practice does not seek to make left-handers right-handed but tries to improve their learning opportunities so that teaching methods and classroom organization do not discriminate against them. The following is a checklist for guidance when teaching left-handers:

- Establish hand preference.
- Encourage triangular grip of pen but ...
- ... ensure hold is slightly further from the end of the pen (cf. Figures 7.16 and 7.17). This enables the child to see the writing emanating from the pen more easily. As it is dragged across the page towards the mid-line the left-hander covers the writing whereas the right-hander's hand is pushing away, leaving the writing clear.
- Demonstrate writing movements with the left hand.
- Sit left-handers on the left-hand side of peers so that they have room for their swing-back arm movements and right-handers have the same.

- Tilt the writing paper ten degrees or more from the vertical – more than for right-handers so that the left-hander has a chance to pull down the page towards the mid-line. Some pupils may need to place the paper horizontally to improve their writing speed and fluency.
- Give plenty of encouragement and ensure that there are left-handed implements such as scissors easily available so that the pupil is comfortable with being left-handed and does not feel different or disabled.

As pupils become a little older encourage all of them to try to draw with their non-preferred hand and use the results as a subject for further study of abilities of the two sides of the brain. The text *Drawing on the Right Side of the Brain* by Edwards (1992) is particularly interesting in this respect.

An exercise in handwriting co-ordination difficulty

It is often not understood that many children in a classroom have mild to severe handwriting difficulties which will hamper neatness and fluency for a considerable time. Such children are not always given the understanding and consideration which they really need. To illustrate this turn on the radio and find some speech and then with the non-preferred hand try to take some detailed notes for five minutes. Most people find this task particularly difficult, they find their spelling deteriorates, their concentration on the meaning goes and their script is a series of uncoordinated scribbles. The amount of effort required to do this task is very great; perspiration, white knuckles, aching fingers and emotional stress are evident. These are some of the problems and some of the feelings which pupils with handwriting difficulties face every day at school.

REMEDIAL METHODS

The problem of pupils learning infant print and then having to change at about 8 years to cursive is a significant one and the change is not achieved without considerable sacrifice in terms of time, which at this stage could more usefully be given to the subject curriculum, by all the pupils. A large number of them will find learning a whole new set of motor programmes difficult and may fail to see the relevance of it. Those who have writing difficulties will probably find it too hard to make the transfer as they have hardly acquired a competent writing form in the first place (see Figure 7.18 for a checklist of errors). In addition it is common practice not to allow pupils who cannot write neatly in print to go

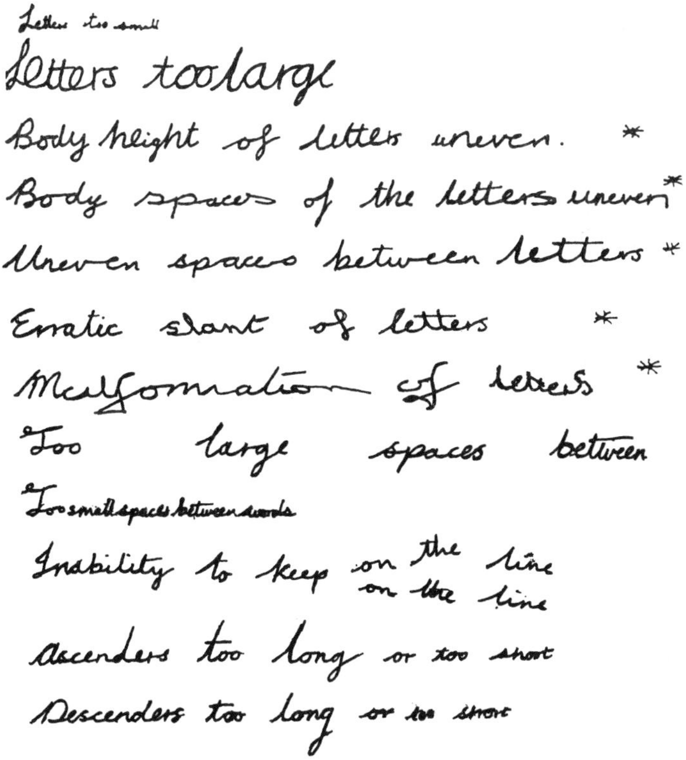

Letters too small

Letters too large

Body height of letters uneven.   *

*Body spaces of the letters uneven**

Uneven spaces between letters *

Erratic slant of letters   *

Malformation of letters   *

Too   large   spaces   between

Too small spaces between words

Inability to keep on the line
on the line

Ascenders too long or too short

Descenders too long or too short

Figure 7.18 *Handwriting checklist: analysing errors in handwriting preparatory to remediation (half of original size). Intervention is needed in body size and slant.*
Source: Montgomery, 1990 (after Waller, 1973)

on to learn cursive. This is particularly punitive for it may well be that it is only through learning a full cursive that they will ever conquer their writing and spelling problems. (We observed these problems in the writing of undergraduate students as well as in school age pupils.) Two examples follow.

Denise has problems with the following:

- making letters stay on the lines (she was using lines);
- she drags in from the margin towards the mid line – a characteristic of co-ordination difficulties;
- spacing between letters being too wide in 'it', 'had', etc.;
- making 's, k, w, m' small enough in size and crossing the 't' in the right place;
- the first three lines show firm pressure but the rest is variable;
- letter strokes and circles are variable and there is a wobble on some.

Denße

monday 24ᵗʰ may

Once upon a Time
There was a Lady
She had a terrible Dream
She saw a monster
it was Black it had
horns it had wings
it was Like a Devil
it had Sharp nails
in her Dreem it wanted
To Kill her. he Took
out a Knife and put
it Back and called
Some men They all
looked The same
They all took out
There nithe and Sed
we will wait and
they Stabbed her then
She woke up

Figure 7.19 *An example of Denise's handwriting problems (7 years) (half of original size)*

Denise's writing (Figure 7.19) shows at least six major signs of handwriting co-ordination problems as well as a spelling difficulty and the use of capital B and D so that she does not confuse the lower case versions. To the casual observer it looks relatively neat but spotted about with capital letters. They might then give training on that area rather than address Denise's inability to write difficult constructions like 'w, s, k' and 't' as small precise letters. Dragging the writing to the middle line and wide rivers of space flowing down the page through the words are also characteristic signs of her difficulty. Even closer attention will show the wobble and shake and the start–stop movements round the letter shapes. It took Denise 50 minutes of concentrated effort to write this story apart from hopping up and down to find the teacher to check spellings in the first few lines. 'Once upon a time' was the beginning of the story-line copied from a chart on the wall. As the fatigue sets in so the writing and the spelling deteriorate.

To complete the checklist of handwriting difficulties we can add:

- non-standard pencil grip in some cases can hamper writing;
- great pressure hampers fluency and makes holes or dents in the paper which can be felt on the reverse side;
- contra-lateral body and arm movements can be observed;
- effort and grip causes whitening of the knuckles;
- tongue may be stuck out;
- fatigue rapidly sets in;
- complains of aches and pains after only short periods of writing.

Mark's writing (Figure 7.20) was diagnosed as mainly a handwriting problem with spelling difficulties which, to a large extent, would clear up as his writing improved. He was given five minutes writing training each day before school for a fortnight. He became so excited by his achievements that he took it home and practised there as well. Figure 7.21 shows his progress after a fortnight, first copying the teacher's model and second writing his own chosen useful words.

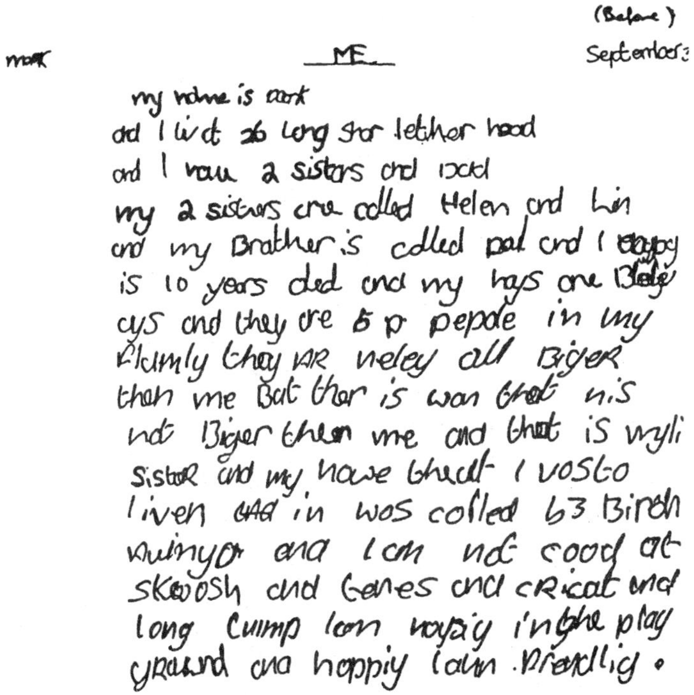

Figure 7.20 *Mark's writing before intervention (10 years 6 months) (two-thirds of original size)*

a) Using the teacher's models

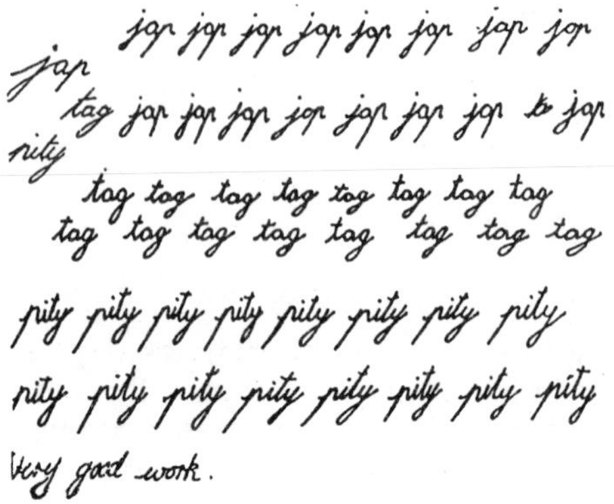

b) Using his own ideas with 'wh' words

Figure 7.21 *Mark's writing after a fortnight (half of original size)*

According to Cripps and Cox (1987) ordinary writers quickly become more confident and are able to write at speed, with legibility and enthusiasm when introduced to cursive, and these findings are widely confirmed. What is also interesting is that the children's spelling also improves. The fluidity of movement enables it more quickly to be acquired as a fluent *automatic* motor programme for each word. These automatic movements seem to flow out of the end of the pen enabling the mind to concentrate more on the story-line or the way the word is assembled for spelling. Using syllable spelling/writing techniques can enhance both.

Simultaneous Oral Spelling (SOS)

Gillingham et al. (1940)

This remedial method was devised by Stillman and used in a preventative experiment in 1932. The child says the name of each letter whilst writing it and then says the total sound. The similarities between this and the Fernald (1943) whole-word tracing method are clear. Stillman's technique involves tracing and writing. The purpose, according to Stillman, is to establish the *feel* of the hand in spelling of any letter sequence such as a phonic unit or word. The 6-year-olds in her 'preventative' class compared each printed letter with the corresponding written form. Then, starting at the same point each time, and always following the same path, they traced over the three-quarters of an inch high letters (each one several times), simultaneously saying its name (SOS) *followed by its sound*. They used this technique to build words and sentences for some time before being introduced to printed text. Stillman taught the method and her rationale for it to Agnes Wolff, a pupil-teacher who worked with her on the preventative programme.

This method, like that of Edith Norrie (see Chapter 8), places stress upon multisensory training, in this instance hand–eye co-ordination in writing with visuo-verbal integration in naming and sounding. Stillman's method is directly addressed to spelling in the early stages.

Wolff (1974)

Wolff brought the SOS technique to Britain, working with Creak (1934–35), at the Maudesley Hospital in London where she taught children with learning difficulties, taking a particular interest in the remediation of writing and spelling problems. She resumed her work in 1964 and practised SOS and her own modified versions of it.

Wolff's (1974) case examples report sufficient progress after as few as 15 lessons for one subject to have caught up to age expectation and 29 lessons for another, with most subjects requiring more than this. All her subjects were taught the flowing cursive form for writing. She explained:

> I work on the assumption that dysgraphia reflects a lack of clarity in the child's mind of the units – phonograms – of which words are composed. So I teach the letters, phonograms and other regular groups by a multisensory approach. The aim is to get them into his [*sic*] system so that he feels the form and sequence in his arm, hand, mouth, ear and sees them in the mind's eye. When he can write words

legibly and space them without attention to his hand, i.e. with eyes averted – he is free to attend to the thoughts he wants to communicate. (Wolff, 1974, p. 74)

This technique is a useful one if the number of words overall is limited but if all new words for spelling had to be learned in this fashion it could become a tedious task. It certainly would seem an advance on the usual classroom teacher's remonstration to 'copy out the correct spelling five times'. Many pupils seem to be able to perform this 'correction' task and yet still make the same misspelling in their very next piece of writing. Spelling from memory and then checking to see if one has got it right, and if not where one went wrong and then trying again, would seem to be a better strategy. The attempt to establish a motor programme bypassing phonology for difficult words is also apparent.

Bradley (1981a)

Bradley used an adaptation of Stillman's SOS in her research to find an effective remediation technique. The method consisted of a series of steps:

1. The pupil proposes the word he or she wants to learn.
2. The word is written correctly for him or her (or made with plastic script letters (ref. Norrie's technique).
3. The pupil names the word.
4. He or she then writes the word, saying the alphabetic name of each letter of the word as it is written.
5. He or she names the word, again, then checks to see that the word has been written correctly: this is important as backward readers are often inaccurate when they copy (Bradley *et al.*, 1979, 1983). Steps 2 to 5 are repeated twice more, covering or disregarding the stimulus word as soon as the pupil feels he or she can manage without it.
6. The pupil practises the word in this way for six consecutive days. The procedure is the same whether or not the pupils can read or write, and whether or not they are familiar with all sound/symbol relationships, but it must not deteriorate into rote spelling, which is an entirely different thing.
7. Learn to generalize from this word to other words in the same sound category. The plastic letters are a good way to do this.

The whole procedure takes only 30 seconds per word, and this one-week consistent training seemed to be so effective that the pupils would often remember the word six months later, provided they followed the instructions correctly (Bradley, 1981a).

Bradley uses the alphabetic naming of the letters in the word and advocates word-building for reading and writing. Although she emphasizes that the system must not be allowed to deteriorate into rote spelling, one can see that there is a considerable amount of routine memorizing attached to it, especially if one has to tackle the same word every day in this way for a whole week. The number of words learnt in this manner would be time-consuming and limiting. It is to be hoped that it will be possible to develop a more efficient system than this from the basic formats suggested by these remediators and researchers; a method, too, which is more cognitively challenging and interesting.

Multisensory whole-word method (Fernald, 1943)

This method was first introduced by Fernald in 1943. She advocated a tracing method with whole words for pupils with severe reading and spelling problems. The pupil decides which word she or he wishes to learn and it is written on a card in large *cursive letters*.

The teacher pronounces the word clearly and the pupil then *traces over* the word with the forefinger of the preferred hand, pronouncing each syllable as it is traced. When the pupil thinks she or he has learned the word, it then has to be written from memory. If this is unsuccessful, it is written once more from memory. If an error is made, the pupil must return to finger-tracing again.

By this means, an attempt is made to establish an automatic motor spelling programme for the whole word, which bypasses phonology. For this reason it is often recommended as a method for teaching irregular words such as 'said' and 'come'.

One of the main problems with this technique is that, after the initial novelty effect, the pupils may easily become bored and fail to pay attention to the tracing. Therefore, the original method has been adapted when incorporated into other schemes (Cowdery *et al.*, 1984). The modification directs the pupils' attention to tracing individual letters in a cursive hand and then to combining these letters immediately to form words.

Another problem found when using the Fernald whole-word technique is that the method is laborious if every word to be spelled has to be learned in this fashion. What the pupils need is a set of strategies for using knowledge of previously learned words to generate new ones. This system does not necessarily ensure that this skill develops, although some pupils do develop such skills spontaneously.

Research evaluations of multisensory training are relatively few but Hulme (1981) in a controlled study found that with early readers and spellers multisensory training was effective *only for those who had learning difficulties* and it did not seem to help those without learning difficulties. This led him to the conclusion that there was little to be gained from multisensory training for all, but that the benefits were obtained when it was applied in remedial programmes. This would seem to be sound advice.

Bradley's (1981a) adaptation of the Stillman SOS strategy showed evidence for enhancement of spelling in her SOS trained groups as opposed to rote copying controls. It is interesting to note, however, that her form of SOS did not incorporate cursive handwriting training. Nor did her method refer to any taxonomy of spelling development which might help the pupils, the only reference is that the pupils should learn to generalize from this word to other words in the same sound category: 'The plastic letters are a good way to do this.' This would seem a similar task to some of Tansley's phonics drills (bat, hat, mat, cat, sat) without reference to an order and structure in orthography and to some extent seems a minor, and even optional, addition after the previous 15 steps are carried out on six consecutive days! Wolff's technique draws closer attention to word structure than Bradley's and makes it an integral part of the programme but hers is also without reference to an orthographic taxonomy. Stillman's (1932) method offers writing in cursive, simultaneous oral spelling, naming, looking at word structure and giving the sounds or phonological basis of the words. To this was linked the early alphabet work and the structured phonological-syllabic-linguistic (APSL) method in the 1940 and later revisions of the programme.

It could be hypothesized that, if Bradley's (1981a) research found significant differences as a result of this low-order remedial spelling strategy, that of Wolff (1974), Gillingham *et al.* (1940) and Gillingham and Stillman (1956 and 1969) should show progressively improved levels of spelling development after training.

Unisensory training (Brown, 1990)

Brown (1990) suggests that unisensory training should be used as an alternative to the 'current dominant phonic-cum-multisensory approach to the remediation of spelling and writing difficulties' (p. 289). He recommends the use of words as icons or ideographs where these have no phonological associations as in the Chinese language. He illustrates this by explaining that a person unable to segment a complex oral word such as 'corporation' into syllables and then into discrete sounds linked to letters may possibly learn the spelling when presented *morphemically* as corp-or-at(e)-ion with clues to the meaning of the particles. This is similar to the approach adopted in the Teaching Reading Through Spelling (TRTS) programme described in Chapter 8 which makes an advanced system beyond basic phonics and is characteristic of most APSL programmes.

Although the approach may be unisensory-visual input there is a strong cognitive input to resource it. The second example described by Brown is the illustrative case of Alex who had difficulties with writing, b d reversals and the graphomotor test (Aston Index) which he could only do shakily and in reverse. The procedure used was to:

- Blindfold Alex (keeping eyes shut and writing was too difficult).
- Guide his hand and pencil through the looped pattern.
- Gradually withdraw guidance when Alex can do it on his own kinaesthetically.
- Remove blindfold, repeat procedure if regressions occur.
- Teach a range of small words in the same way.
- Use a fully cursive script.

Straightforward copying merely caused Alex to become confused. By the sixth lesson Alex had learnt a small range of words, verbs, nouns, prepositions and articles, and was then required to write sentences. This development of automatic motor programmes is regarded as a 'unisensory' approach and can best be facilitated by the cursive form of writing; it is difficult to write well in print with the eyes shut.

Brown reported that tracing sandpaper letters appeared to divert attention from the kinaesthetic memory of the letters. Other pupils attending his clinic were similarly helped; their problems like Alex's could either be avoided or at least ameliorated. The difficulties were described as '*dysgraphic*' rather than dyslexic and were found to correlate highly with low scores on the WISC-R Coding sub-test as well as poor performance on the Aston Graphomotor test.

Further training by Brown using shaded paper to increase the ascender and descender lengths also proved successful. The pupils were asked to write the body of their letter in the unshaded section and to make the other parts of the letter extend fully into the shaded section and to write as rapidly as possible. This is a similar strategy to that recommended by Morse (1984) and which can also be found in the copywriting books of the nineteenth century.

Many similar examples of success have been reported by teachers in the Learning Difficulties Research Project studies. It is particularly effective where the diagnosis of *dysgraphia* with or without dysorthographia or dyslexia is made. The case of Roger, a 10-year-old, is typical; within a dozen short lessons he had become a reasonable writer and speller (Figures 7.22 and 7.23). Older pupils with some spelling skills responded particularly well to this approach. The appeal of learning to use joined-up writing, a mature style instead of their babyish print or capital letter print, was particularly strong (see also the example of Mark's writing in Figure 7.20).

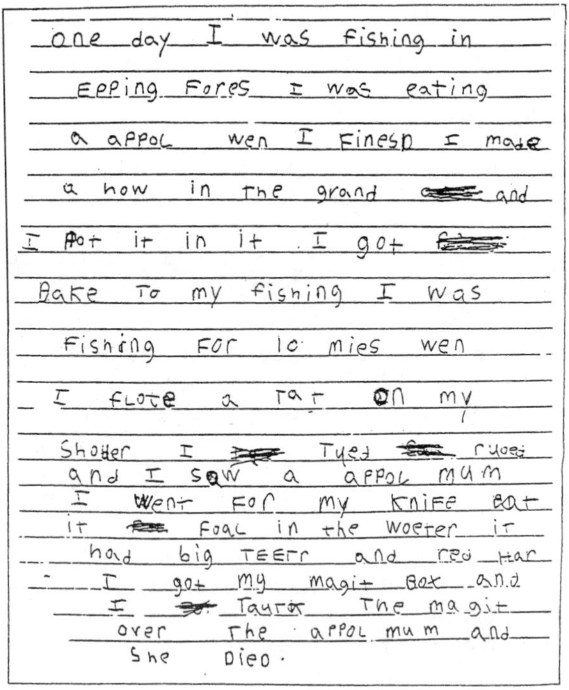

Figure 7.22 *Roger's handwriting before cursive handwriting training (10 years 6 months) (half of original size)*

Cerebellar dyspraxia

Children with severe co-ordination handwriting difficulties should not be forced to wield a pen. They may need several years extra developmental time before they are really able to learn to write more than their own name. A careful assessment of need reveals that such a pupil would be far better occupied in learning to word process in reception class and transfer to some handwriting two or three years later. For some children the transfer may not be possible. The child who has the relatively rare difficulty, cerebellar dyspraxia, which disrupts control over smooth handwriting, will have very shaky, scribbly handwriting (Figure 7.24) which no amount of cursive handwriting training can remediate. The pupil must have access to word processing at home and at school if the difficulty is not to be made into a handicap. An assessment through writing strategy will reveal the intractability of the problem and the teaching strategy can be switched to word processing.

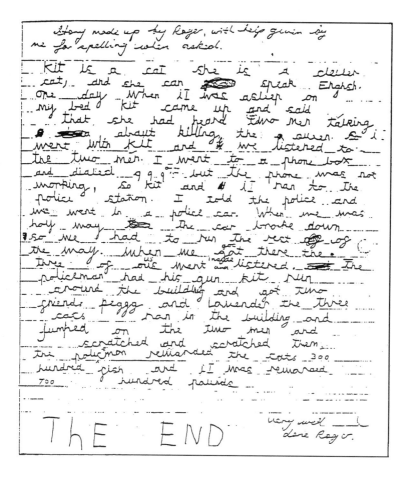

Figure 7.23 *Roger's work during the programme (two-thirds of original size)*

Extreme anxiety

Sometimes there are children who suffer distress and who are
extremely anxious and this can sometimes be seen in their writing
which may be very small, words running together with a tiny
tremor seen in all the strokes. There are, of course, some minor
hand tremors which run in families which also cause handwriting
to wobble. Other signs of anxiety such as sighing and breathless-
ness, beads of perspiration on the upper lip, voicelessness and so
on will enable the teacher to identify the type of problem.

BEHAVIOURAL METHODS

Behavioural methods are based less upon skills development and
linguistics and more upon performance objectives and the specification and achievement of learning outcomes. The methods have
their origins in behavioural psychology, programmed learning and
behaviour control (Nuttall and Snook, 1973). Typical approaches
are task analysis, precision teaching and the assessment through
teaching model. The first significant endorsement of the curriculum defined in terms of the objectives-based model appeared in the
Warnock Report (DES, 1978). The report required pupils with
special educational needs to have 'well-defined' guidelines for
each area of the curriculum, and 'programmes ... planned for individual children with clearly defined short-term goals within the
general plan' (DES, 1978, s. 11.5). The 1981 Education Act endorsed
these practices by defining assessment procedures for statementing in terms of the categorical distinctions made in the
objectives-based/skills analysis approach to the curriculum (Wood
and Shears, 1986). The specification of the National Curriculum,
with its criterion-referenced assessments, subjects defined in terms
of ten levels and targets with programmes of study laid out in
detail and all assessed by standard attainment tasks, carried this
aim further forward. The statutory requirements in the Code of
Practice (DfEE, 1994) and the Individual Education Plans (IEPs)
have set the seal of official approval upon this model.

However, it has been argued that an objectives-based approach
to the wider curriculum is less appropriate in normal class-based
teaching than in the remedial setting where hierarchies of skills
may need to be defined and taught for some of the time in order to
overcome learning blocks or missed experiences. Narrow skills-
based teaching had become the only curriculum that was offered in
some 'remedial' classes (Brennan, 1979), and so the National

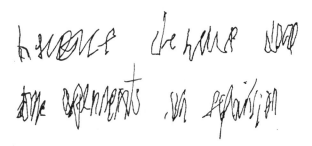

(In science we have done some experiments on expansion) (13 years)

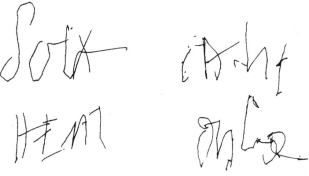

(Such, Heat, Can't, Once) (9 years)

Figure 7.24 *Examples of the writing of pupils with cerebellar dyspraxia (two-thirds of original size)*

Curriculum's implementation has been of benefit to some pupils although some would argue that this has been at the expense of literacy skills – but this need not have been so.

In a three-year, million dollar study of objective assessment and standard attainment tasks Feller (1994) came to one overall conclusion which was that they hurt the educational process. The results showed that many standardized tests and textbooks heavily emphasized lower-level skills and rote memorization instead of measuring higher-level skills such as conceptualizing and reasoning. Feller found that this influenced instructional practices and curriculum content to emphasize the same low-level goals. He concluded that such practices rob time from curriculum activities which could be used to develop higher-order thinking. The current

National Curriculum, though cut by 20 per cent, is still overfilled and teachers are having to hurry through the material to 'cover' the syllabus which can only be to the detriment of learners, particularly those with literacy difficulties. Teachers are often reluctant to allow pupils to be withdrawn from classes for remedial help because they will have missed a crucial piece of content teaching. This can all only contribute to a spiralling down of competence in learning on the wider scale and lead to more problems in the literacy area.

However, matching pupils' needs to the task can significantly reduce attention-seeking and the time off-task which can be used in disruption. Behavioural methods can have a useful part to play when used appropriately.

Task analysis

Task analysis was introduced into the educational field from industrial psychology and the field of programmed learning. Programmed learning was based upon behaviour control principles (Nuttall and Snook, 1973). This label was applied because underlying its concepts is the notion of teaching as a method of controlling the behaviour of students and the conditions of learning. Each task is analysed and broken down into small, manageable units or steps and the learner proceeds from step to step up through the task gradient with each small success being positively reinforced. If there is a failure at any point, the problem area is immediately identifiable, reteaching can occur and the programme rolls forward again. Linear and then branching programmes were developed to teach numerous mathematical and scientific skills and contents. Gagné (1977) did much to promote these techniques in the broader context of task/skills analysis in the classroom, demonstrating the value of breaking down complex tasks into shorter teaching units with regard to his 'hierarchy of learning' and 'conditions of learning', linking both behaviourist and cognitivist approaches.

Descriptions of learning outcomes (Gagné, 1977), or the end products of learning (Grönland, 1970) are often called 'behavioural' or 'performance' objectives and sometimes 'teaching' or 'instructional' objectives. In essence, they describe what the pupil should be able to do after learning has occurred and should be quantifiable and measurable. For example, at the end of the session the pupil should be able to identify the /sh/ digraph in beginning and end positions of words and find it with 95 per cent accuracy in any piece of text at own reading level. This type of behavioural objective conforms to Vargus's (1977) conditions. It contains three components: a verb which describes an observable behaviour from the pupil; a description of conditions for the performance; a description of the criterion to be achieved. The objective, to learn five new sight words from the reading scheme by the end of one week to a 90 per cent criterion, is another example of this type of behavioural objective, and most examples given derive from the basic skills area of reading, spelling and arithmetic, which seem to lend themselves to such programming and are a feature of the technique called 'precision teaching' first developed by Lindsay in the 1960s (Formentin and Csapo, 1980).

Precision teaching and Special Needs Action Programme (SNAP)

Precision teaching is more a method of recording the pupil's responses in a systematic way – recording rate of response, time to completion, graphing cumulative results and testing – than a method of teaching. Precision teaching became widely used in LEAs and was promoted by Ainscow and Tweddle (1979) and Ainscow and Muncey (1983) in their Special Needs Action Programme for Coventry LEA (SNAP, 1981).

Unfortunately, rate of learning under teacher scrutiny is often the only required pupil response and so, where pupils have severe specific learning difficulties, the value of learning five words without the property of generalizing to other words may in the end prove negligible. The time might have been better spent on a structured and coherent programme which was theoretically sound and empirically tested. Studies in the Learning Difficulties Research Project (1990) at Kingston showed that dyslexic pupils often proved incapable of learning two sight words by these techniques, however encouraging the teacher, and however precisely the objectives are framed. What seems to be important in precision teaching is to find out what the pupil's mind is doing whilst he or she stares at the five new words.

A significant motivating factor is the autonomy often afforded by precision teaching to the pupils in being allowed to monitor and record their own daily progress on the assessment and recording charts. As yet no full-scale independent evaluation of such a programme has become available and, although the reports of the users and devisers of SNAP themselves looked very encouraging, by the late 1980s some unease was beginning to be expressed (Woods and Shears, 1986) about programmes in which the learner was passive and lacked any autonomy in the learning process and was a passive recipient whose behaviour is shaped by the teacher. However, Solity and Bull (1987) advocated a range of behaviourally based approaches to the curriculum and in particular recommended DISTAR (direct instructional system for teaching and remediation) as did Turner (1990a) on the basis of his research findings in Somerset schools. DISTAR was developed in the Headstart programme in the USA and includes systematic phonics training.

DATAPAC, DISTAR and direct instruction

DATAPAC (daily teaching and assessment for primary age children) was produced by a group of psychologists (Ackerman *et al.*, 1983) as an assessment-through-teaching package for individual pupils. The materials consist of assessment tools, teaching sheets and teaching instructions in the areas of reading, handwriting, spelling and mathematics. In other words DATAPAC, like DISTAR, had defined teaching programmes. DISTAR had been criticized by teachers in this country for taking the teaching out of their hands: they become the 'pencil and sheet monitors'. Swann (1985) criticized direct instructional (DI) approaches such as these for their lack of relevance to the children's experience outside schools and their narrowness of contents. More recently, task analysis has been introduced on a wide scale into ordinary classrooms to help pupils with special needs, and texts have been produced on the subject to help teachers and in-service trainers, for example, Ainscow and Muncey (1984), Solity and Bull (1987).

An example of precision teaching for spelling

Decision: XXXX will learn to spell AND, THE and FROM.
Action: XXXX has to write the spellings correctly in cursive.
Conditions: The task will be presented multisensorily.
Criterion: XXXX has mastered the skill when the words can be written 100 per cent correctly to dictation (by teacher or tape) at a rate of ten words to the minute.
Probes: The dictation probe will be given daily for one to two minutes as appropriate, the order of the words will be randomized.

Implementing the programme:
• XXXX will be taught to spell the words by Stillman's SOS method for five minutes.
• The probe will be given at the same time each day.
• The format will be HEAR TO WRITE (as opposed to see to say or see to write).

- The number of correct and incorrect responses will be counted and recorded on the ratio chart by XXXX.
- The precision teaching will be discontinued after XXXX has met the criterion on three successive days.
- If the task proves too difficult it will be SLICED (made easier).
- If it still proves too difficult a different teaching method will be introduced such as Norrie's letter case method (multisensory phonics – see Chapter 6).

Special needs individualized programme planning (SNIPP) (Northumberland County Council, 1993)

This is a classroom-based programme for children with special educational needs in reading, spelling, mathematics and handwriting. It was developed as a project over a two-year period by a group of staff within a local authority.

The principles of the programme are based upon those elaborated as Precision Teaching by Ainscow and Muncey (1984). In other words it is not a teaching programme but is an assessment programme directly related to learning outcomes. Suggested resources and activities for teaching accompany each level of the National Curriculum. Associated with these are checklists to record date started, date achieved, and date checked for each item and level.

In relation to spelling there is an 'integrated spelling list' divided into 16 sections. The words are derived from the most frequently used words from 1,600 scripts of 8- to 9-year-olds' spontaneous writing. Successful learning of a spelling is designated as two or more successful tries on successive occasions at least a day apart. On a later check 'Repeat 1' 5 out of 5 is the expected success level. On 'Repeat 2' it is 7 out of 7, for example.

An examination of checklists indicates the rationale behind the programme and also its shortcomings. For example there are the following checklists for spelling:

- letter strings checklist;
- high frequency word checklist.

Examples given for strings are:

OME	THIN
home	think
come	nothing
some	something

As already indicated the letter strings approach needs to be incorporated into a logical-analytical approach to language and word structure. The base word or root and affixing rules are key components in this. Whilst noting the *ome* string may be useful for reading it is not particularly helpful for spelling 'regular' home as opposed to irregular 'cum' and 'sum'.

Learning to say and spell the letter string *thin* is not particularly helpful in either decoding or encoding 'think' whereas the /th/ digraph, the short vowel sound /i/ and the blend –nk are helpful to both. In relation to 'thin' and nothing/something, *thing* is the base word composed of

th	digraph
–ing	(letter string) suffix
no– thing	words changing the meaning of the
some– thing	base words

The only proposed strategy for learning the letter strings and the rest of the spellings was 'look–cover–write–check'. However, the programme recommends a range of *supplementary* activities:

- long vowel sounds – ae ee ie oe ue oo
- short vowel sounds – a e i o u
- long vowel sounds – ar air er or oi ou
- short a and long ae
- short e and long ee
- short i and long ie
- short o and long oe
- short u and long ue oo

Some confusion exists here in what can be considered as long vowel sounds, vowel digraphs, vowels modified and diphthongs.

The programme also makes a number of recommendations about handwriting, its form and development. However, a print script is its recommended form and the analysis of needs of left-handers is incomplete. For example left-handers' pages need to be more sloped for writing than those of right-handers – or the drawings show them to be opposite but the same with right-handers' paper too sloped for easy writing. This could be a problem that has arisen in the development of the artwork rather than originating in the programme but there is no note in the text to correct this interpretation.

In summary, the programme is a characteristic precision teaching format which identifies errors and addresses their correction by a rote learning format.

Where children had made little progress in spelling and a precision teaching approach was adopted to some commonly used words, significant gains in motivation and correct spelling of these common words were obtained. This was sometimes sufficient for the pupil to learn to decode similar words and transferred particularly well to reading. However, there were always specific children who despite precision teaching did not learn to spell more than one or two words on the basic word list, if any at all, and they could become more agitated and distressed at their obvious failure to progress. A number of comparative studies by teachers in the Learning Difficulties Project demonstrated this effect. It was the 'dyslexic' pupils who seemed to have particular problems with the precision teaching approach. Even if they learned a few useful basic spellings they seemed unable to use this knowledge to generate or transfer it to spell new words. This of course is not unexpected when we look at the research which shows they have difficulties in making analogies, rhyming and alliteration, and in learning sound/symbol correspondences.

Peer counselling for spelling (James *et al.*, 1991)

James and her colleagues reported a preliminary study with 12 poor spellers in which they argued that the failure to spell properly is often associated with emotional difficulties. As a consequence they identified peer counsellors, some of whom had also needed support in their earlier years. The counsellors were all given three one-hour sessions in basic counselling skills and then they were to act in a befriending role with one of the Year 7 poor spellers for one hour per week. The counsellors were to help the pupils to help themselves, not tell them what to do. In each case the poor spellers were encouraged to link success to effort and to take responsibility from that point for making the effort. The counselling took place over 20 weeks and at the end of the period significant gains were found in the reading and spelling scores of the experimental group but none for the matched controls. Staff who were unaware of the project remarked on improvements of the counselled group in motivation and effort, handwriting, oral English, self-confidence, attitudes to study, personal cleanliness and social interaction. The peer counsellors also gained from the experience.

This is clearly a valuable approach to supporting children with a range of learning and other difficulties and emphasizes the value of the support teacher and specialist teacher who both need to act in the counselling and advocacy role where a pupil is experiencing difficulties. Recruiting other children in support of the learner is an important strategy with benefits for all.

SUMMARY

In this chapter skills training in writing has been examined and the relative merits of cursive over manuscript or print script have been presented, both for developmental writing from reception class and as a remedial hand in the later stages. The need for a full flowing cursive in which all letters begin on the line was emphasized. This avoids confusion over where to place the pen and prevents orientation problems. The use of lines for writing in the early stages was recommended. It was shown how some pupils have co-ordination difficulties which cursive can help to overcome so that they can produce a legible hand.

Cursive writing as an aid to spelling was also described and different methods such as phonogram training, simultaneous oral spelling, and finger-tracing were discussed as developmental and remedial strategies.

In the final section behavioural approaches to spelling, such as precision teaching, DISTAR and direct instruction, were outlined and some evaluation was offered. The section concluded with a preliminary report on peer support for spelling which seemed to be a promising development.

Specialist remedial strategies

INTRODUCTION

A specialist remedial programme must fulfil a number of criteria according to the expert group of the British Dyslexia Association (BDA) established to review the provision and the available teaching programmes which had proved successful with dyslexics. These criteria were set out as follows:

> For successful teaching of dyslexic children a basic framework is needed with the following essential features:
>
> 1. The programme needs to be *phonic* in the sense that it is necessary for the pupils to learn the correspondence between letters and sounds – it must be related to the existing language requirements of the dyslexic but must also be sufficiently flexible to meet the future needs; and it must be *structured, sequential, cumulative* and *thorough*.
> 2. A *structured programme* is one which has a specific organisation in which the differing parts cohere and contribute to the whole.
> 3. Teaching is carried out *sequentially* when there is a progressive disclosure by the teacher of the correspondence between sounds and letters (or groups of letters) in the English spelling system.
> 4. Teaching needs to be *cumulative* in the sense that each step follows from what went before and cannot be studied in isolation.
> 5. Teaching needs to be *thorough* in the sense that each stage in the programme must be fully understood before the dyslexic passes to the next one.
> 6. Teaching is also multisensory in the sense that it endeavours to establish high level control over skills in visual, auditory, motor and kinaesthetic areas and to form linkages between them. Nothing is taken for granted and rote memory work should be at a minimum.
>
> On this theoretical basis are built sympathetic, stimulating and enjoyable lessons, employing all possible aids such as card, phonic work books, suitably graded readers, etc. to ensure that the teaching results in solid progress as well as entertainment. Such methods have in fact been shown to be effective. (BDA, 1981)

When the programmes used or designed by this expert group are examined they can be seen to be much more than structured cumulative and sequential phonics. They all introduce *alphabet* training. At an appropriate stage they teach the sequence of the alphabet, alphabet skills and the upper and lower case letters' names and sounds. They teach *phonics*, the letter symbols or graphemes which are associated with the sound structure of words in a structured and cumulative order. They teach about *syllables*, their structure and the rules which apply to them in relation to them and their affixes. Within this integrated programme they also introduce knowledge of *linguistics*, the rules and structures, the meanings and origins which change the basic word patterns. Hence the abbreviated form of referring to these programmes and their derivatives is *APSL (alphabetic, phonic, syllabic, linguistic) programmes*. The BDA guidelines are to some extent misleading in that they only refer to phonics and include all the rest as well and this may have caused some remedial teachers to construct programmes based only on phonics.

In addition to the APSL programme successful remedial teachers also use *multisensory teaching* of the sound and its grapheme. This approach is based upon the original design of the Gillingham *et al.* (1940) programme introduced into this country from the USA by Childs in 1969.

SOME DIFFERENTIAL PROGRAMME OUTCOMES FOR DYSLEXICS

Although it is now thought possible to identify the potential for dyslexia in pre-school the indicants become much clearer in reception class and the need for preventative measures becomes urgent. Torgeson (1995), for example, found that 98 per cent of phonological-based reading disabilities can accurately be identified in kindergarten. He said that these were the children who at second grade would have been in the bottom set if nothing had been done for them and whose reading problems at 8 years would have become refractory to treatment.

Torgeson investigated the relative effectiveness of three different forms of intervention with the kindergartners – *Alphabetic Phonics* using a synthetic phonics method, *Recipe for Reading*, an onset and rime method, and *Edmark*, a whole-word method. He found that there was a change in phonological processing abilities in all the groups but there was a significantly higher performance overall from the onset and rime method. He recommended that the curriculum should be changed to incorporate this form of teaching

(Rush, 1996). There was a failure in one-third of Bradley and Bryant's (1985) subjects to appreciate rhyme, who later at 7 years were failing in reading. In dyslexics in general there is a failure to show alphabet knowledge in emergent writing and a failure to demonstrate phoneme awareness in reading and phoneme segmentation skills in spelling (Liberman, 1973; Golinkoff, 1978; Vellutino, 1979, 1987). This failure occurs despite a home background in which books are read to them and despite direct teaching of initial sounds and presumably onset and rime methods.

Nowadays, it is not unreasonable to expect teachers to screen for alphabetic knowledge using tests on a monthly basis to track its development and on a daily basis to record its appearance in open-ended/emergent writing. A folder of each pupil's writing can be kept and the writing scanned for development, failure to learn or failure to apply what has been learned. Classroom aides and teaching assistants can readily be trained to help in this and to focus on rhyming games, syllable beats and reinforcing sounds teaching. Studies by the author, of knowledge of lower case alphabet letters by 200 children in ten reception classes in urban and suburban settings, showed that after three weeks in school the majority of pupils knew between five and ten names or sounds. Those who knew none fell into several groups: one or two were developmentally immature and seemed unable to grasp what they needed to do; one or two were unable to concentrate on the task and had very disturbed backgrounds; the rest tried and made random associations and were unaware how they were making sounds such as l, t, d, a, s, f in their mouths. In a similar study Forsyth (1988) followed up a year cohort given LEA screening in three reception classes and found that failure to develop alphabetic knowledge was the best predictor of later reading and spelling ability at 7 years (although this was not included in the screening inventory and was added by her). Again only a small number of children, 3–4 per cent, appeared to be affected. At this point a failure in specialist teaching to overcome the problem needs to be introduced and this should centre on multisensory training on initial sounds for decoding. A writing and multisensory mouth training technique is described below.

Of great concern are all those pupils well into the system who are perhaps moving through the Code of Practice (the Code) stages towards being statemented and who still cannot expect any specialist help for two or three years until they are four-times failures by which time the condition is refractory to treatment (Schiffman and Clemmens, 1966; Torgeson, 1995). They will steadily be losing hope and motivation and lack of specialist help will hamper their progress in all areas of the curriculum where there is a preponderance of reading and writing.

The peak period for statementing and referral of pupils for specialist help prior to the Code, in an LEA which did recognize dyslexia, was between 10 and 11 years of age. There were 288 dyslexic pupil records examined and the reading and spelling ages of the 30 highly able subjects, mean IQ 127, showed that their skills were 10 points higher than the rest of the sample – mean IQ of 110. Twenty out of the 30 had emotional and behavioural difficulties recorded in their cases which was a significantly higher proportion than the rest of the sample and suggests the greater stress and frustration which their condition engendered in them (Montgomery, 1994). The ratio of boys to girls was 5 to 1 whereas the survey of all Isle of Wight pupils (Rutter *et al.*, 1970) found it to be 4 to 1. The girls in the sample of 288 dyslexics were referred on average 11 months later than boys and their problems tended to be more severe. What we might be observing here is a gender bias in referral processes and a difference in response overall between boys and girls to their difficulties, with boys tending to 'act out' their problems more and girls, perhaps developing more compensatory strategies, prepared to sit quietly at work and rote learn and copy write for longer. Where dyslexia as a condition requiring specialist provision is still disputed provision may not be secured until the parents have taken an LEA to tribunal (Boland, 1995) and won. Not all parents have the time, economic resources or knowledge to take on the whole establishment in this way and the pupil moves through secondary school with the difficulties being compounded, set upon a career in disruption or emotional distress (Edwards, 1994; Montgomery, 1995).

Without a carefully structured programme of help dyslexics cannot recover from this downward spiral, for pupils in general leave secondary school with the same level of skills at which they entered, according to a recent survey. At 15 a pupil may have a reading age of 8 years and a spelling age of 6; some may have no functional literacy skills at all but a marginal ability to copy text. Such pupils may have developed a range of compensatory strategies to conceal and avoid confronting their difficulties. They may also find that withdrawal for specialist tuition as well as their poor written work attracts bullying and victimization from both pupils and teachers (Edwards, 1994). After-school tuition and special clubs may be a partial answer to this. Another may be the payment by the school for out of hours tuition by a specialist; currently it is usually only parents who do this. Such tuition could be given at another school, a curriculum centre or in the pupil's home. Preferably the tuition should be given to a pair of pupils with skills at about the same level who can work well together (Cowdery *et al.*, 1983; Ridehalgh, 1997).

Specialist remedial tuition cannot sensibly be given within the mainstream classroom whilst a pupil is being taught subject knowledge. The specialist programme has a linguistic, cognitive and skills curriculum of its own so it is not reasonable to expect a disabled learner to cope with two conflicting contents at the same time, especially when in one of them he or she may have a barrier to learning which has also to be overcome. Such pupils have to learn this special remedial curriculum in two one-hour sessions per week over two years, when the rest have had the equivalent of two years' full-time study and then three years' part-time study to learn and practise.

Ridehalgh (1997) examined a number of factors such as length of remediation, frequency of sessions and size of tutorial groups in dyslexic subjects taught by three different schemes – Alpha to Omega, Dyslexia Institute Language Programme (DILP), and Spelling Made Easy. She found that when all the factors were held constant the only programme in which the dyslexics gained significantly in skills above their increasing age was Alpha to Omega. It has to be recognized that the devisers of schemes can usually make them work in almost any situation but here Ridehalgh was looking at results from teachers who had followed training courses in the use of the programmes, and this is a more severe test. The courses themselves may have been at fault rather than the programme; accumulating more evidence will clarify these findings.

In contrast, a group of 15 pupils, aged 8 to 9 years and diagnosed as dyslexic by a school, were given individual teaching mainly based upon phonics worksheets and reading miscues rather than a specific programme. After six months of one session per week and one hour of in-class support they showed a mean gain of 0.53 months in reading, which is no real progress at all. Within group differences once again cancelled each other out, for example seven subjects improved their reading over the six-month period by a mean of 8.43 months while eight subjects' scores decreased by 7.4 months in the same period. One subject's reading age was now above age level by one year and three months but the rest remained below chronological age by a mean of 2.1 years. In spelling, five subjects gained 8.4 months over and above the six months and eight subjects regressed by 3.9 months. Total progress made by the group overall was 0.08 months and they were still 1.7 years behind in spelling. Those who had not made progress over increasing chronological age by a ratio over something in the order of two to one would be unlikely ever to catch up under the teaching regime offered – they needed to be switched to a specialist programme.

In a follow-up study of dyslexics on the Alpha to Omega (Hornsby and Shear, 1975, 1985) dyslexia-centred teaching programme, Hornsby and Farrar (1990) showed that the reading gains were 1.91 years per year and 1.94 for spelling per year. These, they reported, were considerably greater than 0.53 years for reading and 0.32 years gain for spelling, representing a regression when compared with their progress on non-APSL programmes. They concluded that 91 out of the 107 dyslexics had more than kept up with the age clock during the remediation period. The earlier the tuition can be given the greater chance there is of bringing them up to grade level and keeping them there, because there is less for them to unlearn and they have more chance to practise spelling skills in infant and the early junior school years. Similar results have been found from the Teaching Reading Through Spelling series (Cowdery *et al.*, 1983–88), another APSL programme. Thirty-eight subjects leaving the programme after an average of 1.3 years and two one-hour sessions per week in tutorial matched pairs showed mean gains in reading of 2.45 years and 2.01 years in spelling (Montgomery, 1993).

Thomson (1989) and Thomson and Watkins (1993) have also found evidence for the success of dyslexia-centred remedial programmes using variations of the APSL approach. They show that progress in reading and spelling can be boosted to compensate for increased delay which occurs as dyslexics grow older and that spelling is more resistant than reading to remediation. Thomson (1984) suggested that there appeared to be an alphabetic barrier in the reading and spelling of regular words at around the 8-year reading age level, which provides a platform for 'take off' for written language learning. He showed that the problems of irregular words were more difficult to remediate. His research, however, was geared to phonic levels of the programmes. He went on to state that one specific technique, that of syllable analysis using the categorizing of syllables based on vowel sounds, can be of considerable help in the spelling of two- and three-syllabled regular words and seemed to circumvent some of the dyslexic's problems in phonemic awareness and phoneme segmentation. These results refer to the AP and SL parts of the APSL programmes and make a strong case for the use of the full programme rather than only a part.

Morphemics awareness training was found by Leong (1995) to have positive effects in reading disability (dyslexia – spelling and reading difficulties) but these were not so great as the effects for phonological awareness training, and so a combination of both was recommended. For any method to be successful with dyslexics it has to take account of the levels of knowledge of the learner and those aspects which now need to be acquired. Henry (1995) for example recommended a hierarchy of intervention for all writers beginning with phonic and alphabetic instruction in kindergarten, the influence of Anglo-Saxon on vowels and vowel digraphs, progressing in second grade to compound words with prefixes and suffixes. In fifth to seventh grade she recommended review and the teaching of the influence of the Romance languages. She stated that 14 base words held the key to a knowledge of 100,000 words in the English language (Rush, 1996). These studies lend support to the view that teaching for remediation of dyslexic difficulties must extend in a careful and structured manner well beyond the basics of phoneme awareness and phonic instruction, although these are essential in the early stages. Unless the programme addresses the syllabic-linguistic as well as the alphabetic-phonic levels, the dyslexic will always remain at a disadvantage.

NEUROLOGICAL FINDINGS UNDERPINNING THE PSYCHOLOGICAL PROCESSES WHICH CAN HELP INFORM DYSLEXIA TEACHING

The paradigm shift in thinking about the origins of dyslexia has already been noted. In the majority of cases the dyslexia is thought to be due to an underlying *verbal processing difficulty* particularly in the *phonological area* which can give rise to:

- inability to appreciate rhyme;
- lack of phonemic awareness;
- poor development of alphabetic knowledge;
- lack of development of symbol to sound correspondence;
- lack of development of phoneme segmentation skills;
- lack of spelling development at the higher levels;
- lack of metacognitive awareness of spelling.

These skills and abilities underlie the development of good spelling and reading and develop incidentally in most pupils. However, even direct teaching in the classroom may not enable a dyslexic to acquire these basic skills. What causes this set of problems is still the subject of debate and these were well reviewed by Miles and Miles (1990) in *Dyslexia: A Hundred Years On*.

The direction in which some of the neurological researchers seem to be moving begins to provide a context for the psychological studies and the early interventions proposed. In summary these are:

- The structure of the cerebral cortex in the visual areas of the left hemispheres seem to be more diffuse in dyslexics (Geschwind, 1979; Galaburda, *et al.*, 1985; Galaburda, 1993). Some neurons in male dyslexics appear to have migrated to the outside cortical layer in the brain; in females there appears to be neuron death. Both appear to occur before six months' gestation (Sherman, 1995). More cases are still needed to confirm these findings but these are, of course, difficult to come by. Geschwind (1979) had first identified these phenomena and proposed that this could cause the dyslexics to be deficient in processing and connecting graphemic symbols to their sounds. It may cause them to switch processing to the other hemisphere (Witelson, 1977) which is not so well set up for verbal processing.
- The auditory capacity of dyslexics is inferior. They find difficulty in processing rapid sounds characteristic of speech (Tallal and Piercy, 1973, Tallal, 1994).
- The angular gyrus where auditory, visual and kinaesthetic information is integrated may not be functioning adequately (Geschwind, 1979) and this might account for some awareness difficulties observed (Montgomery, 1981, 1993).

Any or all of these difficulties might disrupt the easy association between the arbitrary symbols of the alphabet and their sounds which most beginners pick up incidentally during reading. Even in classrooms where sounds are being said slowly and the connections between them and the graphemes are made explicit dyslexics fail to learn them. They do not learn to segment the sound 'c' from 'cat' for example as other children do. Ehri (1979) has suggested that the sound is an abstract perceptual unit which has to be linked to the arbitrary graphemic unit. If the dyslexic does not have the awareness of the articulatory feel of a particular phoneme it will make the sound–symbol association particularly problematic to acquire. As sounds with the same symbols appear in different forms – *allophones* – in syllables this can quickly become confusing. Graphemes represent phonemes not allophones and, so, do not distinguish between different pronunciations. When a word is pronounced by a careful speaker most of its constituent phonemes can be heard or felt. It is this 'citation' form that spellers need to use to support their spelling until a word is learned and can be written automatically by direct reference to the lexicon.

It is the articulatory pattern which is concrete and remains roughly the same and which can be used to connect the sound and symbol in a multisensory triangle. By using articulatory cues a pupil should be able to decode the consonantal structure of a syllable or a word even though vowels might be missed. This could account for the scaffold or skeletal phonics seen in, for example, mstr, ws, bd and so on when beginning spellers and dyslexics have begun to break the alphabetic code. Beginners may often be seen mouthing their words for spelling both aloud and sub-vocally.

Earlier researchers such as Monroe (1932) and Schonell (1943) were most insistent about the articulatory aspect of learning to spell. Edith Norrie (1917) taught herself to spell using articulatory phonics. This is a form of metalinguistic awareness which dyslexics may fail to acquire in reception class but may gradually acquire at a later stage. Training in this area could well enable the reception class dyslexic to overcome the phonological disability. It may then make the acquisition of the higher order aspects of the language far easier for them to learn and they may not, in some cases, become so disabled; others may not become disabled at all. There are cases of undergraduate spellers who remain slow readers, have difficulty in comprehending text which is complexly structured and have difficulty in acquiring new subject vocabulary for writing. With significant extra effort they can overcome these difficulties and function well in degree programmes. With support from the cognitive process strategies the upper levels of linguistics are opened up to them and these students obtain first and upper second class degrees. Where dyslexics have the additional dysgraphic difficulties, handwriting co-ordination problems, they are going to have significantly more problems in writing but not reading. Of much greater concern will be those pupils who have complex learning difficulties which may include orientation difficulties, locomotor inco-ordination (dyspraxia), language and attentional difficulties. These indicate wider and more profound neurological difficulties for which a full-time specialist remedial placement should be considered.

ARTICULATION AND PHONIC AWARENESS TRAINING

Multisensory articulatory phonics: the Edith Norrie letter case (1917, 1946 and 1973)

Edith Norrie was a Danish dyslexic, born in 1888, who at 20 taught herself to read and spell by making a set of letters of the Danish alphabet which she ordered and systemized. In 1939, she established the Word Blind Institute in Copenhagen.

An English version of the letter case is produced by the Helen Arkell Centre (Figure 8.1). There are several lower-case and two capitals of each letter and a small mirror in which only the mouth

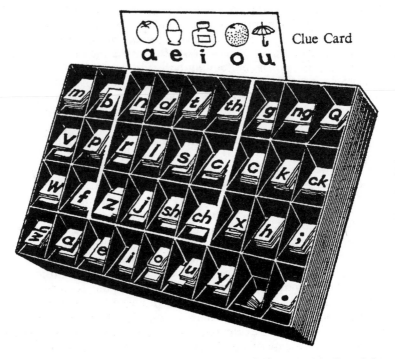

Figure 8.1 *The Edith Norrie letter case. This piece of equipment was originally made for the Danish alphabet but this is the English version. Copyright Helen Arkell Centre.*

can be viewed. The letter case is primarily a spelling aid and consists of a box containing the letters of the alphabet. The box is divided into three compartments, each containing a letter or a consonant digraph. The letters are grouped according to the place of articulation of the sound most frequently associated with it.

When the pupil attempts to spell a word, it is necessary first to work out how the sound is made in the mouth. This, according to Goulandris (1986), increases the awareness of speech sounds and the relationship between phonemes and graphemes, and is most beneficial to pupils with difficulties in this area. The red-coloured vowels enable the pupil to check that every syllable contains a vowel and the black and green coloured consonants help sort out confusions between voiced and unvoiced consonants. The Edith Norrie letter case seems to be most widely used in Helen Arkell Dyslexia Centres and is available from them. They emphasize the speech therapy element in their early training and advocate the use of a mirror so that pupils can see how they are forming the sounds.

This system thus emphasizes both articulation and phonological skills training. The pupils are said to enjoy word-building with the letters so that they can make sure they are producing a correct spelling before copying it down. Errors do not have to be erased or crossed out, the word can be worked on at a concrete operational level and built by successive corrective moves and trials. This same facility has become popular in relation to computer programs offering word-building activities and redrafting facilities in story-writing.

Pollack and Waller (1994) were former teachers at the Helen Arkell Centre and, in their book *Day to Day Dyslexia*, describe the approach to remedial work adopted at the Centre. There are substantial chapters on spelling and handwriting. On spelling they give nine spelling guides covering work on: initial sounds; the order of teaching spelling conventions; silent 'e'; 'murmuring' vowels and digraphs; short vowels and doubling consonants following vowels; –ed endings and –le words following short and long vowels; spelling guidelines for -dge, –tch, –ck, c and k; plurals and when to change y to i and add –es; and, finally, syllable structure, syllable tapping, syllable division, stems (roots), prefixes and suffixes. The order given is very different from the APSL programmes described and there is less detail of structure and methods of training, but the emphasis upon language and speech problems is characteristic of the Helen Arkell Centre as is the use of the Edith Norrie letter case in place of multisensory phonogram training. The book contains useful examples of dyslexics' reading and spelling.

The authors strongly recommend the use of the Edith Norrie letter case and the Hickey multisensory language course, Letterland, Alpha to Omega, Teaching Reading Through Spelling (TRTS) and the Bangor Dyslexia Teaching System, all of which they state (Pollack and Waller, 1994, p. 34) set out a structured approach. They advocate selecting from a structured programme material to suit the needs of a particular child. Whilst this is a sensible strategy for skilled and experienced remediators such as these authors with their detailed knowledge of dyslexics' needs and programmes and no formal structure of their own, this strategy is not recommended for teachers beginning work in this area, nor for those who have never followed in detail and used on a substantial scale one of the structured programmes. It is important that teachers follow a specific programme so that they can learn the intimate details of how it works in practice. Each of the specialist programmes is flexible in that it can be used to match the pupil's needs so that what is known is identified and does not have to be reworked. When familiarity has been achieved with one programme then others can be examined and evaluated against this standard.

Multisensory mouth training for spelling (Montgomery, 1984, 1994)

In dyslexia there is a higher proportion of subjects who have had articulatory and speech problems requiring speech therapy than in the normal population (Nelson and Warrington, 1974; Snowling *et al.*, 1986). Articulation difficulties are usually concerned with motor speech or production problems. Consider, however, the problem of a pupil who is able to pronounce a sound quite clearly and correctly and hear it but be unaware of the key contacts being made by his or her articulators: not being *aware*, for example, when saying the sound /l/ that the tip of the tongue was, for example, touching the roof of his or her mouth, or perhaps not being able to *integrate* this information with visual and/or auditory information. At a milder level, the pupil might have only a vague sensation to this effect, identifiable only with careful consideration. It might be that proprioceptive feedback from the articulators is incomplete; for example, it and in in articulatory terms are produced in similar fashion except that the air is directed through the nasal passage in in and not it which can be detected by trying to say both and holding the nose at the same time. The pupil is able to make the different sounds in speech and discriminate auditorily that the two sounds are different but may not be able to 'feel' these differences in the same way as other pupils and, so, the spelling may contain it, id and in error substitutions. Not all dyslexics have this pattern of difficulty, but some may.

At a different level of processing, depending upon the subtlety of the features analysis which was available, is the obviousness or otherwise of the key features of the phoneme and the level of ability to integrate or use articulatory information. Some forms of remedial training such as Monroe's (1932) grunting, groaning and articulating clearly and precisely might help overcome the problem, as would certain types of speech therapy training and the Edith Norrie letter case method where mirrors to give visual feedback on articulation are used. For awareness articulation training, however, these mirrors would have to be dispensed with at an early stage and concentration given to the 'feel' of the sound. Disability in this specific form of features analysis would have to be in the absence, in most cases, of any overt motor articulation problem which is easily detectable, although McMahon (1982) did detect mild articulation difficulties in all her sample of dyslexic subjects, and Snowling and Stackhouse (1983) maintain that this is more common than is usually believed.

Without 'awareness' of phonemes or of the articulatory skeletal structure of words, learning to read and spell might depend mainly upon visual memory. This may well be a reason for the heavy reliance of dyslexics upon visual strategies as found by Snowling (1985). If there is any difficulty or weakness in this visual area as well, then reading and spelling progress would be severely limited. If the pupil has excellent visual recall, the early phase of acquisition may seem to develop normally but at around 8 years, when normal word attack skills enable new words to be rapidly understood by decoding or analogy, the latent dyslexic may suddenly manifest severe limitations in his or her reading development. It may also give rise to the findings of Frith (1978) that the good reader poor speller is very dependent upon having the word correctly spelt whereas poor readers and poor spellers are not. It is highly probable that this kind of articulatory guided phonemic system with its alphabet markers could arise within the context of a consonantal language. It would be truly remarkable if this were not so at some point. It is also fairly certain that no dyslexic with articulatory 'awareness' problems could have invented such a system.

Consonants are the first that can be identified by 'feel'. The vowels do not cause the articulators to make contacts; they are open-mouthed non-contacting sounds varied by the position of the tongue and the shape of the lips, and are particularly difficult to notice in medial positions. This gives rise early on to the contractions such as bd for bed. Learning to feel the initial sound can give strong support to the onset and rime strategy and can inform a range of phonological awareness and segmentation strategies as well as phonics. Peter, aged 10, was given four 20-minute articulation awareness training support sessions and made two years' reading and spelling progress in a fortnight (McMahon, 1982). This is unusual but it provided the clue he needed to gain metacognitive insight into the whole process of spelling teaching which he was receiving in the TRTS programme.

The reason for delay in development of this refined form of sensitivity or integration of information above the level required not to bite the tongue is just beginning to become clear (Geschwind, 1979; Galaburda, 1993). What has been known for many decades is that visual, auditory and articulatory elements *must be firmly cemented in writing* (Schonell, 1942). In writing the attention is focused and helps reinforce the articulatory and kinaesthetic bridge between the visual and auditory symbols. This makes a four-way relationship – *auditory, visual, articulatory* and *manual kinaesthetic*.

In a series of studies (Montgomery, 1981, 1984, 1994) it was found that dyslexics in comparison with spelling age-matched controls had significantly poorer articulation awareness skills even though they were two and a half years older chronologically. In order to help remediate these difficulties and improve their basic spelling skills a number of strategies termed 'multisensory mouth training for spelling' were developed:

- Encourage pupils to speak clearly and audibly, converse with them, encourage them to speak in small group work and in the larger class. Use collaborative learning strategies (Bowers and Wells, 1985, 1996) to facilitate this.
- Encourage pupils regularly to read aloud to the teacher (not to the class) and into a tape recorder.
- Encourage clear articulation and syllabification of words for spelling, especially concentrating on mouthing and sounding.
- When teaching phonemic awareness, phoneme segmentation and phonics spend some time focusing upon the feel of the letter or letters in the mouth.

Johnson and Myklebust (1967, rev. 1995) illustrated the effect of different forms of dictation on the spelling of a 15-year-old dyslexic as follows:

> When spelling from his own head and no auditory and articulatory stimulation:
> *cabinet* was spelt *kntrs*
> *window* as *wror*
> *recorder* as *rkrrd*
>
> When spelling from words dictated one syllable at a time:
> *hundred*   *hundred*
> *indent*   *indent*
> *represent*   *represent*
>
> When spelling words dictated normally:
> *pencil*   *pnsl*
> *manufacture* *mufnctur*
> *candidate*   *cndati*
>
> (Johnson and Mykelbust, 1967, p. 241)

Teaching clear articulation and syllabification for spelling will help all poor spellers improve their spelling.

Early screening for articulation awareness difficulties

If any 5-year-olds fail to learn their basic sight vocabulary or to develop early reading skills at the same rate as other children and do not appear to be slow learners in any other respect, then select the following letters for testing.

s, a, d, p, f, th, l

Ask the pupil to show mouth open, mouth shut, teeth open, teeth shut, and the tip of the tongue to check he or she can understand the following questions.

Next, ask the pupil to say the sound(s) several times (*do not* let them see your mouth when you say it), *whilst pointing* to the grapheme 's'. Then ask:

1. Are your lips open or shut when you say that sound? (Do not let them touch the mouth area or tongue.)
2. Are your teeth open or shut, or very nearly shut?
3. Where is the tip of your tongue touching?

The pupil who has clear perception will answer these three questions accurately but make sure *and look to see* exactly how the individual makes the sound. There are certain differences between individuals which mean that the pupil correctly perceives his or her own pattern but it is not the same as most other pupils'. It should be counted as correct for that pupil.

An example of an articulation, letter name and sound checklist is shown in Figure 8.2.

Multisensory mouth training protocol

This protocol was incorporated into the foundations of the TRTS programme in 1984 to facilitate the development of sound symbol awareness and knowledge by providing an articulatory bridge between the two. As each letter is introduced any articulation awareness difficulties can be checked as follows:

Present the grapheme l for the pupil to say /l/ then ask whether lips are open or shut, the teeth open or shut and where the tip of the tongue is touching. If there is any doubt ask the pupil to shut his or her lips and try to say /l/. If the pupil cannot answer, check other sounds and find out if it is the lips, teeth or tip of the tongue which is problematic. Practise detecting when saying other sounds /b/, /t/, /p/, etc. whether the lips are open or shut. *At first*, a mirror might be necessary to help get the feel and touching the mouth with the hand to check. Most often, *a few direct questions* will cue the pupil to start thinking about this aspect, and the uncertainty and some of the errors will diminish. Practise the *articulation awareness training with each sound* as it is introduced in the programme, or go over sounds already known visually and auditorily if the pupil is more advanced.

Copy Sheet:
Name: _____
Date: _____

Letter	Sound	Name	Letter	Sound	Name
s			c		
a			w		
t			q		
m			r		
b			o		
e			k		
r			z		
d			i		
l			v		
x			f		
g			y		
p					
u					
h					
n					

* Denotes articulation difficulty

Teaching notes:

Figure 8.2 *An articulation, letter name and sound checklist*

Since we *cannot hear the sequence* of sounds in a syllable when reconstructing spellings phonetically, we need to rely on the *articulatory sequence* to remind us of the order of letters. Pupils who do not learn to do this very early on will become prone to spelling problems (unless they have excellent visual recall) and make sequencing errors and vowel omissions. Older pupils, who have had spelling problems, still find that they have difficulty in saying, reading and spelling polysyllabic words – especially new words from a specialist vocabulary. Early training in syllabification would have helped them overcome some of their difficulties and, again, concentration on the articulatory sequence would assist them in getting the basic structure of the word at the phonemic level.

Multisensory awareness and handwriting training

As each grapheme is introduced in any handwriting and phonic level of a programme it should be accompanied by articulation awareness training, thus ensuring the four-way development of skills for eye, ear, mouth and hand, with articulation and articulatory awareness forming the bridge between the other three. Over the last 50 years the significance of these kinaesthetic links has been lost. Perhaps in the new millennium focus will be upon spelling and a comprehensive approach to its development based upon a measured intervention integrating past and recent methods.

ALPHABETIC, PHONIC, SYLLABIC, LINGUISTIC (APSL) PROGRAMMES

APSL programmes are all derivatives of the original work of Bessie Stillman and Anna Gillingham, and the Samuel Orton research programme of the 1930s and 1940s. APSL has undergone several revisions – 1940, 1956, 1960 – and has been supplemented and revised by Childs (1968) resulting in the Gillingham–Stillman–Childs version which was introduced into the UK in 1969.

Kathleen Hickey language training programme (1977)

Kathleen Hickey began her interest in the area when she found a way to teach a group of young cerebral palsied children, who had previously been thought to be ineducable, to read and write. Later, she became head of the Clayhill Centre for remedial education in Epsom and was helped in her work by Jean Augur, who ran the local authority remedial centre and later became director of the

BDA. Of all the pupils she taught there, the group who interested Hickey most was made up of those pupils who, even after they had achieved a high level of reading, still showed failure in spelling and fluency of written expression. For them, she developed a system of teaching spelling through writing. In 1969, she attended a course by Sally Childs who demonstrated to her the value of the Gillingham–Stillman method. She followed this up by attending a course of language teaching at the Texas Scottish Rites Hospital, Dallas for which she was sponsored by the Bath Association for Dyslexia.

What she learned there from Aylett Cox and Lucius Waites, the course directors, was their detailed, systematic and cumulative remedial programme based upon the original course of Gillingham and Stillman. Hickey decided to adapt this programme for teachers in this country. She substituted English terms for American ones, revised the spelling to British English from American English, and anglicized the pronunciation and diacritical marking. Her multi-sensory techniques for learning the regular part of language are adapted from the teacher-centred techniques of Gillingham and Stillman to her own child-centred ones. For learning irregular words, she introduced the Fernald multisensory tracing techniques. Her emphasis in the programme was for the learner to become self-directed and to be able to aid his or her own recovery through self-learning. She maintained that, if the method was adapted for use in schools, the dyslexic's problems could actually be prevented.

It was Hickey's (1977) experience that not all pupils attending for remedial education would need this specialist approach but that many would benefit from its use, particularly in the early stages. Those she thought would also benefit were pupils who had missed opportunities for learning at infant level because of 'general imma-turity, changes of teacher, prolonged absences from school, undiscovered sensory disabilities such as ear and eye defects, and the slow learners who need all their school subjects geared to their general rate of learning' (Hickey, 1977, p. viii). She found that those pupils who were late in reading would make progress with extra practice with the usual school approach of the 'look and say' reading schemes and some supporting use of phonics suited to their age and maturity. The dyslexic, however, needed to be identi-fied at an early age and the systematic, cumulative language training approach used so that he or she never experienced failure and became a remedial candidate. This is an important point made by an experienced remedial practitioner.

For diagnosis, Hickey recommended the Schonell reading and

spelling tests and, in addition, the Schonell Silent Reading test A for reading speed and comprehension. In 1972 Hickey ran courses from Gipsy Hill College of Education in Kingston and the following process was observed in development.

Hickey's multisensory phonogram training

In the language training programme itself each new phonogram is introduced by a stimulus response training routine (SRR). This involves the teacher presenting, for example, reading pack card 'i'. Pupil responds and says /i/. The teacher shows the clueword igloo and asks for the sound beginning the word. The pupil responds /i/. The teacher says and shows the name of the letter on the reading pack card, I. The pupil responds 'igloo, /i/'. The teacher makes the sound /i/ and asks for the clue word and name of the letter. The pupil responds 'igloo, I'. The teacher says /i/ and asks pupil to repeat this and give the letter's name. The teacher says 'igloo' and asks for the initial letter's sound and name. The teacher says /i/ and asks pupil to repeat the sound and give the I name and now also write the letter. The teacher writes the letter I in the air, on a surface, or on the pupil's back and asks for clueword, sound and name of the letter. The pupil responds.

When the first phonogram is securely learnt, the second reading card is introduced in the same way until the response to the card is automatic. The order of the first letters is i, t, p, n, s. After learning the phonogram in this way it is only necessary for step 4 to be rehearsed for the reading pack, i.e. show learner the *reading pack card* I, ask for the clueword and sound, and step 8 for the spelling pack, i.e. make the sound /i/, ask learner to repeat sound and name of letter and write it down.

The *reading pack* consists of 84 small pocket-sized cards. On the face of each card is a phonogram (a symbol representing a spoken sound) printed in lower case letters. At the bottom right of the card is its capital form (Figure 8.3). On the reverse side of each card are the keywords for sound and name, plus a picture. All vowel cards have two lines drawn across the top to distinguish them from other phonograms. It is recommended that the reading pack is used once a day by the learner alone in spare moments.

The *spelling pack* comprises 51 cards. The written sound is presented, read by teacher or learner, then repeated by learner. It is then spelled by naming the letter(s) 'i', 'y'. The letters are then written and each one is named just before writing. Later irregular spellings –igh and 'ie' are added to the 'i' card as they are learnt.

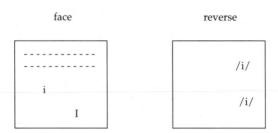

face   reverse

Figure 8.3 *A reading pack card*

The reading and spelling packs are crucial parts of the programme and are presented in detail with letters, cluewords and pictures as shown. The first 16 letters of the programme are as follows:

i, t, p, n, s, a, d, h, e, c, k, ck, b, r, m, y.

Word-building begins as soon as two letters are learnt.

i, t, (it), i, t, p, (pit, tip, pip), i, t, p, n, (nip, pin, tin, tint).

These regular words are presented for both reading and spelling from dictation.

In addition to word-building in this way with phonograms, the position of a phonogram in a word is taught and the pupil is trained to expect to find a particular phonogram at the beginning, middle or end of a word.

Alphabet work is introduced for five minutes at the beginning of each lesson. This is presented so that the pupil can learn to use a dictionary and add to word knowledge and understanding. First, 2-inch high wooden capital letters are presented to be laid out in an arc from A to Z for multisensory training in naming, feeling shape and sequential ordering. It is quite startling to discover that the majority of dyslexics who can read and spell falter and fail at first in this task and have to receive detailed training. They are also taught to find the quartile into which a dictionary word falls: A–D, E–M, N–R, S–Z; and exercises in looking up words in '3, 4 or 5 moves' are practised. Alphabet games are devised and practised.

The *handwriting* training system is based upon that of Anna Gillingham and alternatives to the form recommended are accepted provided that the letter is made all in one movement and has a lead in and a follow on stroke, e.g. *p* or *p* . The pupil is encouraged to verbalize the directions in the letters as they are made, e.g. 'over and back'. Lines are recommended for writing upon, with a faint line above to indicate the size of the main body of the letter in the early stages. Fluency and speed of writing are developed and practised often with a timer to 'beat the clock'.

Thus far the system can be seen to be *multisensory alphabetic phonics*.

After the first 16 phonograms, 'i–e' as in pipe and vowel 'y' (number 20) are introduced and Hickey suggests that, at this point, when long vowel sounds have been introduced more sensible reading material can be studied. She suggests that, by the time the thirty-ninth phonogram in the course has been introduced, the pupil will have a large number of regular and irregular words in his or her reading vocabulary. At this stage, a published scheme can be introduced: Hickey recommends that one of the best is the Royal Road Readers Scheme by Daniels and Diack (produced by Philip and Tacey, 1954–71) because it has a phonic emphasis and gives systematic practice when introducing a new word.

Syllable structures are explained by Hickey and the six common types are detailed and their order of introduction is also specified. The types of syllable are:

1. syllables which are also words;
2. closed syllables;
3. open syllables;
4. regular final syllables;
5. suffixes (usually a syllable);
6. prefixes.

To these are added the spelling rules for adding affixes, e.g. when to 'Add' (flying), 'Double' (hopping), 'Drop' (hoping), 'Change' (tying).

Composition recommendations are given in section 8 by Hickey: how to assist the pupil with continuous prose writing and the use of story schema are shown including the simple notions of beginnings, middles, ends and cartoon sequences with captions to illustrate story ideas.

Section 9 of the training pack shows *games* which can be made to illustrate particular teaching points and many of these are drawn from Childs (1968), her original tutor and also the teachers who attended her courses.

As previously noted, Hickey's contribution was to bring the Gillingham–Stillman programme to this country and, like Childs, Cox and Waites before her, to introduce her own modest improvements and additions to what was basically a well-tried and well-structured remedial programme. The course extends well beyond basic phonics and extends to linguistic structures of the language to meanings and origins. This is why this type of programme has been designated APSL – alphabetic, phonic, structural, linguistic. It also includes multisensory training especially in its early stages when new phonograms are introduced. Later exponents and students of Hickey describe the scheme as alphabetic, phonic, syllabic, linguistic.

In 1991 a second and revised edition was published, *The Hickey Multisensory Language Course: 2nd Edition*, edited by Jean Augur and Sue Briggs. Jean had worked with 'Miss Hickey' as she was always known, on the original language course at the North Surrey Dyslexia Institute. Both had had dyslexic children and had only finally found help for their children when they discovered Miss Hickey. Revision of the original programme had already been started four years before Miss Hickey's death in 1984. The purpose was to make the second edition more user-friendly. The original was a step-by-step format which included a large amount of information that was often complicated and difficult to follow unless the user had been fully trained. Training courses became popular events and a regular feature once a secure base had been established at Staines. The organization became the basis for the Dyslexia Institute and branches have been established throughout the UK.

The second edition divides the programme into three sections. Part One comprises chapters on the theory and background to the multisensory approach to teaching and the basic techniques of the programme such as how to introduce the phonograms using the stimulus–response routine in nine steps; the first 12 phonograms are detailed as follows i, t, p, n, s, a, d, h, e, c /k/, k, and -ck /k/. To these are added concepts, spelling rules and vocabulary, the basic language programme, alphabet work, cursive handwriting training, reading and spelling, story-writing and self-directed learning activities. These chapters are essential reading before embarking on the teaching programme according to Augur and Briggs, and this is certainly true. The early chapters are short, clearly laid out and extremely easy to read providing the reader has an understanding of the principles and practices of the programme. The copyright holder did not permit new insights from research to be included and so the book remains true to the ideas and principles of its originator.

Parts Two and Three are both divided into three sections and demonstrate in a carefully ordered sequence the teaching of the 84 phonograms which comprise the programme and the associated rules and structures. A range of teaching games are presented, with ideas for others also provided, and each section is carefully cross-referenced for ease of use. The new edition is correct in its claims, it is user-friendly. Teachers with an interest in the area could well follow the programme even if they had not had the benefit of a training programme. The danger as always would be the tendency to try to take short cuts and move the pupils through the course too quickly.

Dyslexia Institute language programme (DILP)

This programme is produced in a two-folder format and is only available to those who have attended one of the Institute's training courses. It is not surprising that it is fundamentally based upon the original Hickey language training programme and the courses which she ran at Staines, which is acknowledged in the manual. The programme has been extended to include more example worksheets, games, study skills and language training by its co-editors.

Teaching Reading Through Spelling (Cowdery, 1987; Cowdery *et al.*, 1983, 1984, 1985; Morse, 1986, 1988; Prince-Bruce, 1986)

Teaching Reading Through Spelling (TRTS) is another APSL-type programme. Its authors were all trained by Hickey in the early 1970s. TRTS is based upon the original Gillingham and Stillman programme, is influenced – as was Hickey – by the work of Cox and Waites, but tries to incorporate more in the way of systematic and cumulative structure on the basis of the teachers' experience with their pupils. In TRTS the nature of syllable structure is given greater weight and importance at an early stage. The pupils are taught about the nature of short vowels in closed syllables and the effect therein of the short vowel sound with related affixing rules. Only much later, in the fourth level of the programme, is the long vowel sound for spelling introduced, and the structure and rules related to this. This is a crucial point of departure from the practice in Alpha and Omega and in the Hickey training programme. It is maintained that this preserves better the system and structure of the cumulative requirements of the learner. Similarly, soft 'c' considerations are dealt with at a later stage, although the ramifications of this are of minor significance in relation to the syllable structure points. This all means that there are no published reading schemes to which the dyslexic can easily be introduced and so the system adopted is the linguistic one where the pupil, to a large extent, is writing his or her own reading material and reading any book from any scheme which is deemed appropriate and interesting. Again, the programme includes multisensory training on phonograms, syllables and words, and where appropriate includes nonsense units, and covers alphabet training and story schema. A further difference between the teacher-directed American models and Hickey's work is that the pupils themselves are issued with blank cards upon which they build their own reading and spelling packs. The teacher writes the clueword given by the pupil and the pupil then draws the picture.

The TRTS programme is presented in a series of slim A4 books originally published as Series Two in the Learning Difficulties Research Project at the former Kingston Polytechnic and now by Frondeg Hall for the authors. *Diagnosis Book 2A* details the process of making an assessment and compiling a case profile. The profile contains interview data, criterion-referenced, norm-referenced and diagnostic data from tests and information from the psychologist's report and speech therapist if available. Now, of course, the profile would be supplemented by data from the Statement. Much of the book is about trying to gain a direct insight into the young person's needs and difficulties from direct observation, with the test data as a background.

In the first phase the parent(s) and child are interviewed – the child alone and then the parents alone. An informal relaxed atmosphere is promoted. Guidance on the interview suggests that the child should lead the way from the waiting area to the interview room and the interviewer says, for example, 'go through the last door on the right'. As the pupil does so the interviewer notes the child's gait, any directional confusions and then whether movements are well co-ordinated or if progress is unsteady, lurching, lacking fluency or veering to one side. Can he or she walk in a straight line or is progress aided by contact with the wall? These are indicants of some weaknessess in gross motor control and, possibly, wider difficulties and neurological involvement than dyslexia alone. There may also be difficulties found in handwriting co-ordination on the spelling, dictation and open-ended writing exercises which will give rise to more difficulties in learning. The gross motor difficulties may be accompanied by additional difficulties in attentional set and attention span so that the pupil has difficulty settling down to learning or sitting still long enough to learn. Readers are asked to note any flicking eye movements and seeming constant random ocular movements which may accompany this. This pattern of wider difficulties is suggestive of a pupil with complex learning difficulties and there may also be language difficulties. (Such a pupil may need more than a remedial withdrawal programme. He or she may find progress possible only in a full-time specialist programme.)

In the same interview the teacher asks the pupil for name, address, telephone number, age and birthday, and must not let the parent(s) provide the answers. The pupil is also asked for the name of the school, class teacher and if he or she is receiving special help. The child's interests and likes are also discussed and how he or she feels about the difficulties and how they affect school work.

Explanations of what to look and listen for are detailed and factors such as if the child sits back and allows the parent to step in, or if the parent jumps in too quickly, giving clues to personality and motivation, interests and attitudes are all explored. Assessments made in the classroom are similarly analysed for useful indicants and an informal hearing–reading inventory (Montgomery, 1983, 1986) is included as well as a chart of error types and indicants on the spelling tests and open-ended writing. In the final section are case study examples and notes on understanding the psychologist's report.

In the *Foundations of the Programme Book 2B* (Cowdery *et al.*, 1984) the four essential elements of the programme are described – *alphabet* work, the *reading* and *spelling* packs and the cursive *handwriting* style and training method.

The first section covering the *alphabet* work (written by Cowdery) is similar to that found in Hickey and other APSL derivatives. It consists of using wooden capital letters which the pupil has to lay out in alphabetical order in an arc, tracing over their shape and saying the letter and saying the alphabet in the correct order to the point where an error is made. Each teaching session begins with five or ten minutes of this alphabet work starting from the letter preceding the one where the first error was made until the whole alphabet has been learnt. The pupil finds the letters and lays them out touching and naming, not sounding, them. The procedures involve tracing, naming, visualizing and verbalizing three times before they are put away, and all the letters are named as this is done. A range of games is included on alphabet work – mazes, 'soup', dominoes, battle, crosswords and codes. More advanced work centres upon dictionary use and the four quartiles, with an explanation of how the pupil should be helped to uncover them using a problem-solving strategy. These can then be recorded as A (apples), E (eggs), N (nuts), and S (sausages) or whatever code the pupils invent for themselves to denote the quartiles. One pupil produced 'African Elephants Need Sun'. A series of problem-solving activities on the quartiles is introduced such as 'Find the word DOG in four moves in the dictionary', 'Which quartile is G in?' etc. The words used are those known to be within the pupil's spelling repertoire.

In Section Two the *reading* and *spelling* packs are introduced (this section is written by Prince-Bruce). The purpose of the two packs is to establish a secure relationship between symbol and sound, beginning with single letters and progressing through blends and vowel combinations to complex letter groupings such as –igh and –ough. Every sound is presented through the three main senses so that associations between visual, auditory and kinaesthetic areas can be established. The practice with the packs ensures that the visual stimulus 'a' must immediately evoke the sound /a/ and the automatic writing of 'a' when required. The articulatory feel of the letter is also used as the bridge between these. This systematic and multisensory approach ensures that the pupil has the opportunity to learn anything missed at an earlier stage.

The main linguistic terms are explained and the first five single letters of the scheme which are introduced are i, t, p, n, s. These are the same as in the Hickey programme because they are the most frequently occurring letters in text. Thereafter the order of introduction differs significantly and is based upon an earlier publication by Prince-Bruce (1978) for Kingston LEA. The reading pack is introduced with its relevant general features, such as red-coloured borders on vowel cards so that those with experience of Norrie's letter case can carry their knowledge forward and others will have theirs supported by this extra clue. A simple diacritical marking system to aid pronunciation is used which includes the macron to denote the long vowel sound and the breve for the short vowel sound. The reading pack is built up as the pupil learns the letters and blends for reading. The letters are printed by the pupil on the blank cards, which are playing-card size, and on the reverse a drawing or picture is made of the clueword which the pupil has selected to unlock the sound, e.g. a – apple. On presentation of the letter or blend on the front of the card the pupil says the keyword and sound(s) the letter(s) make.

The spelling pack is built up in a similar fashion. The teacher articulates the sound, the pupil repeats it, noting the articulatory 'feel', writes the appropriate grapheme down from memory, reads what has been written and then checks by looking at the card whether this is correct. 'The use and practice of the Spelling pack is the key to the programme' (Cowdery *et al.*, 1984, p. 25). Brackets round the written letters on the spelling cards indicate the sound or sound 'picture'. On the back of the spelling cards the sound picture is repeated on the left in brackets and on the right of the card the letters that make up that sound. Over time other letters making the same sound are added and these appear on the back of the card in order of frequency of use, e.g. /t/ on the front and on the back /t/

Every letter has an *approach stroke* and a *carry-on stroke*. This means that the pupil can join his or her letters as soon as he or she has learned two or three. It also gives directional flow from left to right and the same starting-point for every letter and word. When writing on lined paper he or she should be asked to place his or her pencil or pen on the line to start, every time, with an approach stroke. (This is invaluable for the pupil whose writing floats all over the page. The use of this 'anchoring point' helps to overcome this problem very quickly.)

Using this procedure the letter shapes will be introduced in the order given.

EXAMPLE: TEACHING THE LETTER 'i'
1. Teacher *writes the shape* fairly large (about 15 cm) on the blackboard saying (ι) as he or she makes the shape.
2. Pupil stands *square to the board*, places different coloured chalk on the beginning of the approach stroke and goes over the *ι* in chalk, saying (ι) as he or she does so.

3. Pupil moves along to the right and copies another *ι* on the blackboard.*
4. Pupil cleans board *from left to right* and writes *ι* on his or her own.*
5. Pupil moves to right again, places chalk on board (or cleans board again) *closes his or her eyes* and writes *ι* .*
   * Child says (ι) each time.

(1) TEACHER WRITES*	(3) CHILD COPIES*	(4) CLEAN BOARD CHILD WRITES* ON HIS OWN	(5) CHILD WRITES WITH EYES CLOSED*
ι	ι	ι	ι
(2) CHILD GOES OVER* (with different coloured chalk).		* saying (ι) ι each time	

(Some children may need to repeat Step 2 several times.)

(Morse, pp. 33, 36)

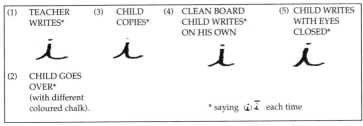

Instantly recognizable as looking and sounding like a snake. (Can use alternative ∂).

The open ∩ helps to avoid confusion with ɑ and q . The ∩ upstroke must be no higher than the body line of the letter or this could lead to confusion with an h .

Figure 8.4 *An example of how to introduce the first letters of the TRTS programme*
Source: Morse, 1984. Copyright P. Morse. Used with permission.

to the left and 't' to the right. On the next line underneath will appear /t/ to the left and –ed to the right. As –ed is a suffix it is written in green. If a keyword is needed this is written on the back in pencil.

In the third section the *handwriting* training system is described (Morse, 1984), and her rationale for this has already been given in Chapter 7. The format for the introduction of each letter, particularly in the early stages, is shown in Figure 8.4.

In Section Four Morse also provides useful guidance for those pupils who have wider difficulties in the motor co-ordination area. These include strategies for writing patterns, notes on the use of lines and some examples.

Section Five contains some records of written progress through the scheme of three pupils and the final section (Montgomery, 1984) describes multisensory mouth training which was discussed earlier in this chapter (pp. 199–201).

The third book in the series is *The Early Stages of the Programme* (Prince-Bruce *et al.*, 1985). This book gives an overview of the whole programme, the structure, the terms used in the first part of the programme and example lessons of particular aspects of children with specific difficulties, e.g. initial consonant blend (Prince-Bruce, 1985, pp. 8–10). The rest of the book explains the linguistics of the early stages, sound pictures, how English words are constructed, syllable division rules, the meanings of prefixes and suffixes, plurals, Simultaneous Oral Spelling, the l-f-s rule and then provides a range of games to reinforce the teaching points made.

The method of using the programme for teaching is explained and there are charts for easy access, and are all cross-referenced. The final section of the book provides 16 pages of dictation related to the teaching order to enable the teacher to check that the sounds and structures have been learned thus far, and there are another set of games linked to the early stages.

What becomes apparent is the tightly structured nature of a teaching session which is highly intensive and demanding of both pupil and teacher. One-hour sessions are conducted with pairs of pupils matched for sociability and in terms of skills and needs. A typical teaching session has the following work order pattern:

• alphabet work;
• reading pack;
• spelling pack;
• words for reading;
• words for spelling;
• dictation;

- pupil uses new words in own open-ended writing;
- games and activities to reinforce learning.

The words for reading and spelling comprise the sounds introduced in the reading and spelling packs plus any sounds previously learned, a generative activity. Sounds which have not been learnt are not included at this stage. An example of part of such a lesson plan to teach /k/ ck illustrates the necessary detail.

Suggested lesson plan to teach /k/ ck (Book 2c, 1985)

The pupil will know about short vowels, consonants, syllables and will have covered /-sk/, /-lk/, /-nk/ in a multisensory way and used these final consonant blends in spelling and dictation.

Teacher: I want you to write some words in a column on the left of your page. Listen – desk. How many sounds can you hear after the short vowel (ĕ) in desk?
Pupil: Two /sk/.
Teacher: Lovely, now write 'desk' on your page. Say it as you write it on the left-hand side of the page.

Pupil writes 'desk'.
Similarly the teacher dictates 'silk' and 'bank' to be written by the pupil under 'desk'.

Teacher: How many syllables have these words?
Pupil: One each.
Teacher What letter makes the /k/ sound at the end of these one-syllable words?
Pupil: /k/ k.
Teacher: (with emphasis) At the end of a word with ONE syllable use /k/ k for the /k/ sound. The stick on the k is like a number one – one syllable k. Use a red pen and draw down the stick on the k at the end of desk, silk and bank. One syllable k.

Helpful addition to the Reading Pack

FRONT   BACK

At the end of a word with one syllable use /k/ k. One syllable k.

Teacher: Now I want you to write some words in a column to the right of the first one, Listen 'deck' – how many sounds can you hear after the short vowel /ĕ/ in 'deck'?

Pupil: Just /k/.
Teacher: That short vowel needs all the help it can get so you use
            both the letters that can make a /k/ sound. You use /k/ *ck*
            directly after a short vowel. Write 'deck' in your book, say
            it as you write.

Pupil writes 'deck' in the second column on the page.
Teacher dictates 'sick', 'back' to be written by the pupil under 'deck'.

Teacher: What kind of vowels have these words?
Pupil: Short.
Teacher: Directly after a short vowel use /k/ *ck*. Take another colour,
            mark the short vowel in 'deck' and write over the *ck*, say the
            word as you do so. Then do the same for 'sick' and 'back'.

Pupil marks short vowels and writes over the *ck*.

Teacher: Now take the red pen and draw down the stick of the *k* to
            show that you use /k/ *k* at the end of these one syllable
            words.

If the pupil can read words such as 'look', 'beak', 'perk' and 'soak',
these can be used as further explanation of the short vowel *ck*
pattern.

Teacher: Why is there just /k/ *k* at the end of 'look'?
Pupil: 'Look' has one syllable but there are two vowels, you only
            use /k/ *ck directly* after *one short vowel*.

A worksheet using similar words can be used even if the pupil
cannot read them to get them to isolate the *ck* pattern from the
others.

The pupil writes across the page:
        ck   lk   nk   sk
The teacher dictates words such as silk, sink, sick, link, lick, sulk,
suck, and the pupil writes them in the correct column.
The activity can be extended later to illustrate the use of the /k/
spelling card.
The pupil writes the spelling card across the page thus:
     c   k   ck   –ke   – – – c

Source: Prince-Bruce *et al.*, 1985. Copyright M. Prince-Bruce. Used with permission.

The Programme: The Later Stages, 2D Part One (Prince-Bruce *et al.*,
1986) gives an overview of the whole programme and the purpose
of its structure. The full set of diacritical marks are explained but

only the breve and micron are suggested for the pupil's use. There then follows the full teaching order of the programme in a chart cross-referenced to rules, packs and pages. There are 17 detailed pages of this and then pages 23–75 contain the phonemes still to be introduced, the rules and generalizations associated with them, and related vocabulary and dictations, beginning with for example:

(a) a Use (a) a in an open syllable e.g. ba / con

- -

apron, bacon, fatal, vacant, April
1. Ted will tax his van in April
2. Mum will put on an apron
3. I will give Ted my bacon
4. It is a fatal crash
5. The hut is vacant

Pages 76–137 introduce more sounds and rules and each is accompanied by a set of exercises and games.

The Programme: The Later Stages 2D Part Two (Prince-Bruce, 1986) introduces the higher-order end of linguistics teaching with more emphasis on open and closed syllables, vowel digraphs and diphthongs. Silent letters, word families and stable final syllables appear with example lesson plans, alternative approaches to suffixing work (*Book 2C*), prefixes and possessive rules, and the programme element finishes with accented syllables, accents in English and patterns and procedures for finding the accented syllables in a word. There are then a series of related games on pages 57–80. The complete reading and spelling pack cards are then shown in full in the final pages.

The three final books in the series – *The Handwriting Copy Book* (Morse, 1986), the *Infant Handwriting Copy Book* (Morse, 1988) and *The Spelling Notebook* (Cowdery, 1987) – are reference works.

The *Spelling Notebook* contains a summary of all the linguistic rules and teaching points governing English spelling which a teacher and pupil might conceivably need. It is an indispensable companion to the series but is also useful as a reference book and sourcebook for anyone interested generally in spelling.

The diagram 'Fishing for Sounds' (Cowdery, 1987) (Figure 8.5) shows most of the key aspects to the TRTS programme. As the pupil learns each part so she or he colours in the fish as a record of progress.

Figure 8.6 shows the results of some remedial work with Steven based upon TRTS. He received six 20-minute tutorials over a

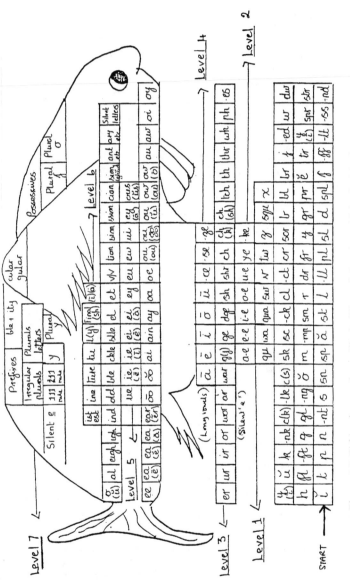

Figure 8.5 *Fishing for sounds: pupil's checklist and chart (two-thirds of original size) Copyright L.L. Cowdery. Used with permission.*

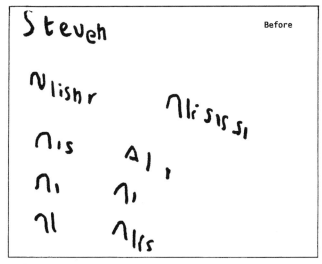

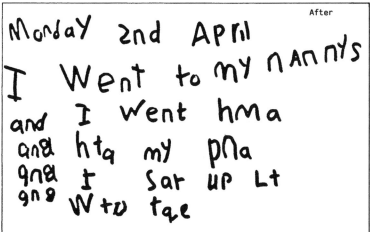

Figure 8.6 *Examples of Steven's progress to literacy, before and after six TRTS tutorials (two-thirds of original size)*

period of six weeks from a student in initial training in a setting where he was not permitted to learn cursive writing. He can be seen clearly to have cracked the alphabetic code and now has some chance of making progress.

Figures 8.7 and 8.8 are from the programme itself and show the work of John at 8 years and 6 months and then again at 9 years 10 months. In his case it can be seen that he has a wider difficulty with motor co-ordination. At chronological age 8 years John had no score on the Daniels and Diack Tests for reading and spelling. His writing and reading problems were severe. He had missed a lot of time at school due to illness and was still physically weak suffering from kidney disease. Figure 8.7 is written from a tape on '–nd' at age 8 years and 6 months. He wrote many letters from right to left and, therefore, was unable to join them. He confused b and d and reversed 'in' completely to 'ni' in writing the n from right to left.

At age 9 years and 10 months John's writing (Figure 8.8) is still not beautiful but he is now able to form all his letters going round in the right direction and join them up. For an initial period of some months when writing his spelling pack he had to pause after saying each sound and think carefully which shape he had to make to reproduce that sound on paper. He still has to listen to the order in which sounds are spoken to get the letters sequenced correctly plus checking the direction of every 'b' and 'd' he writes. He is pleased that he can now do this much unaided. John's reading age is now 8.0 years, using the Daniels and Diack Standard Test of Reading Skill.

STRAND's Spelling then reading: Approaching the needs of dyslexic students (Hampshire LEA)

This programme is a looseleaf file of worksheets produced by a team of Hampshire teachers, P. Pentote, N. Clark and A. Naylor, with the support of their former Adviser for Special Needs, Gill Tester, who has been Inspector (SEN) in Kingston. The STRAND worksheets are designed to teach spelling and reading as support materials and should *not be used in isolation* warn the accompanying guidelines. The materials support the training courses based upon the Teaching Reading Through Spelling (APSL) programme as taught by Cowdery, Morse and Prince-Bruce; thus recognizing that theory and practice should go hand in hand and that pupils with reading and spelling problems should not simply be set to complete an endless stream of worksheets from which they invariably learn little. Teaching the pupil is an essential prerequisite; a worksheet is then used to reinforce that which has been learned. Worksheets cannot be used both to teach and to reinforce when pupils already have difficulties in learning by all usual methods. The worksheets are designed for a range of difficulties in spelling and reading, not specifically confined to dyslexic problems.

When teachers do not have the advantage of having attended a programme designed to illustrate the rationale and the method of use of materials, and a manual does not supply this, then the best

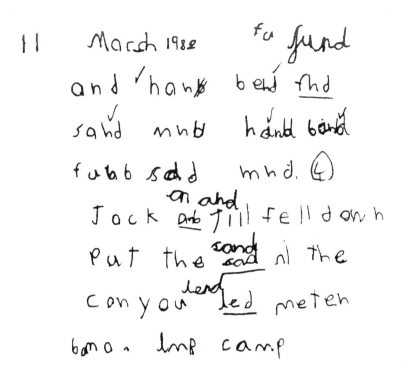

Figure 8.7 *John's writing and spelling (8 years 6 months) (two-thirds of original size)*
Source: Cowdery et al. (1983). Used with permission.

11 th July 1983

It will be fun to dump mud in the tub.
Rub the dust off the black drum.
Bang the drum but do not eat the skin.
The big pig is in the pen. Tip it in the bin.

Figure 8.8 *John's writing and spelling (9 years 10 months) (two-thirds of original size)*
Source: Cowdery et al. (1983). Used with permission.

and most effective use cannot be made of them. Special educational needs (SEN) resource centres across the country regularly order such packages but rarely can provide the teaching back-up for their use. One illustrative lecture is not sufficient for this purpose; it is usual for such a programme to require at least one week of intensive in-service training or the equivalent in part-time provision, if the best results are to be obtained.

A phonetic-linguistic programme: Alpha to Omega (Hornsby and Shear, 1976, 1985)

According to Hornsby (1985), a structured phonetic-linguistic method of remediation is used in all centres where dyslexia is taken seriously. She argues that, unfortunately, phonics approaches are frequently misunderstood and often involve teaching the association between letter shapes and single sounds without using letter names. She insists that letter names need to be taught in order (Figure 8.9) to describe how a word such as 'betting' is spelled, for b – e – t can be sounded out and makes sense but betting cannot. Letter names are also constants whereas sounds change according to context in a word. It is notable that all APSL variants teach letter names and sounds together by some system of

1st	b p m w h
2nd	d t n g k ŋ (ng)
3rd	f s z
4th	v TH voiced [ʤ] sh [ʒ] l ch j
5th	y qu [kw] r th [θ] x [ks] or [gz]
6th	Consonant blends

Figure 8.9 *The order of introduction of Hornsby and Shear's letters*

phonogram training as described by Hickey (1977) after Gilling-ham *et al.* (1940).

To the order of letter introduction, Hornsby and Shear add a final activity, 'Pupil writes letter eyes closed', thus emphasizing the sensory motor programming aspect although cursive is not insisted upon. Alpha to Omega, according to its authors, is a highly structured, multisensory and cumulative reading, writing and spelling programme moving from single letters through to single-syllabled and multisyllabled words using cards in a reading and spelling pack as previously described by Hickey's programme. It is suggested that the reading pack cards can show more advanced patterns for this accelerates faster than spelling and it will also serve to familiarize the pupils with the spelling patterns by the time they are expected to spell them.

The programme, on close inspection, lacks some of the system-atic and cumulative structure that is claimed, such as that illustrated in the other two schemes. For example, although the associations between single letters, sounds and shapes are trained first, the first basic vowels are introduced more or less simultane-ously and then 'y', the semi-vowel. Many of the dyslexic pupils I have met who have been taught in this way become completely confused and cannot remember the sounds, keywords or names of any of the vowels. James was a case in point. His 'remedial' teacher had done just this, given him each vowel to draw and a clue picture to illustrate the sound which he also had to draw. In the labour of all this, with his co-ordination problem, he recalled nothing, although he had practised it many times.

Another major departure from the original model is for Hornsby to say that there are no hard and fast rules about handwriting. In the original schemes, great emphasis was laid upon teaching cursive script of an economic kind at the outset as part of the motor training programme to aid spelling. The authors of Alpha to Omega, however, do insist that the pupils must be taught to form the letters correctly and be shown where each letter should start. Another departure, and a crucial one in terms of Cowdery *et al.*'s TRTS programme, is the introduction of open and closed syllables and the short and long vowel sounds at more or less the same point. This is also found to lead to confusion in many dyslexics.

Consonant blends and digraphs including what are called vowel consonant digraphs, er or ar, are taught in sections and final syl-lables such as –tion –sion –cion and –tail in a manner resembling phonics systems rather than meaning-orientated syllable division structures, rules and derivations. This, perhaps, is not surprising since the programme is called phonetic-linguistic. What it appears to do is to preserve what teachers expect to do and see in a reading and spelling programme, extending basic phonics without being too controversial and thus, at the time of publication, was a welcome addition to the field.

The programme has also been revised (Hornsby and Shear, 1985, 3rd edition) and supplemented with Alpha to Omega stories and dictations. The linguistic basis of the programme is also detailed. The dictations are recommended to begin early to help structure the language, and useful examples of sentence structures are given, beginning with SAAD, the Simple Active Affirmative Declarative sentences, e.g. 'The man ran to the red van' is given as an early example of dictation, using regular words. 'A black cat jumped on the table' shows a later more advanced level dictation using SAAD. A multisensory approach to dictation is suggested in which:

1. The whole sentence is dictated.
2. The pupil repeats it.
3. The teacher dictates it again slowly and clearly.
4. The pupil writes it down.
5. The pupil reads aloud what is written and self-corrects it if necessary.
6. The teacher helps correct it if necessary.
7. The pupil reads the sentence again 'with expression'.

The sentence structure taught is also structured and cumulative, leading from affirmatives to negatives, compound sentences, complex sentences with main and subordinate clauses, cause and effect structures, passive affirmative and negative passive construction. In free writing, remediators and parents are warned that the pupil will make more errors because the mind is more on content than form.

The claims of Alpha to Omega to be a phonetic-linguistic programme have foundations but the programme has its origin in a reduced and modified version of the Gillingham and Stillman programme. The claims to be structured and sequential are, by comparison, less well founded as already detailed but the scheme is popular and has many supporters. Of interest are the comments made by Hornsby (1989) on a set of errors made by one of her pupils:

famel (family)	punshment (punishment)	pont (point)
perhas (perhaps)	continu (continue)	poshon (portion)
constucted (constructed)		

'His spellings of family and punishment indicate his tendency to omit syllables when writing words. It is interesting that the final syllable –tion has been partly mastered but without good sequencing skills words with this ending cannot be spelled accurately' and 'pronunciation needs sharpening', in dis drif (disc drive) and chrismas (Christmas) (Hornsby, 1989, pp. 130–1). As one example, it is arguable that an ending such as –tion can best be learnt by a dyslexic through training in the sequence of its sounds for it is variously spelled –sion, –cian and sounded –shun as in attention, mansion, magician. What might be a more effective means of learning would be some knowledge of these particular suffix forms and the situations in which they are appropriate. These may be found detailed in the APSL/psycholinguistic programmes and are a cognitive approach to remediation in an area in which rote training can be overburdensome and eventually self-defeating if applied to every situation. The multisensory rote training for words is reserved in the other programmes of Hickey etc. for those 15 per cent of words for which no definite rule or cognitive structure can be found, e.g. 'said'; even these are grouped where possible into families and a cue sentence or ditty is invented and learnt, incorporating them.

The Bangor dyslexia teaching system (Miles, T.R., 1978 and 1989; Miles, E., 1992)

The basic system is a phonological-linguistic one. The original teaching manual was produced in 1978 for teachers at the Dyslexia Unit, University College of North Wales, Bangor. Part One of the new version is intended for teaching primary age pupils and Part Two is for secondary school pupils although Miles states some secondary pupils may need to be started on Part One as their skills are so poor. Miles recommends that as dyslexics have a problem with the phonological aspects of language or 'phoneme deafness' according to Frith (1985) then the remedial programme needs to address this directly. She also recommends multisensory teaching using any of the Alpha to Omega or Hickey phoneme-grapheme cards or the Edith Norrie letter case. The handwriting style illustrated is a print script (Miles, 1992, p. 40) although it is stated that dyslexic pupils may be taught cursive from the outset because they can become confused at the changeover stage which is always too easily forgotten.

The pupil must have a book in which to record the spelling patterns he or she has learnt, another for practices and dictations. Miles recommends an emphasis upon *patterns* rather than rules, plenty of practice, using mnemonics where necessary, teaching reading and spelling together as decoding and encoding activities, using phonic reading books for the first six months, and encouraging plenty of oral work trying words aloud and saying sentences before writing them down. The compilation of the pupil's 'dictionary' is a central theme or system of the book and sample pages are given.

Part One is organized in six sections:

1. Single letter sounds and single syllable words with short vowel sounds; ar, or, and er are at the end of this section.
2. Commonest long vowel patterns including final 'e', vowel digraphs and vowel 'w' or 'y'.
3. A checklist of irregular words to be learnt.
4. More patterns such as –ight, ir, ur and ought, aught, ough.
5. Silent consonant patterns.
6. Word endings, common grammatical endings and changes to base words when affixing.

The teacher is advised to check all the consonants and their second sounds; knowledge of names at this stage is optional. The five short vowels to be taught gradually as a, i, o, u, e and the short sound is marked with the breve (˘). Work on alphabet and dictionary skills can start quite soon. Singing the alphabet in letter groups is recommended and the display of the whole alphabet 'as in a rainbow formation or some similar arrangement is a useful way for pupils to become more proficient in its use' (Miles, 1992, p. 40; see also Hickey, 1977). Learning the quartiles is mentioned and tracking exercises are advocated. These recommendations on handwriting and alphabet work are in an appendix and appear not to be integral to the scheme. In the original 1984 text it was recommended (p. 26) that letters should be grasped for handwriting according to their starting-point, for example:

> those on the right a c d g o q s
> those on the left r m n p i j v w x y z u
> and at the top of the 'stick' l h b k t f
> and 'starts in the middle'

In both the original text and in the revised and updated versions the building of the personal dictionary is paramount. The advice begins with 'Begin by checking that your pupil knows most of the usual sounds of *all* the consonants including y qu and the hard sounds of c and g' (Miles, 1992, p. 9), and 'Knowledge of sound can be optional at this stage' (*ibid.*). This knowledge is to be recorded in the *first* page of the dictionary, the inside cover, and then three letter words with short vowel sounds are taught and recorded. This is followed by tracing of consonant digraphs and consonant blends, doubling with l–f–s, –ck, –ld, –dge, doubling with polysyllables, hop hopping, silent e, stress and much more.

The pupil's dictionary should contain all vowels, consonants and blends, digraphs and –ng and –nk. Page one of the dictionary lists short vowel words; all combinations of beginning and ending blends including three-letter ones appear here. Page two – sample second page (Miles, 1992, p. 19) – includes long vowel sounds, final 'e' patterns, silent 'w' as in write and final 'e' patterns as –ee, –ie, –oe, -ue and appropriate lists. Hard and soft 'c' and 'g' information is included here.

The Bangor dyslexia teaching system seems to be one which is based upon the logical analysis of the language but which includes too much too soon for the dyslexic. It needs a great deal of interpretation and revision by the teacher in interaction with the pupil. To be fair this is recommended by the author as part of the sensitive and flexible approach needed by the teacher in interaction with the individual pupil. A teaching course may well be necessary to learn to use it well, rather than just as a more extensive phonic-linguistic programme.

An illustration of this point exemplifying the problems which may arise can be seen where the text says:

> check for the sound the pupil knows and then teach the ones not known. As they are learnt they should be written by the pupil in the dictionary.
>
> a e i o u

This could indicate that the teacher should teach this group together or one after the other by sight and sound. This will quickly confuse the dyslexic still in logographic mode.

Plastic letter shapes are recommended for alphabet work and the Norrie letter case (Norrie, 1973) and Bradley (1981b) are referred to. However, wooden letters are recommended by Cowdery *et al.* (1984) because of the additional tactile information from the surface of the wood and the lack of colour which can be used as clues by the dyslexic. Alphabet training needs to be systematic and detailed taking place on a regular basis over many weeks and used as a starting-point for a few minutes each lesson. The order of introduction of new material needs to be more sequential and cumulative if the dyslexic is to benefit from it. Alternatively, the training has to provide for this and there are supplementary editions to the book showing how teachers use the scheme. Frequency of appearance of common forms such as ee and oo ensures that these come early in the scheme.

Multisensory teaching is now recommended but only goes so far as to advise teachers to use:

- The Alpha to Omega or Hickey cards or the Edith Norrie letter case.
- A book for the client to record the spelling patterns as he or she learns them.
- Dictation for reading and writing.
- Use of work books, exercises and computer activities which include saying the words.

The system is not so much a system but a scheme and a context through which teacher and pupil must plot a course. Experienced remedial teachers would find it useful as it would extend their knowledge of phonics into linguistics in a more substantial way. Too many of the basics seem to be omitted which could indicate a difference in the Bangor clientele who may be older or have better reading and spelling skills than in the samples with which other remediators have to deal.

The original book *Help for Dyslexic Children* (Miles and Miles, 1983, repr. 1992) contained a large number of dictation exercises to accompany the scheme. These are referred to in the present book and are replaced by longer explanations of linguistic points and lists of words in specific groups.

A companion volume, *Tackling Dyslexia the Bangor Way* by Cooke (1992), is essential reading for those using the system and for those interested in teaching dyslexics by any scheme. Cooke explains that the Bangor system is basically *phonological* not visual or linguistic. She details ways in which Miles and Miles's (1992) recommendations are operationalized, and it becomes clear that alphabetic work and cursive writing using multisensory learning are secondary to the main thrust of the programme. Perhaps they are a more recent addition and have not yet been fully integrated into the system. There is still a choice to be made over print versus cursive and all the children's examples are in print script. A very useful chapter on 'the use of computers in lessons with dyslexics' is also included and there is an excellent appendix on materials, games and books for teaching.

SUMMARY AND CONCLUSIONS

In this chapter specialist articulation training programmes and strategies were discussed and a range of alphabetic, phonic, syllabic, linguistic programmes and APSL derivatives were outlined along with the reasons which suggested why they might work. These are all specialist techniques and programmes for use with learners with disability and are not necessary for use with the majority of readers and spellers. A 'pick and mix' approach to the teaching of dyslexics can actually be harmful. Dyslexics need a structured, cumulative and sequentially ordered programme in which the phonogram teaching is multisensory. It is important that the programmes teach not only phonics, but also all the levels of linguistics within the remedial session. This is a detailed curriculum in itself which other children have had five or six years' advantage in acquiring in ordinary lessons. Because of the detailed nature of the work these children should be taught in a separate tutorial environment, for such tuition cannot successfully be given within other lessons. At present under the Code of Practice it is common for pupils up to Stage Three, if they are withdrawn from lessons, to receive their 'remedial' support in groups of at least eight. As will be inferred from the examples in this chapter it is not possible for the teacher to work in a detailed interactive way with more than two pupils in a session. This can only mean that the dyslexic pupil's needs will remain unmet for a further period of years, becoming exacerbated and possibly intractable in some cases.

It is clear that there are the appropriate knowledge and programmes in this country and no need to import further untested strategies from other countries. Investment in practice-related remediation research in England and Wales is still needed. This would establish clear evidence for the most appropriate specialist methodology and the most effective method of training for the teachers as well as assessment and referral processes. Substantial funding has never been allocated to this area of need and for many years this highly structured approach has been regarded as unsuitable; it is unsuitable for the majority but this should not blind us to the needs of the few. Reading research and reading teaching has dominated this field and it is time this balance was redressed.

It was a great pity that LEA centres of excellence in this area were disbanded following the changes in funding arrangements for schools and LMS (Local Management of Schools). Their skills in specialist teaching and in-service training are being diluted as they become peripatetic tutors and in-class support teachers.

Able children frustrated by their inability to acquire literacy skills will become disruptive and disturbed as they fall further behind waiting for the system to grind through its procedures until it catches up with them. Places in Emotional and Behavioural Difficulties (EBD) units and schools will be filled inappropriately by these pupils whose needs should have been met in other ways.

APSL programmes, especially those which incorporate multisensory phoneme awareness and phonogram training and linguistics, appear to be the most capable of enabling the dyslexic to crack the alphabetic code. The problem could be identified and addressed in reception classes, and then we might find that in a significant proportion of cases the whole pattern of delay leading to deficits in reading and writing might not then occur. If a number of longitudinal pilot studies could be established this could make a significant contribution to knowledge and skill in this area. Too often remedial research has consisted of insufficient input of a specialist nature – the inappropriate techniques leading to nil results.

In North America investment in this area of research exceeds $10 million per year. In England and Wales the Government has just proposed the establishment of 20 specialist *reading* training centres to address literacy problems but there has been no investment over the previous ten years to establish what is effective. The Chief Inspector for Schools, C. Woodhouse, has just announced (1996) that there must be no more trendy methods of teaching from the 1960s and 1970s. There must be formal teaching to whole-class groups for all subjects just as in the Pacific-rim countries. This no doubt will also mean a return to phonic drills and in ten years' time there will be another bee in someone's bonnet to switch it all back again. Meanwhile the professionalism of teachers is being undermined as those who have no recent and relevant experience of teaching children or teaching teachers to teach can change the course of education and damage children's lives.

> ... it has become customary to delay the institution of corrective programmes until third grade or later when the dyslexic will have segregated himself from the 'late bloomer'. This undoubtedly effects an economy from the standpoint of the administrator ... but this economy is accomplished at a heavy cost to the dyslexic child. For by the time the remedial programme is offered to him [sic], he has had several years of failure, with consequent development of aversion to reading and related activities as well as of emotional problems related to feelings of inadequacy. (Eisenberg, 1962, pp. 4–5)

Is it too much to expect that dyslexics can expect to get a fair deal in the new millennium?

Epilogue

The history of spelling difficulties has been inextricably linked with the history of dyslexia and both have suffered from an almost exclusive attention to reading and reading difficulties. Teaching interest began 100 years ago when Morgan (1896) described the case of Percy, a young boy referred to him because of his 'atrocious' spelling. He wrote his name as Precy, Percy or Pecry and at 14 was a very poor reader. Morgan described this problem as 'congenital word blindness'. As a result of reading about this case Hinshelwood, a surgeon at the Glasgow Eye Infirmary, became very interested in such problems and tried to establish their scientific basis. He later referred to them as 'congenital dyslexia' (Hinshelwood, 1917) and used the term 'word blindness' to refer to acquired cases, for example after strokes and head injuries. He located the lesion in the acquired cases, with some accuracy for those days, as in the left angular gyrus. For congenital or developmental dyslexics he recommended a system of remediation by spelling words out letter by letter so that the visual, auditory and speech movements would be trained simultaneously. Under this system his protégé made more progress in 13 months than he had in the preceding seven years. When researching in the UK, Orton came across the work of Morgan and Hinshelwood and with his team in the 1930s adapted the systematic sequential phonics widely used in England and added to it a version of Hinshelwood's alphabetic, multisensory system, and this became the basis of the first Gillingham *et al.* (1940) programme.

Thus the wheel has come full circle in this 100 years. Alphabetic – phonic, now plus syllabic – linguistics is again a recommended method of teaching but this time for dyslexics and not the whole population, unless another Government edict dictates a wholesale return to this method. Reading teachers and reading experts have always resisted these methods, for obvious reasons, but it should be the right of the few who need such methods to be given access to them at the earliest stage possible.

In order to help the rest, the generally poor spellers, the subject of teacher education needs to be readdressed. In 1983 the Government took over control of the curriculum in all teacher education courses through the Committee for the Accreditation of Teacher Education (CATE) and by 1989 had removed 'irrelevant theory', that is, the background to teaching practice, as outlined in this book, in relation to spelling. It was replaced with the expansion of time for the academic studies of subjects such as English, geography and so on. English specialists took over the leadership of the language (and reading) courses, and reading teaching was coped with by importing teachers and advisers in to do a few sessions of practical work. This practical work could often be more of the same that was already failing spellers. In a survey undertaken by the NFER for CATE (1992) it was found that on the whole primary BEd courses gave 80 hours language contact time and PGCE courses 60 hours. The significance attached to spelling in *Training Teachers to Teach Reading: A Review* can be seen in the report's heading. This same bias can be seen on the cover of this book. The actual time given to the teaching and learning of literacy skills within the contact hours umbrella was a much smaller proportion, 34 hours in BEds and 21 hours in PGCEs. The survey confirmed data from an earlier HMI report (DES, 1987) that the assessment of reading progress received very little attention and so the teachers were unable to assure themselves that their teaching strategies had been effective. All the ITT initial teacher training institutions involved practising teachers in supporting, monitoring and assessing student's school based work. Many brought teachers in to teach elements of the courses and thus demonstrated the lack of expertise within those institutions and raised questions about the planning and structure of the courses. Students themselves felt the need to have more course time devoted to the teaching of reading and especially to helping those with special needs.

The data on secondary courses were less extensive but there was evidence that in the mainly subject-based programmes the development of reading was not given sufficient attention. 'Secondary trained graduates' awareness of the need to develop reading other than in terms of literature was relatively low' (CATE, 1992, B4.4, p. 7).

Staff in the survey insisted that they offered an eclectic approach to teaching reading integrating writing, spelling and oracy, which must have gone over the students' heads for they claimed that they had little or no teaching about phonics. Presumably separate sessions on spelling and handwriting did not figure at all.

A very different picture existed during the 1980s in some ITT and in-service programmes which could have been used as models for good practice for literacy and learning difficulties teaching. CATE requirements caused these to be closed and the expertise dispersed. One can only suggest that the Government has 'sown the wind and is now reaping the whirlwind' as pupils become more alienated from school work and their teachers less able to help them. It should never have been necessary to import Reading Recovery nor set up 20 specialist literacy teaching centres round the country. The expertise needs to be drawn back together and the initial training of teachers should be revised and based upon good practice models rather than on ideology of 30 years ago.

Perhaps as a first step the Department for Education (leaving Employment) should be closed down since the errors have emanated from there and piecemeal attempts to correct them are a further waste of money. After this:

- Cut all reception classes to no more than 15 children so that the teacher can work on an individual basis with pupils each day as well as with groups and the whole class.
- Train all infant teachers as specialists in the teaching of literacy as a main subject instead of English, history, geography, etc. This would give academic challenge at the highest levels, for at the moment one can only study literacy and linguistics as masters and PhD programmes.
- Compulsorily retrain all infant teachers and special needs co-ordinators who do not have an additional qualification in the area for the equivalent of a one-year part-time study programme leading to a post-graduate certificate in literacy teaching. Reward those who have re-educated themselves by giving an equivalent study period or additional money.
- Buy in independent assessment, statementing and assessment services so that recommendations are not dependent upon LEA cash restraints and perceived career progression of members of the hierarchy.
- Make certain that referral for specialist tuition takes place by the beginning of Year One for dyslexics.
- Make child-rearing, parenting and the development of language and literacy skills a compulsory GCSE or equivalent programme for all pupils in secondary schools.
- Establish a committee of experts to advise upon appropriate programmes of the study of literacy teaching (not just reading) in higher education.
- Establish a substantial budget similar to that in other countries for a systematic programme of research to evaluate literacy

teaching methods and the effectiveness or otherwise of the proposed training changes.

In the long term addressing these issues could improve the quality of teaching and learning at all levels, produce a better skilled and qualified workforce, and keep many people out of prison.

Bibliography

Ackerman, I., Gunelt, D. and Kenwood, P. (1983) *DATAPAC. An Interim Report*. Birmingham: Birmingham University.

Ainscow, M. and Muncey, J. (1981) *Special Needs Action Programme*. Coventry: Coventry LEA.

Ainscow, M. and Muncey, J. (1983) 'Learning difficulties in primary schools, an inservice training initiative'. *Remedial Education* 3, 116–24.

Ainscow, M. and Muncey, J. (1984) *Special Needs Action Programme (SNAP)*. Swansea: Drake Education.

Ainscow, M. and Tweddle, D.A. (1979) *Preventing Classroom Failure*. Chichester: Wiley.

Alston, J. (1993) *Assessing and Promoting Writing Skills*. Stafford: NASEN.

Alston, J., and Taylor, J. (1987) *Handwriting Theory and Practice*. London: Croom Helm.

Alston, J., Taylor, J. and Jarman, C. (1985) *The Handwriting File: Diagnosis and Remediation of Handwriting Difficulties*. Wisbech: Learning Development Aids.

Amano, I. (1992) 'The light and dark sides of Japanese education'. *Royal Society of Arts Journal* **145** (5424).

Annett, M. (1983) 'Handedness'. In M. Jeeves (ed.) *Psychology Survey No. 3*. London: Allen and Unwin, 1–15.

APU (Assessment of Performance Unit) (1991) *Assessment of Writing Skills*. London: Further Education Unit.

Arkell, H. (1973) *The Edith Norrie Letter Case*. London: Helen Arkell Centre.

Attneave, F. and Arnoult, H.D. (1956) 'The quantitative study of shape and pattern perception'. *Psychological Bulletin* **53** (6), 452–71.

Augur, J. and Briggs, S. (eds) (1991) *The Hickey Multisensory Language Course*. 2nd edn. London: Whurr.

Bakker, D.J. (1972) *Temporal Order and Disturbed Reading*. Rotterdam: Rotterdam University Press.

Bakker, D.J. (1990) *Neuropsychological Treatments of Dyslexia*. Oxford: Oxford University Press.

Bannatyne, A.D. (1971) *Language, Reading and Learning Disabilities*. Illinois: Charles C. Thomas.

Barker-Lunn, J.C. (1986) *Report of NFER Survey on Teaching Basic Skills in Primary Schools*. Windsor: NFER-Nelson.

Barnard, H.C. (1961) *A History of English Education*. 2nd edn. London:

London University Press.

Baron, J. and Strawson, C. (1976) 'Use of orthographic and word specific knowledge in reading words aloud'. *Journal of Experimental Psychology, Human Perception and Performance* **2**, 386–93.

BDA (British Dyslexia Association) (1981) *BDA Guidelines for Teaching Dyslexic Children*. Reading: British Dyslexia Association.

BDA (British Dyslexia Association) (1990) *Papers of the Education and Training Committee of the BDA*. Reading: British Dyslexia Association.

Bender, L. (1957) 'Specific reading difficulty as a maturational lag'. *Bulletin of the Orton Society* **7**, 9–18.

Bezant, D., Combley, B. and Hinchcliffe, M. (1993) *Sheffield Structured Material – Sight, Sound, Movement Multisensory Resource Materials*. Sheffield: Sheffield Support Services.

Birch, H.G. (1962) 'Dyslexia and the maturation of visual function'. In J. Money (ed.) *Reading Disability*. Baltimore: Johns Hopkins Press.

Birch, H.G. and Belmont, L. (1964) 'Auditory-visual integration in normal and retarded readers'. *American Journal of Orthopsychiatry* **34**, 851–61.

Birkett, R. (1993) *Sounds Easy*. Baldock, Herts: Egon.

Bishop, D.V.M. (1989) 'Unfixed reference, monocular occlusion, and developmental dyslexia – a critique'. *British Journal of Ophthalmology* **73**, 209–15.

Blagg, N. (1989) *Somerset Thinking Skills Course*. Revd 1993. Taunton: N. Blagg Associates and Somerset County Council.

Blakeslee, S. (1994) 'New clue to cause of dyslexia seen in mishearing of fast sounds'. An interview with Dr P. Tallal. *New York Times* 16 August, p. 21.

Boder, E. (1971) 'Developmental dyslexia: prevailing diagnostic concepts and a new diagnostic approach'. In H. Myklebust (ed.) *Progress in Learning Disabilities, Vol 2*. New York: Grune and Stratton.

Boland, H. (1995) 'An investigation into the reasons why parents of children with complex SpLD wish to place their children in specialist schools'. Unpublished MA Dissertation, London: Middlesex University.

Bowers, S. and Wells, L. (1985, rev. 1996) *Ways and Means: An Approach to Problem Solving*. Kingston upon Thames: Kingston Friends Workshop Group.

Bradley, L. (1980) *Assessing Reading Difficulties: A Diagnostic and Remedial Approach*. Basingstoke: Macmillan.

Bradley, L. (1981a) 'The organisation of motor patterns for spelling: an effective remedial strategy for backward readers'. *Developmental Medicine and Child Neurology* **23**, 83–97.

Bradley, L. (1981b) 'A tactile approach to reading'. *British Journal of Special Education* **8** (4), 33–36.

Bradley, L. (1982) 'An experimental evaluation of effective remedial techniques for the learning disabled'. *Thalamus* **2** (1), 43–60.

Bradley, L. and Bryant, P. (1980) 'Why children sometimes write words which they cannot read'. In Frith (1980).

Bradley, L. and Bryant, P.E. (1985) *Children's Reading Problems*. Oxford: Blackwell.

Brady, S., Shankweiler, D. and Mann, V. (1983) 'Speech perception and memory coding in relation to reading ability'. *Journal of Experimental Child Psychology* **38**, 345–67.

Brand, V. (1993) *Spelling Made Easy*. 14th edn. Baldock, Herts: Egon.

Brennan, W.R. (1979) *Curriculum Needs of Slow Learners, Working Paper No. 63*. London: Methuen Education.

Brooks, P. et al. (1995) *Phonological Assessment Battery – Research Edition*. London: University College.

Brown, N.E. (1990) 'Children with spelling and writing difficulties: An alternative approach'. In P. Pumfrey and C.D. Elliott (eds) *Children's Difficulties in Reading, Spelling and Writing*. London: Falmer, 289–304.

Brown, G.D.A. and Ellis, N.C. (eds) (1994) *The Handbook of Spelling*. London: Wiley.

Brown, G.D.A. and Loosemore, R.P.W. (1994) 'Computational approaches to normal and impaired spelling'. In G.D.A. Brown and N.C. Ellis (eds) *Handbook of Spelling*. Chichester: Wiley, 319–36.

Bryant, P.E. (1975) 'Crossmodal developments and reading' In D. Duane and M.E. Rawson (eds) *Reading, Perception and Language*. Baltimore: York.

Bueckhardt, G. (1988) Unpublished thesis on learning difficulties, Kingston upon Thames: Kingston Polytechnic.

Burnhill, P., Hartley, J., Fraser, L. and Young, D. (1975) 'Writing lines: an exploratory study'. *Programmed Learning and Educational Technology* **12** (2), March.

Cashdan, A. and Pumfrey, P. (1969) 'The effects of remedial teaching of reading'. *Educational Research* **11**, 138.

CATE (1992) *Training Teachers to Teach Reading: A Review*. London: HMSO.

Chall, J. (1967) *Learning to Read: The Great Debate*. New York: McGraw Hill.

Chalmers, G.S. (1976) *Reading Easy 1800–1850. A Study of the Teaching of Reading*. London: Broadsheet King.

Chedru, F.V. and Geschwind, N. (1972) 'Writing disturbance in acute confusional states'. *Neuropsychologica* **10**, 343–53.

Child Education (1991) 'Reading survey confirms structured teaching approach'. *Child Education*, (68), January.

Childs, S. (1968) 'Education of specific language disabilities. The papers of Anna Gillingham (1919–1963)'. *Monograph No 3*. Pomfret County: Orton Society.

Chomsky, C. (1971) 'Write first, read later'. *Childhood Education* **47** (6), 296–99.

Chomsky, N. and Halle, M. (1968) *The Sound Pattern of English*. New York: Harper and Row.

Clarke, L.K. (1988) 'Invented versus traditional spelling in first grader's writing and effects on learning to spell and read'. *Research on the Teaching of English* **22**, 281–309.

Clay, M.M. (1972) *The Early Detection of Reading Difficulties: A Diagnostic Survey*. Auckland: Heinemann.

Clay, M.M. (1979) *The Early Detection of Reading Difficulties*. London: Heinemann.

Clay, M.M. (1989) 'Observing young children reading texts'. *Support for Learning* **4** (1), 7–11.

Clements, S.D. (1966) 'Learning disabilities – Who?' *Special Education Strategies for Educational Progress*. Washington, DC: Council for Exceptional Children.

Cooke, A. (1992) *Tackling Dyslexia the Bangor Way*. London: Whurr.

Cotterell, G.C. (1974) 'A remedial approach to a spelling disability'. In B. Wade and K. Wedell *Spelling Task and Learner*. Birmingham: Educational Review No. 5, University of Birmingham, 51–55.

Cotterell, G.C. (1985) *Cotterell Checklist and Diagnostic Spelling Test*. Wisbech: Learning Development Aids.

Cowdery, L.L. (1987) *Teaching Reading Through Spelling (TRTS): The Spelling Notebook*. Kingston upon Thames: Kingston Polytechnic, Learning Difficulties Research Project.

Cowdery, L.L., McMahon, J., Montgomery, D. (ed.), Morse, P. and Prince-Bruce, M. (1983) *Teaching Reading Through Spelling (TRTS): Diagnosis Book 2A*. Kingston upon Thames: Kingston Polytechnic, Learning Difficulties Research Project.

Cowdery, L.L., Montgomery, D. (ed.), Morse, P. and Prince-Bruce, M. (1984) *Teaching Reading Through Spelling (TRTS): The Foundations of the Programme Book 2B*. Kingston upon Thames: Kingston Polytechnic, Learning Difficulties Research Project.

Cowdery, L.L., Morse, P. and Prince-Bruce, M. (1985) *Teaching Reading Through Spelling (TRTS): The Early Stages of the Programme Book 2C*. Kingston upon Thames: Kingston Polytechnic, Learning Difficulties Research Project.

Cox, A.R. (1975) *Structures and Techniques of Remedial Language Training: Multisensory Teaching for Alphabetic Phonics (Rev)*. Cambridge, MA: Educators Publishing Service.

Cramer, P.L. (1976) 'Diagnosing skills by analysing children's writing'. *The Reading Teacher* **30** (3), 276–79.

Cripps, C. (1988) *A Hand for Spelling*. Wisbech: Learning Development Aids.

Cripps, C. (1988) *Joining the ABC*. Wisbech: Learning Development Aids.

Cripps, C. and Cox, R. (1987) Data reported in Cripps, C. (1989) *Joining the ABC*. Wisbech: Learning Development Aids.

Critchley, M. (1970) *Developmental Dyslexia*. 2nd edn. London: Heinemann.

Crystal, D., Fletcher, P. and Garman, M. (1976) *A Language Assessment, Remediation and Screening Procedure (LARSP)*. London: Arnold.

Daniels, J.C. and Diack, H. (1958) *The Standard Reading Test*. London: Chatto and Windus. (Reprinted by Hart Davis Educational, 1979.)

Dearing, R. (1994) *The National Curriculum Revised Orders*. London: HMSO.

Dechant, E.D. (1968) *Diagnosis and Remediation of Reading Disability*. New York: Parker.

Delpire, R. and Monory, J. (1962) *The Written Word*. London: Prentice Hall.

DES (1971) *Education Act: Handicapped Children*. London: HMSO.

DES (1972) *Children with Specific Reading Difficulties: The Tizard Report*. London: HMSO.

DES (1978) *Children with Special Educational Needs: The Warnock Report*. London: HMSO.

DES (1981) *Education Act: Children with Special Educational Needs*. London: HMSO.

DES (1983) *Assessment and Statements of Special Educational Needs: Circular 18/3*. London: DES.

DES (1989) *English for Ages 5–16*. London: HMSO.

DES and Welsh Office (1990) *English in the National Curriculum (No. 2)*. London: HMSO.

DfE (1990a) *Education (Special Educational Needs) Assessment Regulations No. 1524*. London: HMSO.

DfE (1990b) *The Teaching and Learning of Reading in Primary Schools: HMI Report*. London: HMSO.

DfEE (1994) *The Code of Practice on the Identification and Assessment*. London: HMSO.

Diack, H. (1965) *In Spite of the Alphabet*. London: Chatto and Windus.

Di Carlo (1965) In P. Groff (1975) *The Reading Teacher* **28** (8), 742–74.

DILP (1993) *Dyslexia Institute Language Programme*. Staines: Dyslexia Institute.

Dombey, H. (1994) 'Reading recovery research, an evaluation'. *British Educational Research Journal* **20** (2).

Downing, J. (1964) *The Initial Teaching Alphabet*. 2nd edn. London: Cassell.

Downing, J. and Thackray, D. (1970) *Reading Readiness*. London: Unibooks.

Dunlop, D.P. (1974) 'Orthoptic assessment of children with learning difficulties'. *Australian Journal of Ophthalmology*, **2**.

Durrell, D.D. and Murphy M.H.A. (1953) 'The auditory discrimination factor in reading readiness and reading disability'. *Education* **73**, 556–60.

Dyche, T. (1707) *Guide to the English Tongue*. London.

Early, G.H. (1976) 'Cursive handwriting, reading and spelling achievement'. *Academic Therapy* **12** (1), 67–74.

Edwards, B. (1992) *Drawing on the Right Side of the Brain*. London: Souvenir Press.

Edwards, J. (1994) *Scars of Dyslexia*. London: Cassell.

Ehri, L.C. (1979) 'Linguistic insight: threshold of reading acquisition'. In T.G. Waller and G.E. Mackinnon (eds) *Reading Research: Advances in Theory and Practice*. New York: Academic Press.

Eisenberg, L. (1962) 'Introduction' In J. Money (ed.) *Reading Disability, Progress and Research Needs in Dyslexia*. Baltimore: Johns Hopkins Press, 4–5.

Elbro, C. (1995) 'The role of morpheme recognition and morphological awareness in dyslexia'. Annual Conference of the Orton Society. Houston, Texas, 1 November.

Elliott, C.D. (1992) *B.A.S. Spelling Tests*. Windsor: NFER-Nelson.

Elliott, C.D., Murray, D.J. and Pearson, L.S. (1983) *The British Ability Scales (BAS)*. Windsor: NFER-Nelson.

Ellis, A.W. (1993) *Reading, Writing and Dyslexia* 2nd edn. Hove: L. Erlbaum.

Ellis, N.C. (1994) 'Longitudinal studies of spelling development'. In G.D.A. Brown and N.C. Ellis (eds) *Handbook of Spelling*. Chichester: Wiley, 155–77.

Erwin and Miller (1963) Cited in P. Groff (1975) 'Reading ability and auditory discrimination: are they related?' *The Reading Teacher* **28** (8), 742–74.

Evans, J.W. (1993) 'Dyslexia: The Dunlop test and tinted lenses'. *Optometry
Today* 28 June, 26–30.

Farnham-Diggory, S. (1978) *Learning Disabilities*. Harmondsworth:
Penguin.

Fassett, J.H. (1929) *The New Beacon Readers: Teacher's Manual*. Revd edn.
London: Ginn.

Feller, M. (1994) 'Open book testing and education for the future'. *Studies
in Educational Evaluation* **20** (2), 235–8.

Fernald, G.M. (1943) *Remedial Techniques in Basic School Subjects*. New York:
McGraw-Hill.

Ferreiro, E. (1978) 'What is written in a written sentence? A developmental
answer'. *Journal of Education* **160** (4), 25–39.

Ferreiro, E. and Teberosky, A. (1982) *Literacy Before Schooling*. Exeter, NH:
Heinemann Education.

Fish, J. (1985) *Educational Opportunities for All. Fish Report*. London: Inner
London Education Authority.

Fisher, J.R. (1984) 'The formulation of a language enrichment programme
for two low progress readers and an evaluation of its effectiveness'.
Unpublished Dissertation, Kingston upon Thames: Kingston Polytechnic.

Flavell, J.H. (1979) 'Metacognitive development'. In J.M. Scandura and C.J.
Brainerd (eds) *Structural Process Theories of Complex Human Behaviour*.
Netherlands: Sitjtoff Noordhoff.

Formentin, T. and Csapo, M. (1980) *Precision Teaching*. Vancouver: Vancouver Centre for Human Development.

Forsyth, D. (1988) 'An evaluation of an infant school screening instru-
ment'. Unpublished Dissertation, Kingston upon Thames: Kingston
Polytechnic.

Francis, H. (1982) *Learning to Read: Literate Behaviour and Orthographic
Knowledge*. London: Allen and Unwin.

Frith, U. (1974) 'Internal schemata for letters in good and bad readers'.
British Journal of Psychology **65** (2), 223–33.

Frith, U. (1978) 'Spelling difficulties'. *Journal of Child Psychology and Psychiatry* **19**, 279–85.

Frith, U. (ed.) (1980) *Cognitive Processes in Spelling*. London: Academic
Press.

Frith, U. (1982) 'Specific spelling problems'. *NATO Advanced Study Institute
Conference*. Mimeo, Maratea, October.

Frith, U. (1985) 'Beneath the surface of developmental dyslexia'. In K.
Patterson and M. Coltheart (eds) *Surface Dyslexia*. London: Routledge
and Kegan Paul.

Frostig, M. (1963) *Developmental Test of Visual Perception*. Palo Alto, CA:
Consulting Psychologists Press.

Frostig, M. and Horne, D. (1964) *The Frostig Programme for the Development
of Visual Perception*. Chicago: Follett.

Gagné, R.L. (1977) *Conditions of Learning and Theory of Instruction*. 2nd edn.

London: Holt Rinehart and Winston.

Galaburda, A.M. (1993) *Dyslexia and Development*. Cambridge, MA: Harvard University Press.

Galaburda, A.M., Signoret, J.C. and Ronthal, M. (1985) 'Left posterior angiomatous anomaly and developmental dyslexia. Report of five cases'. *Neurology* **35**, Supplement 198.

Gelb, I.J. (1963) *A Study of Writing*. 2nd edn. London: University of Chicago Press.

Gentry, J.R. (1981) 'Learning to spell developmentally'. *The Reading Teacher* **34** (4) 378–81.

Gentry, J.R. and Richardson, E.H. (1978) 'Three steps to teaching beginning readers to spell'. *The Reading Teacher* **31** (6), 632–36.

Geschwind, N. (1979) 'Specializations of the human brain'. *Scientific American* **241** (3), 158–67.

Gibson, E.J. and Levin, H. (1975) *The Psychology of Reading*. Cambridge, MA: MIT Press.

Gillingham A.M. and Stillman, B.U. (1956) *Remedial Teaching for Children with Specific Disability in Reading, Spelling and Penmanship*. 5th edn. New York: Sackett and Williams.

Gillingham A.M. and Stillman, B.U. (1969) *Remedial Training for Children with Specific Disability in Reading, Spelling and Penmanship*. 5th edn reprint. Cambridge, MA: Educators Publishing Service, and in the UK by Better Books, Bath, 1983.

Gillingham, A.M., Stillman, B.U. and Orton, S.T. (1940) *Remedial Training for Children with Specific Disability in Reading, Spelling and Penmanship*. New York: Sackett and Williams.

Gittelman, R. and Feingold, I. (1983) 'Children with reading disorder'. *Journal of Child Psychology and Psychiatry* **24** (2), 169–93.

Golinkoff, R.M. (1978) 'Phonemics awareness skills and reading achievements'. In F.B. Murray and J.J. Pikulski (eds) *The Acquisition of Reading*. Baltimore: University Park Press.

Goodacre, E.J. (1971) *Reading in Infant Classes*. 2nd edn. Windsor: NFER.

Goodenough, F.L. (1942) *The Mental Growth of Children from Age 2–14 Years*. Minneapolis: Minneapolis University Press.

Goodman, K.S. (1969) 'Analysis of oral reading miscues: applied psycholinguistics'. *Reading Research Quarterly* **5**, 8–30.

Gorman, T. and Fernandes, C. (1993) *Reading in Recession*. Windsor: NFER-Nelson.

Goswami, U. (1992) 'Orthographic analogies and reading development'. Spearman Medal Address to the British Psychological Society. In *The Psychologist*, July 1993, 313–15.

Goswami, U. (1994) 'The role of analogies in reading development'. *Support for Learning* **9** (1), 22–25.

Goswami, U. and Bryant, P.E. (1990) *Phonological Skills and Learning to Read*. Hove: L. Erlbaum.

Goulandris, N.K. (1986) 'Speech perception in relation to reading skill. A developmental analysis'. *Journal of Experimental Child Psychology* **41**, 489–507.

Gray, W.S. (1963) *The Teaching of Reading and Writing.* Geneva: UNESCO.

Gregory, R.P. (1988) *Action Research in the Secondary School: The Psychologist as Change Agent.* London: Routledge.

Groff, P. (1975) 'Reading ability and auditory discrimination: are they related?' *The Reading Teacher* **28** (8), 742–74.

Groff, P. (1986) 'The maturing of phonics instruction'. *The Reading Teacher* **39**, May, 919–23.

Grönland, N.E. (1970) *Stating Behavioural Objectives for Classroom Instruction.* New York: Macmillan.

Grundin, N. (1980) Cited in A.E. Tansley and J. Pankhurst, *Children with Specific Learning Difficulties.* Windsor: NFER.

Gubbay, S.S. (1975) *The Clumsy Child.* London: W.B. Saunders.

Hanna, P.R., Hanna, J.S., Hodges, R.E. and Rudorf, E.H. (1966) *Phoneme-Grapheme Correspondence as Cues to Spelling Improvement.* Washington, DC: US Office of Education.

Hatcher, P. Hulme, C. and Ellis, N.C. (1993) 'How children best learn to read'. *British Psychological Society Annual Conference Proceedings.* Leicester: British Psychological Society.

Henry, M.K. (1995) 'The importance of roots in the English spelling system'. Annual Conference of the Orton Society Houston, Texas, 2 November.

Hickey, K. (1977) *Dyslexia: A Language Training Course for Teachers and Learners.* 19 Woodside, Wimbledon, London, SW9.

Hinshelwood, J. (1917) *Congenital Word-Blindness.* London: Lewis.

Hinson, M. and Smith, P. (1993) *Phonics and Phonics Resources.* Stafford: NASEN.

HMI (1981) *Slow Learning and Less Successful Children in Secondary Schools.* London: HMSO.

HMI (1990) *The Teaching and Learning of Reading in Primary Schools.* London: HMSO.

Hornsby, B. (1989) *Overcoming Dyslexia.* London: MacDonald.

Hornsby, B. and Farrar, M. (1990) 'Some effects of a dyslexia-centred teaching programme'. In P.D. Pumfrey and C.D. Elliott (eds) *Children's Difficulties in Reading, Spelling and Writing.* London: Falmer Press, 173–96.

Hornsby, B. and Shear, F. (1976) *Alpha to Omega.* London: Heinemann.

Hornsby, B. and Shear, F. (1985) *Alpha to Omega.* Revd edn. London: Heinemann.

Hulme, C. (1981) *Reading Retardation and Multisensory Teaching.* London: Routledge and Kegan Paul.

Hulme, C. and Snowling, M. (1988) 'The classification of children with reading difficulties'. *Developmental Medicine and Child Neurology* **30**, 391–406.

Irlen, H.L. (1983) 'Successful treatment of learning disabilities'. Paper presented to the American Psychological Association. August.

Irlen, H.L. (1988) 'The use of the Irlen lenses in the remediation of scotopic sensitivity syndrome'. Paper delivered on behalf of H.L. Irlen by P. Clayton, 6th Annual Learning Difficulties Conference. Kingston upon

Thames: Kingston Polytechnic.
Irlen, H.L. and Lass, M.J. (1989) 'Improving reading problems due to scotopic sensitivity using Irlen Lenses and overlays'. *Education* **109**, 413–17.
i.t.a. Federation (1992) *United Kingdom i.t.a. Federation Annual Report.* London: Hotline Printers/i.t.a. Federation.
James, J., Charlton, T., Leo, E. and Indoe, D. (1991) 'A peer to listen'. *Support for Learning* **6** (4), 165–69.
Jarman, C. (1979) *Development of Handwriting Skills.* Oxford: Blackwell.
Johnson, D. and Myklebust, H. (1967, rev. 1995) *Learning Disabilities: Principles and Practices.* New York: Grune and Stratton.
Kappers, E.J. (1990) 'Neuropsychological treatment of dyslexic children'. *Euronews Dyslexia* **3**, 9–15.
Kimura, Y. and Bryant, P.E. (1983) 'Reading and writing in English and Japanese'. *British Journal of Developmental Psychology* **1**, 129–44.
Kinsbourne, M. and Warrington, E.K. (1963) 'Developmental factors in reading and writing backwardness'. *British Journal of Psychology* **4**, 145–56.
Klein, C. and Millar, R.R. (1990) *Unscrambling Spelling.* Sevenoaks: Hodder and Stoughton.
Knowles, S. and Masidlover, M. (1982) *Derbyshire Language Programme.*
Kolb, D.A. (1984) *Experiential Learning: Experience as a Source of Learning and Development.* New York: Prentice Hall.
Koppitz, E.M. (1971) *Children with Learning Disabilities: A Five Year Follow Up Study.* New York: Grune and Stratton.
Koppitz, E.M. (1977) *The Visual-Aural Digit Span Test.* New York: Grune and Stratton.
Koppitz, E.M. (1981) 'The VADS test for seventh grades. A normative study'. *Journal of Learning Disabilities* **14** (2), February, 93–95.
Lane, C.H. (1978) 'The ARROW approach for aural rehabilitation'. *The Volta Review* **80**, 149–54.
Lane, C.H. (1986) *The ARROW Manual.* Cambridge: The Cambridge System Ltd.
Lane, C.H. (1990) 'Alleviating children's reading and spelling difficulties'. In P. Pumfrey and C.D. Elliott (eds) *Children's Difficulties in Reading, Spelling and Writing.* London: Falmer Press, 237–54.
Lane, C.H. and Chinn, S.J. (1986) 'Learning by self voice echo'. *Academic Therapy* **21** (4), 477–82.
Lazslo, M. (1987) 'Children with perceptuo-motor difficulties in schools'. *Times Educational Supplement* 3 September, 22.
Learning Difficulties Research Project (1990) *Learning Difficulties Research Project Publications and Reports.* Maldon: Learning Difficulties Research Project.
Lennox, C. and Siegal, L.S. (1994) 'The role of phonological and orthographic processes in learning to spell'. In G.D.A. Brown and N.C. Ellis (eds) *Handbook of Spelling.* Chichester: Wiley, 93–110.
Leong, C.K. (1995) 'Summary of presentations and additional information'. Annual Conference of the Orton Society Houston, Texas, 1 November.

Lerner, J.W. (1971) *Children with Learning Disabilities*. Boston: Houghton Mifflin.

Liberman, A.M., Shankweiler, D.P., Cooper, F.S. and Studdert-Kennedy, M. (1967) 'Perception of the speech code'. *Psychological Review* **74** (6), 431–61.

Liberman, I.J. (1973) 'Segmentation of the spoken word and reading acquisition'. *Bulletin of the Orton Society* **23**, 365–77.

Liberman, I.J. and Shankweiler, D. (1972) 'Speaking the alphabet and teaching to read'. In L. Beswick and P. Werbner (eds) *Theory and Practice of Early Reading*. New York: L. Erlbaum.

Lintern, L. (1992) *Leighway Readers. i.t.a. Graded Readers Reillustrated*. Doncaster: Nightingale Primary School, Balby.

Lloyd, S. (1992) *The Phonics Handbook*. Chigwell: Jolly Learning.

Luria, A.R. (1973) *The Working Brain*. Harmondsworth: Penguin.

McMahon, J. (1982) 'An analysis of the spelling problems and remedial interventions with a group of dyslexic children'. Unpublished Dissertation, Kingston upon Thames: Kingston Polytechnic.

McNally, J. and Murray, W. (1962) *Key Words to Literacy*. London: Schoolmaster.

Makita, K. (1968) 'The rarity of reading disability in Japanese children'. *American Journal of Orthopsychiatry* **38**, 599–614.

Marsh, G., Friedman, M.P., Welch, V. and Desberg, P. (1980) 'The development of strategies in spelling'. In U. Frith (ed.) *Cognitive Processes in Spelling*. London: Academic Press, 339–54.

Marsh, G., Friedman, M.P., Desberg, P. and Saterdahl, K. (1981) 'Comparison of reading and spelling strategies in normal and reading disabled children'. In M.P. Friedman, J.P. Das and N. O'Connor (eds) *Intelligence and Learning*. New York: Plenum.

Miles, E. (1989) *The Bangor Dyslexia Teaching System*. London: Whurr (2nd edn 1992).

Miles, T.R. (1978) *Understanding Dyslexia*. Sevenoaks: Hodder & Stoughton.

Miles, T.R. (1982) *The Bangor Dyslexia Test*. Wisbech: Learning Development Aids.

Miles, T.R. (1983) *Dyslexia: The Patterns of Difficulty*. Oxford: Blackwell.

Miles, T.R. (1993) *Dyslexia: The Patterns of Difficulty*. 2nd edn. London: Whurr.

Miles, T.R. (1996) 'A hundred years of dyslexia in Britain. In *The Dyslexia Handbook*. Reading: British Dyslexia Association, 15–23.

Miles, T.R. and Miles, E. (1990) *Dyslexia: A Hundred Years On*. Buckingham: Open University Press.

Miles, T.R. and Miles, E. (1983) *Help for Dyslexic Children*. London: Methuen (rev. edn 1992).

Mittler, P. (1990) 'Foreword: Towards education for all'. In D. Montgomery, *Children with Learning Difficulties*. London: Cassell, ix–xxiv.

Money, J. (1962) *Reading Disability, Progress and Research Needs in Dyslexia*. Baltimore: Johns Hopkins Press.

Monroe, M. (1932) *Children Who Cannot Read*. Chicago: Chicago University Press.

Montgomery, D. (1977) 'Teaching pre-reading through training in pattern recognition'. *The Reading Teacher* **30** (6), 216–25.

Montgomery, D. (1979) *Visual Pattern Recognition Test and Manual*. Windsor: NFER.

Montgomery, D. (1981) 'Do dyslexics have difficulty accessing articulatory information?' *Psychological Research* **43**, 235–43.

Montgomery, D. (1984) 'Multisensory mouth training'. In Cowdery *et al.* (1984), 80–7.

Montgomery, D. (1986) 'Hearing reading inventory' Copy page in D. Montgomery and A. Rawlings (1986) *Classroom management*. Leamington Spa: Scholastic. 103

Montgomery, D. (1989) *Managing Behaviour Problems*. Sevenoaks: Hodder and Stoughton

Montgomery, D. (1990) *Children with Learning Difficulties*. London: Cassell.

Montgomery, D. (1993) 'Underfunctioning: The problems of dyslexics and their remediation'. In K.A. Heller and E.A. Hany (eds) *Competence and Responsibility, Vol. 2*. Toronto and Göttingen: Hogrese and Huber, 224–36.

Montgomery, D. (1995) 'Social abilities in highly able disabled learners and the consequences for remediation'. In M.W. Katzko and F.J. Monks *Nurturing Talent: Individual Needs and Social Abilities*. Assen, Netherlands: Van Gorcum, 226–38.

Montgomery, D. (1996) *Educating the Able*. London: Cassell.

Moreney, G. (1968) Cited in P. Groff (1975).

Morgan, W.P. (1896) 'A case of congenital word blindness'. *The British Medical Journal* 7 November. Also reprinted in *The Dyslexia Handbook*. Reading: British Dyslexia Association, 11–149.

Morse, P. (1984) 'Handwriting and handwriting difficulties'. In L.L. Cowdery, D. Montgomery, P. Morse and M. Prince-Bruce *Teaching Reading Through Spelling (TRTS): Foundations of the Programme*. Kingston upon Thames: Kingston Polytechnic, 32–68.

Morse, P. (1986) *Teaching Reading Through Spelling: The Handwriting Copy Book*. Kingston upon Thames: Kingston Polytechnic Learning Difficulties Research Project.

Morse, P. (1988) *Teaching Reading Through Spelling: The Handwriting Copy Book*. 2nd edn. Clwyd: Frondeg Hall.

Morse, P. (1991) 'Cursive in Kingston upon Thames' *Handwriting Review* **5**, 16–21.

Morse, P. (1992) 'Getting it right from the start: beginner writers'. *Handwriting Review* **6**, 24–26.

Moseley, D.V. (1988) 'New approaches to helping children with spelling difficulties'. *Educational and Child Psychology* **5**, (4), 53–58.

Moseley, D.V. (1989) 'How lack of confidence in spelling affects children's written expression'. *Educational Psychology in Practice* **5** (1), 42–46.

Moseley, D.V. (1994) 'From theory to practice'. In G.D.A. Brown and N.C. Ellis (eds) *Handbook of Spelling*. Chichester: Wiley, 459–79.

Moseley, D.V. and Nicol, C. (1988) *Aurally Coded English: The ACE Spelling Dictionary*. Wisbech: Learning Development Aids.

Myklebust, H.R. (1965) *Developmental Disorders of Written Language: Volume One, The Picture Story Language Test.* London: Grune and Stratton.

Myklebust, H.R. (1973) *Development and Disorders of Written Language: Volume Two, Studies of Normal and Exceptional Children.* London: Grune and Stratton.

Naidoo, S. (1972) *Specific Dyslexia: Research Report of ICAA (Invalid Children's Aid Association.* London: Pitman.

NCC (National Curriculum Council) (1989) *Non Statutory Guidelines in English.* York: NCC.

Neale, M.D. (1958) *Neale Analysis of Reading Ability: British Adaptation.* London: Macmillan. (New edn, 1977)

Neale, M.D., Christophers, U. and Whetton, C. (1994) *Neale Analysis of Reading.* Rev. edn. Windsor: NFER-Nelson.

Nelson, H.E. (1974) 'The aetiology of specific spelling disabilities, a neurologist's approach'. *Educational Review* **5**, 31–39.

Nelson, H.E. and Warrington, E.K. (1974) 'Developmental spelling retardation and its relation to other cognitive abilities'. *British Journal of Psychology* **65** (2), 265–74.

Newton, M. and Thomson, M. (1976) *The Aston Index.* Birmingham: Aston University.

Nicholson, R.I. and Fawcett, A.J. (1994) 'Spelling remediation for dyslexic children: a skills approach'. In G.D.A. Brown and N.C. Ellis *Handbook of Spelling: Theory, Process and Intervention.* Chichester: Wiley, 505–28.

Norrie, E. (1917) Cited in the (1973) *Edith Norrie Letter Case Manual.* London: Helen Arkell Centre.

Norrie, E. (1946) *The Edith Norrie Letter Case.* London: Word Blind Institute.

Norrie, E. (1973) *The Edith Norrie Letter Case.* London: Helen Arkell Centre, Fulham.

Northumberland County Council (1993) *Special Needs Identification and Programme Planning.* Northumberland: Northumberland County Council.

Nuttall, G. and Snook, I. (1973) 'Contemporary models of teaching'. In R.M.W. Travers (ed.) *Second Handbook of Research on Teaching.* Chicago: Rand McNally, 40–76.

O'Connor, J.D. (1978) *Phonetics.* Harmondsworth: Penguin.

Orton, S.T. (1937) *Reading, Writing and Speech Problems in Children.* New York: W.W. Norton.

Parrant, H. (1986) 'An investigation of remedial approaches to children's spelling difficulties'. Unpublished Dissertation, Kingston upon Thames: Kingston Polytechnic.

Paul, R. (1990) 'Critical thinking'. In *Critical Thinking Handbook.* Sonoma: Sonoma State University, Centre for Critical Thinking and Moral Critique.

Pavlidis, G.Th. (1978) 'The dyslexic's erratic eye movements'. *Dyslexia Review* **1** (1), 22–28.

Pavlidis, G.Th. (1981) 'Sequencing, eye movements and the early objective diagnosis of dyslexia'. In G.T. Pavlidis and T.R. Miles *Dyslexia Research and Its Application to Education.* Chichester: Wiley, 99–164.

Pavlidis, G.Th. (1986) 'The role of eye movements in the diagnosis of dyslexia'. In G. Th. Pavlidis and D.F. Fisher (eds) *Dyslexia: Its Neuropsychology and Treatment*. Chichester: Wiley, 97–110.

Perera, K. (1984) *Children's Writing and Reading: Analysing Classroom Language*. Oxford: Blackwell.

Peters, M.L. (1967, rev. 1985) *Spelling: Caught or Taught?* London: Routledge and Kegan Paul.

Peters, M. and Smith, B. (1993) *Spelling in Context*. Windsor: NFER-Nelson.

Pirozzolo, F.J. and Raynor, K. (1980) 'Disorders of oculomotor scanning and graphic orientation in developmental Gerstmann syndrome'. *Brain and Language*, **5**, 119–26.

Pitman, Sir I. (1961) *The Initial Teaching Alphabet*. London: Pitman.

Pollack, J. (1975) *Dyslexia: The Problems of Spelling*. London. Helen Arkell Dyslexia Centre.

Pollack, J. and Waller, E. (1994) *Day to Day Dyslexia*. London: Routledge.

Prince-Bruce, M. (1978) *Structured Spelling Programme*. Kingston upon Thames: Kingston Education Authority.

Prince-Bruce, M. (1986) *Teaching Reading Through Spelling (TRTS): The Later Stages of the Programme Vols 1 and 2*. Kingston upon Thames: Kingston Polytechnic Learning Difficulties Research Project.

Prince-Bruce, M., Morse, P. and Cowdery, L.L. (1985) *Teaching Reading Through Spelling (TRTS): The Early Stages*. Kingston upon Thames: Kingston Polytechnic Learning Difficulties Research Project.

Pumfrey, P.D. and Elliott, C.D. (eds) (1990) *Children's Difficulties in Reading, Spelling and Writing*. London: Falmer Press.

Pumfrey, P. and Reason, R. (1991) *Specific Learning Difficulties (Dyslexia) Challenges and Responses: A National Inquiry*. Windsor: NFER-Nelson.

Rack, J.P. (1996) 'Differential diagnosis of dyslexia'. *Proceedings of the British Psychological Society* **4** (1), February, 62.

Rack, J.P., Snowling, M. and Olson, R.K. (1992) 'The non-word reading deficit in developmental dyslexia: a review'. *Reading Research Quarterly* **27**, 28–33.

Radaker, L.D. (1963) 'The effect of visual imagery upon spelling performance'. *Journal of Educational Research* **54**, 370–72.

Rayner, K. (1986) 'Eye movements and the perceptual span'. In G. T. Pavlidis and D.F. Fisher (eds) *Dyslexia, Its Neurology and Treatment*. Chichester: Wiley.

Read, C. (1975) *Children's Categorization of Speech Sounds in English*. Urban, IL: National Council of Teaching English.

Read, C. (1986) *Children's Creative Spelling*. London: Routledge and Kegan Paul.

Reason, R. and Boote, R. (1993) *Learning Difficulties in Reading and Writing: A Teacher's Manual, Revised*. London: Nelson. (Reprinted London: Routledge)

Reber, A.S. and Scarborough, D.L. (eds) (1977) *Towards a Psychology of Reading: The Proceedings of the CUNY Conference*. Hillsdale, NJ: Erlbaum and J. Wiley.

Reid, J.F. (1971) 'Dyslexia; a problem of communication'. *Educational Research* **10** (2), 126–33.

Resnick, L.B. (1989) *Knowing, Learning and Instruction: Essays in Honour of Robert Glaser*. Hillsdale, NJ: Erlbaum.

Richardson, M. (1935) *Writing and Writing Patterns*. New Education Fellowship Conference Papers, St Andrews Silver Jubilee Exhibition.

Ridehalgh, N. (1995) 'An evaluation of Reading Recovery in New Zealand'. International Module in MA SpLD, Mimeo. London: Middlesex University.

Ridehalgh, N. (1997) 'A comparative study of the effectiveness of three dyslexia teaching programmes'. Unpublished MA dissertation. London: Middlesex University.

Rosner, J. (1974) 'Auditory analysis training with pre-readers'. *The Reading Teacher* **27**, 279–381.

Rozin, P. and Gleitman, L.R. (1977) 'The structure and acquisition of reading 11. The reading process and the acquisition of the alphabetic principle'. In A.S. Reber and D.L. Scarborough (eds) *Towards a Psychology of Reading*. Hillsdale, NJ: Erlbaum and Wiley.

Rubin, N. and Henderson, S.E. (1982) 'Two sides of the same coin. Variations in teaching methods and failure to learn to write'. *Special Education* **9** (4), 14–18.

Rumelhart, D.E. and McClelland, J.L. (eds) (1986) *Parallel Distributed Processing Vol. 1: Foundations*. Cambridge, MA: MIT Press.

Rush, S. (1996) 'Dyslexia the American way'. International Module Report of MASpLD (mimeo) of the 1995 Annual Conference of the Orton Society. London: Middlesex University.

Rutter, M., Maugham, B., Mortimore, P. and Ouston, J. (1979) *Fifteen Thousand Hours: Secondary Schools and Their Effect on Children*. London: Open Books.

Rutter, M., Tizard, J. and Whitmore, K. (eds) (1970) *Education, Health and Behaviour*. London: Longmans.

Rutter, M. and Yule, W. (1973) 'Specific reading retardation'. In L. Mann, W. Yule and D. Sabatino (eds) *The Second Review of Special Education*. Philadelphia: Buttonwood Farms.

Sassoon, R. (1983a) *The Practical Guide to Children's Handwriting*. London: Thames and Hudson.

Sassoon, R. (1983b) 'Writing wrongs, the neglect of handwriting in schools in depriving pupils of an essential tool for life'. *Times Educational Supplement*, March, 23.

Sassoon, R. (1989a) *Handwriting – A New Perspective*. Cheltenham: Stanley Thornes.

Sassoon, R. (1989b) *Handwriting – How to Teach It*. Cheltenham: Stanley Thornes.

Schiffman, G. (1972) 'Table to show percentage gains after two years of remedial education at different ages of identification'. In H.K. Goldberg and G.B. Schiffman *Dyslexia: Problems of Reading Disabilities*. London: Grune and Stratton, 66.

Schiffman, G. and Clemmens, R. (1966) *Observations on Children with Severe Reading Problems, Learning Disorders*. Seattle, WA: Special Child Publications.

Schonell, F.J. (1934) 'The relationship between defective speech and disability in spelling'. *British Journal of Educational Psychology* **4** (2), 123–89.

Schonell, F.J. (1942) *Backwardness in Basic Subjects*. Edinburgh: Oliver and Boyd.

Schonell, F.J. (1943) *Schonell Graded Word Reading Test*. Edinburgh: Oliver and Boyd.

Schonell, F.J. and Schonell, E.E. (1946) *Diagnostic and Attainment Testing*. 4th edn. Edinburgh: Oliver and Boyd.

SED (Scottish Education Department) (1978) *The Education of Pupils with Learning Difficulties in Primary and Secondary Schools: A Progress Report by H.M.I.* Edinburgh: HMSO.

Sherman, G.F. (1995) 'The anatomical basis of dyslexia'. Annual Conference of the Orton Society Houston, Texas, 3 November (reported in S. Rush, 1996).

Shore, B.M. and Tsiamis, A. (1986) 'Identification by provision'. In K.A. Heller and J.F. Feldhusen (eds) *Identifying and Nurturing the Gifted*. Berne: Huber.

Simon, D.P. and Simon, H.A. (1973) 'Alternative uses of phonemic information in spelling'. *Review of Educational Research* **43**, 115–37.

Singleton, C. (1990) *Computers and Literacy Skills*. Hull: British Dyslexia Association Resource Centre.

Singleton, C. (ed.) (1994) *Computers and Dyslexia*. Hull: University of Hull.

Singleton, C. (1996) 'Computerised cognitive profiling and early diagnosis of dyslexia'. *Proceedings of the British Psychological Society* **4** (1), February, 63.

Skinner, B.F. (1958) *Science and Human Behaviour*. New York: Macmillan.

Smith, F. (1973) *Psycholinguistics and Reading*. New York: Holt Rinehart and Winston.

Smith, F. (1978) *Understanding Reading*. (Reprint.) New York: Holt Rinehart and Winston.

Smith, F. (1985) *Reading*. Cambridge: Cambridge University Press.

Smith, F. (1988) *Understanding Reading: A Psycholinguistic Analysis of Reading and Learning to Read*. Hillsdale, NJ: Erlbaum.

Smith, J. and Bloor, M. (1985) *Simple Phonetics for Teachers*. London: Methuen.

Smith, P.A.P. and Marx, R.W. (1972) 'Some cautions on the use of the Frostig Test'. *Journal of Learning Disabilities* **5** (6), 357–62.

SNAP (1984) See Ainscow. M. and Muncey, J. Special Needs Action Programme (SNAP). Swansea: Drake Education.

Snow, R. (1973) 'Theory construction for research on teaching'. In R.M.W. Travers (ed.) *Second Handbook of Research on Teaching*. Chicago: Rand McNally, 77–112.

Snowling, M.J. (1981) 'Phonemic deficits in devlopmental dyslexia'. *Psychological Research* **43** (2), 219–34.

Snowling, M.J. (ed.) (1985) *Children's Written Language Difficulties*. Windsor: NFER-Nelson.

Snowling, M.J. (1987) *Dyslexia: A Cognitive Developmental Perspective*. Oxford: Blackwell.

Snowling, M.J. and Stackhouse, J. (1983) 'Spelling performance of children with developmental dyspraxia'. *Developmental Medicine and Child Neurology* **25**, 430–37.

Snowling, M.J., Stackhouse, J. and Rack, J.P. (1986) 'Phonological dyslexia and dysgraphia. A developmental analysis'. *Cognitive Neuropsychology* **3**, 309–39.

Solity, J. and Bull, S. (1987) *Special Needs: Bridging the Curriculum Gap*. Milton Keynes: Open University.

Southgate-Booth, V. (1986) 'Teachers of reading: planning the most effective use of their time'. In B. Root (ed.) *Resources for Reading: Does Quality Count?* London: UKRA/Macmillan, 80–98.

Spache, G.D. (1940) 'Characteristic errors of good and poor spellers'. *Journal of Educational Research* **34** (3), 182–89.

Spalding, R.B. and Spalding, W.T. (1957) *The Writing Road to Reading*. New York: Whiteside and Morrow.

Spalding, R.B. and Spalding, W.T. (1967) *The Writing Road to Reading*. Republished. New York: Whiteside and Morrow.

Sprague (1963) In M. Frostig and D. Horne *Manual of the Frostig Programme and Test*. Chicago: Follett.

Stackhouse, J. (1982) 'An investigation of reading and spelling performance in speech disordered children'. *British Journal of Disorders of Communication* **17**, 52–59.

Stainthorp, R. (1990) 'The handwriting of a group of teacher education students'. Lecture presentation at the United Kingdom Reading Association Conference (UKRA), July. Unpublished paper.

Stein, J.F. and Fowler, S. (1981) 'Diagnosis of dyslexia by means of a new indication of eye dominance'. *British Journal of Ophthalmology* **66** (5), 322–26.

Stein, J.F. and Fowler, S. (1985) 'Effect of monocular occlusion on visuomotor perception and reading in dyslexic children'. *Lancet* 13 July.

Stephens, T.M. (1976) *Directive Teaching of Children with Learning and Behavioural Handicaps*. 2nd edn. New York: Merrill.

Stern, C. and Gould, T. S. (1965) *Children Discover Reading. An Introduction to Structured Reading*. New York: Random House.

Stillman, B. (1940) Cited in A. Gillingham *et al.*, 1940.

STRANDS (1991) *Spelling Teaching for Reading and Needs of Dyslexic Students*. Winchester: Hampshire LEA.

Surrey County Council (1980) *Remedial Teaching in the Middle School*. Ewell: Glyn House, Surrey County Council.

Swann, W. (1985) 'Is the integration of children with special needs happening?' *Oxford Review of Education* **11**, 3–18.

Talbot, J. (1707) *Christian Schoolmaster*. London.

Tallal, P. (1980) 'Auditory temporal perception, phonics, and reading disabilities in children'. *Brain and Language* **9**, 182–98.

Tallal, P. (1994) 'New clue to cause of dyslexia seen in mishearing of fast sounds. An interview with Dr Tallal by S. Blakeslee', *New York Times* 16 August, 24.

Tallal, P. and Piercy, M. (1973) 'Developmental aphasia: impaired rate of non verbal processing' as a function of sensory modality'. *Neuropsy-*

chologia **11**, 389–98.

Tallal, P., Stark, R.E. and Mellitts, E.D. (1985) 'Identification of language impaired children on the basis of rapid perception and production skills'. *Brain and Language* **25**, 314–22.

Tansley, A.E. (1967) *Reading and Remedial Reading*. London: Routledge and Kegan Paul.

Tansley, A.E. (1971) *Sound Sense, Books 1–8*. Leeds: E.J. Arnold.

Tansley, A.E. and Pankhurst, J. (1981) *Children with Specific Learning Difficulties: Critical Review*. Windsor: NFER.

Thomas, D. (1996) 'An evaluation of phonological awareness training. A report of school based work' for MA in Specific Learning Difficulties. London. Middlesex University.

Thomas, L.F. and Harri-Augstein, E.S. (1985) *Self Organised Learning*. London: Routledge and Kegan Paul.

Thomson, M.E. (1984) *Developmental Dyslexia*. 1990, 3rd edn. London: E.J. Arnold.

Thomson, M.E. (1989) *Developmental Dyslexia: Its Nature, Assessment and Remediation*. London: Cole and Whurr.

Thomson, M.E. (1990) 'Evaluating teaching programmes for children with specific learning difficulties'. In P.D. Pumfrey and C.D. Elliott (eds) *Children's Difficulties in Reading, Spelling and Writing*. London: Falmer Press, 155–71.

Thomson, M.E. and Watkins, E.J. (1993) *Teaching the Dyslexic Child*. London: Whurr.

THRASS (1995) *Teaching Handwriting, Reading and Spelling Skills*. Sheffield LEA Reading Recovery Teams Project. London: Collins Educational.

Torgeson, J.K. (1985) 'Memory processes in reading disabled children'. *Journal of Learning Disabilities* **18**, 350–57.

Torgeson, J.K. (1995) 'Instructional alternatives for children with severe reading difficulties'. Annual Conference of the Orton Society, Houston, Texas, 1 November (reported in S. Rush, 1996).

Treiman, R. (1994) 'Sources of information used by beginning spellers'. In G.D.A. Brown and N.C. Ellis (eds) *Handbook of Spelling*. Chichester: Wiley, 75–92.

Turner, M. (1990a) 'Positive responses' (to DISTAR). *Times Educational Supplement* 9 January, 7.

Turner, M. (1990b) *Sponsored Reading Failure*. Surrey: Warlingham Park School, E.A. Unit.

Turner, M. (1991) 'Finding out'. *Support for Learning* **6** (3), 99–102.

Van Nes, F.L. (1971) 'Errors in the motor program for handwriting'. *I.P.O. Annual Progress Report* **6**, 61–63.

Vargus, J.S. (1977) *Behavioural Psychology for Teachers*. New York: Harper and Row.

Vellutino, F.R. (1977) 'Alternative conceptualizations of dyslexia: evidence in support of a verbal deficit hypothesis'. *Harvard Educational Review*, Special Issue **47**, 334–54.

Vellutino, F.R. (1979) *Dyslexia: Theory and Research*. London: MIT Press.

Vellutino, F.R. (1987) 'Dyslexia'. *Scientific American* **256** (3), 20–27.

Vellutino, F.R., Steger, J.A., Harding, C. and Phillips, F. (1975) 'Verbal versus non verbal paired associate learning in poor and normal readers'. *Neuropsychologica* **13**, 75–82.

Vincent, C. (1983) 'A study of the introduction of cursive writing'. Unpublished Dissertation. Kingston upon Thames: Kingston Polytechnic.

Vincent, D. and Claydon, J. (1983) *Dianostic Spelling Test.* Windsor: NFER-Nelson.

Wallach, L., Wallach, M.A., Dozier, M.G. and Kaplan, N.E. (1977) 'Poor children learning to read do not have trouble with auditory discrimination but do have trouble with phoneme recognition'. *Journal of Educational Psychology* **69**, February 36–39.

Waller, E. (1973) *The Problems of Handwriting.* London: Croom Helm.

Warnock, M. (1978) *Children with Special Educational Needs: The Warnock Report.* London: HMSO.

Wedell, K. (1973) *Learning and Perceptuomotor Disabilities in Children.* Chichester: Wiley.

Wendon, L. (1984) *The Pictogram System.* Barton, Cambs: Pictogram Supplies.

Wepman, J.M. (1958) *Auditory Discrimination Test.* Chicago, IL: Language Research Associates.

Wilson, J. (1993) *P.A.T. Phonological Awareness Training: A New Approach to Phonics.* London: Educational Psychology Publishing.

Wilson, J. (1994) 'Phonological awareness training. A new approach to phonics'. *PATOSS Bulletin* November, 5–8.

Wing, A.M. and Baddeley, A.D. (1980) 'Spelling errors in handwriting'. In U. Frith (ed.) *Cognitive Processes in Spelling.* London: Academic Press, 251–86.

Wisby, A. (1984) 'Preventing waste'. *Industrial Society* June, 22–24.

WISC-R (1974) *Wechsler Intelligence Scale for Children-Revised.* New York: Psychological Corporation.

Wise, B.W. and Olson, R.K. (1994) 'Using computers to teach spelling to children with learning disabilities'. In G.D. Brown and N.C. Ellis (eds) *Handbook of Spelling.* Chichester: Wiley, 481–504.

Witelson, S.F. (1977) 'Developmental dyslexia: two right hemispheres and one left'. *Science* **195**, 309–11.

Wolff, A.G. (1973) 'The dyslexic and the code'. *Dyslexia Review* (10), 7–9.

Wolff, A.G. (1974) *The Assessment and Teaching of Dyslexic Children.* London: Invalid Children's Aid Association.

Wood, S. and Shears, B. (1986) *Teaching Children with Severe Learning Difficulties: A Radical Reappraisal.* London: Croom Helm.

Wray, D. (1991) 'A chapter of errors: A response to Martin Turner'. *Support for Learning* **6** (4), 145–49.

Wright, A. and Prance, J. (1993) 'The Reading Recovery programme in Surrey Education Authority'. *Support for Learning* **7**, 103–10.

Ysseldyke, J.E. (1987) 'Annotation'. *Journal of Child Psychology and Psychiatry* **28** (1), 21–24.

Yule, W. (1967) 'Predicting reading ages on Neale's Analysis of Reading Ability'. *British Journal of Educational Psychology* **347**, 252–5.

Index